大学实用英语综合教程

主 编 马海旭 邢 舫 韩 芳
副主编 杨 平 赵 喆 戴 冕

北京理工大学出版社
BEIJING INSTITUTE OF TECHNOLOGY PRESS

内 容 提 要

本教程是为满足全日制普通民办本科院校艺术类专业大学英语教学以及艺术类学生个性化发展的需要而编写的。教程分为上、下册两部分，其总目标是通过打好"基础"、应用"生活"、传播"文化"，最终服务"专业"，培养国际化艺术类人才。教程以项目的实施过程为主体，引出各个知识点；能采取恰当的教学方法和手段满足项目教学的需要，调动学生的积极性，有效拓展项目。依据教学目标、成果导向及子项目要求进行教程中不同内容的选材，为项目目标服务。

版权专有　侵权必究

图书在版编目（CIP）数据

大学实用英语综合教程/马海旭，邢舫，韩芳主编 . —北京：北京理工大学出版社，2021.1
　ISBN 978 – 7 – 5682 – 9464 – 5

　Ⅰ . ①大… 　Ⅱ . ①马… ②邢… ③韩… 　Ⅲ . ①英语 – 高等学校 – 教材 　Ⅳ . ①H319.39

中国版本图书馆 CIP 数据核字（2021）第 012949 号

出版发行 / 北京理工大学出版社有限责任公司	
社　　址 / 北京市海淀区中关村南大街5号	
邮　　编 / 100081	
电　　话 /（010）68914775（总编室）	
（010）82562903（教材售后服务热线）	
（010）68948351（其他图书服务热线）	
网　　址 / http：//www.bitpress.com.cn	
经　　销 / 全国各地新华书店	
印　　刷 / 唐山富达印务有限公司	
开　　本 / 787毫米×1092毫米　1/16	
印　　张 / 19	责任编辑 / 时京京
字　　数 / 446千字	文案编辑 / 时京京
版　　次 / 2021年1月第1版　2021年1月第1次印刷	责任校对 / 刘亚男
定　　价 / 58.00元	责任印制 / 李志强

图书出现印装质量问题，请拨打售后服务热线，本社负责调换

前 言

为全面实施《大学英语教学指南》，贯彻"分类指导、因材施教"的原则，满足全日制普通本科院校艺术类专业大学英语教学的需求，以及艺术类学生个性化发展的需要，编者团队专门编写了《大学实用英语综合教程》。

一、编写依据

本教程在充分考虑艺术类专业学生的基础水平、学习习惯、兴趣爱好、认知规律等特点的基础上，适当调整语言难度、丰富题材体裁，提高学生的学习兴趣，科学合理地精选了各类文章，内容涵盖文化、音乐、设计、美术、影视等领域。

教学要求为《大学英语课程教学要求》中的"一般要求"。通过本教程的学习，学生能听懂日常使用的结构简单、发音清楚、语速较慢的英语对话和与生活、专业相关的对话，能够就艺术类专业话题、中国传统文化话题、日常话题进行简单的英文交谈，能读懂一般题材及与未来职业相关的基础英文资料，理解基本正确，能完成一般性写作，能借助工具书翻译一般性的英文资料。

二、教材特色

本教程分为上、下两册，总目标：通过打好"基础"、应用"生活"、传播"文化"，最终服务"专业"，培养国际化艺术类人才。

本教程能采取恰当的教学方法和手段满足项目教学的需要，调动学生的积极性，有效拓展项目；依据教学目标、成果导向及子项目要求进行教材中不同内容的选材，为项目目标服务。

另外，在子项目设置中加入了文化版块。随着中国文化走出去战略的实施，作为新时代大学生，尤其是将来可能从事文化艺术类工作的学生，传播和传承中国文化是其神圣的使命。因此，教会学生用英文介绍有特色的中国传统文化，既可与西方文化对比，又让学生学会"用英语讲好中国故事"。

本教程将语言学习、专业学习、通识教育三者并重，培养学生的语言能力；并结合专业知识来提高学生的人文素养、国际化视野，这也是本教材和特色所在。

三、教材构成

本教程每册都分为四个项目体系，详细如下：

1. 根据艺术类专业学生的知识水平及学习习惯，首要任务是打好语言基础，即进行"基础知识"项目，包括字母、音标、发音规则、词性、时态、基础语法、国家、百科、节日等内容，使其爱上英语。

2. 在基础知识打好的前提下，进行第二个子项目的学习，即"生活情境"项目的学习。语言是生活中的工具，离不开生活场景，包括日常情景会话、校园生活、移动生活、现代生活、科技生活等。此部分内容为每册的前两个单元。

3. 为了更好地为专业服务，本教程加入"中国文化"项目学习。随着中国文化走出去战略的实施，作为新时代大学生，尤其是将来从事文化艺术类工作的学生，传播和传承中国文化是其神圣的使命。因此，让学生学会"用英语讲好中国故事"，既可与西方文化对比，又能将中国传统文化元素应用到专业、职业之中。此部分内容为每册的中间两个单元。

4. 在进行了基础、生活、文化项目后，学生已有一定知识积累，能够更好地进行"专业英语"项目的学习，包括舞台剧、歌唱、绘画、设计、动画等专业英语文章，以及专业英语词汇、英文简历写作、面试基本问答等未来职业相关内容的学习。此部分内容为每册的后两个单元。

每单元的 Dialogue Samples 部分提供了音频，学生均能扫码即看、扫码即听。本教材中的图片均来自网络，仅用于本教材教学使用。

四、编写团队

本教程在编写过程中得到了北京理工大学出版社的大力支持。编写团队来自沈阳工学院及沈阳理工大学，主编为马海旭、邢舫、韩芳，副主编为杨平、赵喆、戴冕，每人负责两个单元的编写工作。外籍教师 Jason Current 参与了录音工作及教材部分内容的审稿工作。

由于编者水平有限，书中难免有错误及疏漏之处，敬请广大读者及同行专家不吝赐教。

编者

2020 年 3 月

目 录

上 篇

Unit 1　My College Life ······· 3

  Warm-up Activities ······· 4
    Text A　How to Spend College Career ······· 5
    Text B　Two famous Chinese's Early Lives and Their Careers ······· 17
    Grammar　Verbs ······· 22
    Culture　Introduction of American Culture ······· 24

Unit 2　Technology ······· 26

  Warm-up Activities ······· 27
    Text A　The Book *A Brief History of Time* ······· 28
    Text B　Virtual Reality Making It Possible to Travel in Time ······· 40
    Grammar　Passive Voice ······· 45
    Culture　Uncle Sam ······· 47

Unit 3　Calligraphy and Painting ······· 49

  Warm-up Activities ······· 50
    Text A　Calligraphy ······· 51
    Text B　Chinese Ancient Painting ······· 62
    Grammar　Non-finite Verbs ······· 67
    Culture　The American Spirit of "Do-It-Yourself" ······· 70

Unit 4　World Heritage Sites ······· 71

  Warm-up Activities ······· 72
    Text A　World Cultural Heritage in China ······· 73
    Text B　Mount Taishan ······· 84

  Grammar Subjunctive Mood ································· 89
  Culture Thanksgiving ····································· 91

Unit 5 Animated Film and Oil Painting ························ 92

  Warm-up Activities ··· 93
  Text A *Loving Vincent* ··································· 94
  Text B Is she really smiling? ···························· 105
  Practical Writing Note for Leave ························ 110
  Culture The self-made man ······························ 113

Unit 6 What is Good Design? ··································· 115

  Warm-up Activities ·· 116
  Text A Ten Principles for Good Design ················ 117
  Text B The logo designs for 24 solar terms shine at the UN headquarters ·············· 128
  Practical Writing Letter of Invitation ···················· 133
  Culture Halloween ······································· 136

附录 I 词汇表 ·· 138

附录 II 短语表 ··· 146

下 篇

Unit 7 Environment Protection ································· 151

  Warm-up Activities ·· 152
  Text A Low-carbon Life Cutting a College Student's Budget ······················· 153
  Text B Green Economy：Farming in the Sky in Singapore ······················· 164
  Grammar Attributive Clauses ··························· 169
  Culture British Social Life（Section A） ················ 170

Unit 8 Modern Life ··· 172

  Warm-up Activities ·· 173
  Text A Taking the Sweat Out of Online Shopping ····· 174
  Text B The Dangers of Cell Phone Use ················ 185
  Grammar Emphatic Pattern ···························· 190
  Culture British Social Life（Section B） ················ 191

Unit 9 Chinese Festivals ··· 193

  Warm-up Activities ·· 194

  Text A Chinese Qixi Festival ·········· 195
  Text B The Spring Festival ·········· 206
  Grammar Subject-Verb Agreement ·········· 211
  Culture Talking About the Weather ·········· 213

Unit 10 Chinese Kung Fu ·········· 214

 Warm-up Activities ·········· 215
  Text A The Schools of Chinese Kung Fu ·········· 216
  Text B Chinese Kung Fu ·········· 227
  Grammar Adjective and Adverb ·········· 232
  Culture Three Royal Traditions ·········· 233

Unit 11 Designers and Musicians ·········· 235

 Warm-up Activities ·········· 236
  Text A The Golden Age of Design ·········· 237
  Text B Different Types of Composers ·········· 249
  Practical Writing Letter of Complaining ·········· 254
  Culture Three Don'ts ·········· 256

Unit 12 Dreams and Career ·········· 258

 Warm-up Activities ·········· 259
  Text A From a Tattoo* Artist to a Fashion Designer ·········· 260
  Text B Derivative Occupation ·········· 271
  Practical Writing Resume ·········· 276
  Culture Love of Privacy ·········· 280

附录Ⅲ 词汇表 ·········· 282

附录Ⅳ 短语表 ·········· 290

参考文献 ·········· 293

上篇

Unit 1

My College Life

Warm-up Activities

Ⅰ. Matching

Learn the following words and phrases about different types of design, and match them to the pictures.

1. lecture hall(　　)   2. library(　　)   3. experiment centre (　　)
4. gymnasium (　　)   5. canteen(　　)   6. classroom (　　)

A.

B.

C.

D.

E.

F.

Ⅱ. Reading

brilliant future 宽广的未来
younger generation 年轻一代
responsibility n. 责任，担当

　　A nation will be full of hope and a country will have a brilliant future when its younger generations have ideals, ability, and a strong sense of responsibility.

　　青年一代有理想、有本领、有担当，国家就有前途，民族就有希望。

　　（习近平总书记给北京大学援鄂医疗队全体"90后"党员的回信）

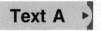

How to Spend College Career

Li Kaifu* (Extract)

Dear Daughter:

1. As we drove off from Columbia, I wanted to write a letter to you to tell you all that is on my mind.

....

2. I will always remember the first moment I held you in my arms. I felt a **tingling** feeling that directly touched my heart. It was an **intoxicating** feeling I will always remember. When I put you down, it was always with both **relief**(she finally fell asleep!) and **regret**(wishing I could hold you longer). You were so cute and **adorable**, and that is why everybody loved you so.

3. You have been a great kid ever since you were born, always quiet, **empathetic**, **attentive**, and **well-mannered**. I remember when we built our house, you were three and you happily ate hamburgers every meal in the car, sang with Barney until you fell asleep.

......

4. College will be the most important years in your life. You often question "what good is this course". I encourage you to be **inquisitive**, but I also want to tell you: "**Education** is what you have left after all that is taught is forgotten." What I mean by that is the **materials** taught isn't as important as you gaining the abality to learn a new subject, and the ability to **analyze** a new problem. That is really what learning in college is about—this will be the period where you go from teacher-taught to master-**inspired**, after which you must become self-learner. So do take each subject seriously, the skills of learning will be something you cherish forever.

......

5. Follow your **passion** in college. Steve Jobs* says when you are in college, your passion will **create** many **dots**. In his great speech given at Stanford **commencement**, he gave the great example where he took calligraphy (writing), and a decade later, it developed into desktop publishing, and brought wonderful tools like Microsoft Word to our lives. His **attempt** taken for pleasure into calligraphy was a dot, and the Macintosh became the connecting line. So if you like some subject, go for it, even if you think "it's not useful".

......

6. I told your mom I'm writing this letter, and asked what she wanted me to say. She thought and said: "just ask her to take care of herself."Simple but deeply caring-that is how your mother is, and that is why you love her so much. Please listen to your mother and take care of yourself.

7. College is the four years where you have: the most **flexibility** to change.

......

8. May Columbia become the happiest four years in your life, and may you **blossom** into just what you dream to be.

Love,
Dad (& Mom)

New Words

tingle[ˈtɪŋgl] v. to have a feeling as if a lot of sharp points are being put quickly and lightly into your body 激动

intoxicate[ɪnˈtɒksɪˌkeɪt] v. fill with high spirits; fill with optimism 使陶醉

relief[rɪˈliːf] n. a feeling of happiness that something unpleasant has not happened or has ended 减轻

regret[rɪˈgret] n. sadness associated with some wrong done or some disappointment 遗憾

adorable[əˈdɔːrəbəl] adj. lovable especially in a childlike or naive way 迷人的

empathetic[ˌempəˈθetɪk] adj. showing empathy or ready comprehension of others' states 移情作用的；感情移入的

attentive[əˈtentɪv] adj. giving care or attention 周到的

well-mannered[ˈwelˈmænərd] adj. of good upbringing 行为端正的

inquisitive[ɪnˈkwɪzɪtɪv] adj. showing curiosity, inquiring or appearing to inquire 好学的

education[ˌedʒʊˈkeɪʃən] n. the gradual process of acquiring knowledge 教育

material[məˈtɪərɪəl] n. the tangible substance that goes into the makeup of a physical object 材料

analyze[ˈænəˌlaɪz] v. consider in detail and subject to an analysis in order to discover essential features or meaning 分析

inspire[ɪnˈspaɪə] v. heighten or intensify, supply the inspiration for 启发；鼓舞；激励

passion[ˈpæʃ(ə)n] n. strong feeling or emotion 热情

create[krɪˈeɪt] v. make or cause to be or to become 创造

dot[dɒt] n. a very small round mark 小点

commencement[kəˈmensmənt] n. an academic exercise in which diplomas are conferred (美)学位授予典礼；毕业典礼

attempt[əˈtempt] n. earnest and conscientious activity intended to do or accomplish something 尝试

flexibility[ˌfleksəˈbɪləti] n. the property of being flexible 柔韧性；灵活性

blossom[ˈblɒsəm] v. produce or yield flowers; develop or come to a promising stage 开花

Useful Expressions

Phrases	Examples
drive off 驾车离去	He drove off without saying goodbye. 他不辞而别驾车离去
on my mind 在我心里	The loss of the ticket to the concert has been a weight on my mind. 丢失音乐会入场券的事压在我心里
put up with 忍受	You will have to put up with Grace's absent-mindedness. 你得忍受格蕾丝的心不在焉
take sth. seriously 认真对待	When people ask you to do something, you should take it seriously. 人家托你的事，你别不在意
go for it 尝试	When she heard about the chance for performance, she decided to go for it. 当她听到有表演的机会时，她决定一试

 Background Information

1. Li kaifu: 李开复，1961年12月3日出生于台湾省新北市中和区，祖籍四川成都，曾就读于卡内基梅隆大学，获计算机学博士学位，后担任副教授、信息产业的经理人、创业者和电脑科学研究者，曾在苹果、SGI、微软和Google等多家IT公司担当要职。2009年9月从谷歌离职后创办创新工场，任董事长兼首席执行官。2013年9月对外宣布罹患淋巴癌。2015年，李开复在患病离开北京17个月后回到创新工场的北京办公室。2017年1月，参演《奇葩大会》。

2. Steve Jobs: 史蒂夫·乔布斯（1955年2月24日—2011年10月5日），生于美国旧金山，苹果公司联合创办人。1976年和朋友成立苹果电脑公司，2011年8月24日辞去苹果公司行政总裁职位。计算机业界与娱乐业界的标志性人物，经历了苹果公司几十年的起落与兴衰，先后领导和推出了麦金塔计算机（Macintosh）、iMac、iPod、iPhone、iPad等风靡全球的电子产品，深刻地改变了现代通信、娱乐、生活方式。同时也是前Pixar动画公司的董事长及行政总裁。2011年10月5日，因胰腺癌病逝，享年56岁。美国加州将每年的10月16日定为"乔布斯日"。

Reading Comprehension

Ⅰ. **Decide whether the following statements are True (T) or False (F).**
(   ) 1. When I (the father) put you (the daughter) down, it was always with both relief and regret.
(   ) 2. You were so pretty, and that is why everybody loved you so.
(   ) 3. You have been a great kid ever since you were born.
(   ) 4. College will be the most important years in your life.
(   ) 5. Education is what you have left after all that is taught is forgotten.
(   ) 6. The materials taught is as important as you gaining the ability to learn a new subject, and the ability to analyze a new problem.
(   ) 7. You have to do take each subject seriously, and even if what you learn isn't critical for your life.

Ⅱ. **Complete the answers to the following questions.**
1. What good is this course? (Para. 4)
   Gaining the ability to _____ a new subject, and the ability to _____ a new problem.
2. What is really about learning in college? (Para. 4)
   A change from teacher-taught to _____, after which you must become _____.
3. In his great speech given at Stanford commencement, What example did Steve Jobs give about learning in college? (Para. 5)
   He take _____ as an example.
4. What may be the relation between the passion in college and the development later in life? (Para. 5)
   The passion in college was _____, and the development later in life became _____.
5. What did the mom say to her daughter when she knows the father is writing the letter? (Para. 6)
   "Just ask her to _____."

Vocabulary and Structure

Words and Phrases to Drill

drove off	on my mind	tingle	intoxicate	relief
adorable	empathetic	dot	inquisitive	inspire
take sth. seriously	go for it	put up with	flexibility	commencement

Ⅰ. Choose the appropriate explanation from Column B for each of the words in Column A.

A	B
_____ 1. relief	a. to have a feeling as if a lot of sharp points are being put quickly and lightly into your body
_____ 2. flexibility	b. fill with high spirits; fill with optimism
_____ 3. tingle	c. a feeling of happiness that something unpleasant has not happened or has ended
_____ 4. inquisitive	d. lovable especially in a childlike or naive way
_____ 5. dot	e. showing empathy or ready comprehension of others' states
_____ 6. adorable	f. showing curiosity, inquiring or appearing to inquire
_____ 7. commencement	g. heighten or intensify, supply the inspiration for
_____ 8. empathetic	h. a very small round mark
_____ 9. inspire	i. an academic exercise in which diplomas are conferred
_____ 10. intoxicate	j. the property of being flexible

Ⅱ. Fill in the blanks with the correct forms of the words in Column A of the above table. Change the form if necessary.

1. Don't be so _____. It's none of your business!
2. These _____ tree-hugging animals feed on tree leaves.
3. I felt a sudden _____ of excitement.
4. I am sensitive, _____, and artistic.
5. We are all fellow passengers on a _____ of earth.
6. To their great _____, the missing world famous painting Sunflower was found.
7. We're trying to _____ him with confidence.
8. At _____, academic degrees are officially given.
9. Cherishing a rose means to _____ yourself on her beauty.
10. _____ is also an extremely important quality for an art communication.

Unit 1 My College Life

III. Compare each pair of words and choose the correct one to fill in each blank.

1. adore   adorable
   a. The kids _____ their father and confide in him.
   b. Men only adore women who are _____ .
2. commence   commencement
   a. The second term _____ in March.
   b. He made a speech at the _____ .
3. flexible   flexibility
   a. We need a foreign policy that is more _____ .
   b. Online education gives students enough _____ .
4. relief   relieve
   a. This medicine will _____ your headache.
   b. The pills gave her some _____ .
5. inspire   inspiration
   a. You _____ me with admiration.
   b. Many poets and artists have drawn their _____ from nature.

IV. Add the prefix "dis-" to the following words in brackets. Then complete the sentences with the words formed.

> **Tips:** 前缀 dis – 加在形容词、动词前面，表否定意义，如 dis + loyal→disloyal(不忠诚的)，dis + like→dislike(不喜欢)，dis + appoint →disappoint(失望)。

Sample: She was <u>disabled</u> to solve the problem. (able)

1. He was _____ after the accident. (able)
2. The king disgraced the _____ courtier. (loyal)
3. Gradually the heavy footsteps _____ . (appear)
4. His hopes have been repeatedly _____ . (appoint)
5. I _____ to be so inquisitive with other's matters. (like)

V. Choose the best phrase to complete each sentence.

1. He was just about to _____ when the secretary ran out to him.
   A. drive off   B. drive on   C. drive at   D. drive out
2. It can melt the ice in one's heart and blow away the dust _____ one's mind.
   A. off   B. away   C. from   D. on
3. My girlfriend is a saint to put _____ with me.
   A. down   B. up   C. off   D. on
4. The children are always complaining that they are hungry to death. Don't _____ it seriously.
   A. put   B. make   C. take   D. have
5. Can you introduce yourself in two minutes? _____ for it!
   A. Go   B. Come   C. Make   D. Put

11

VI. Complete the following sentences by translating the Chinese given in brackets into English.

1. You can't quit now! You're almost there! _____(去争取吧！)
2. _____(你认为可信吗) his prediction of a government defeat?
3. Developing countries won't _____(容忍这一情况) for much longer.
4. The couple loaded up their red sports car and _____(疾驰而去).
5. This game has been _____(我一直想着) all week.

VII. Translate the following sentences into Chinese.

1. When I put you down, it was always with both relief (she finally fell asleep!) and regret (wishing I could hold you longer). (Para. 1)

2. Education is what you have left after all that is taught is forgotten. (Para. 4)

3. The materials taught isn't as important as you gaining the ability to learn a new subject, and the ability to analyze a new problem. (Para. 4)

4. That is really what learning in college is about—this will be the period where you go from teacher-taught to master-inspired, after which you must become self-learner. (Para. 4)

VIII. Combine the following sentences using the structure "It is far... than..."

> It is far adj. / adv. 比较级（to do）A than (to do) B. 结构用于连接两句陈述对象相关、含义相反的句子，表示"A 远比 B……"far 后加形容词或副词比较级。
>
> Sample: It is honorable to fail. It is not so honorable to cheat.
> It is far more honorable to fail than to cheat.
> 失败远比欺骗光彩。

1. It is cold today. It was not so cold yesterday.

2. It is easy to recognize an error. It is not so easy to correct an error.

3. It is good to read aloud. It is not so good to read in silence.

4. It is easy to start something. It is not so easy to finish it.

5. It is advisable to do preparation before give a speech.
   It's not advisable to know nothing before a speech.

IX. Combine the following sentences using the conjunction "since".

> since 连词，引导让步状语从句，意味"既然"，表示原因。
> Sample: He refused to help us.   There is no reason for us to help him when he's in trouble.
>   Since he refused to help us, there is no reason for us to help him when he's in trouble.
>   既然他拒绝帮助我们，他有麻烦时我们也没理由帮他。

1. We would ask someone else.   You didn't say anything.

2. I shall go home now.   It is late.

3. He'll believe you.   You have got evidence.

4. You have to get up early.   The school bus leaves at 7 a.m.

5. Let's try another method.   This method doesn't work.

Dialogue Samples

Listen and read the samples carefully, and then complete the communicative tasks that follow.

Dialogue 1　College Life in the Library

Billy: Good morning, Sir.

Librarian: Morning. Can I help you?

Billy: Yes, I'd like to know how to use the library. You know, I'm a new student here.

Librarian: All you need to check out books is your student identification card.

Billy: OK. Here's my identification.

Librarian: That's all you need.

Billy: Thank you very much. By the way, how many books am I allowed to check out?

Librarian: You can check out two books at a time. But you can't check out newspapers, magazines and periodicals; they must be read within library.

Billy: How long can I keep the books?

Librarian: For two weeks. After that you must renew the books if you wish to keep them longer.

Billy: I want a book on physics. Could you show me where I can find it?

Librarian: Yes, over there on your left.

Dialogue 2　College Life in the Dormitory

Billy: Alright, we need to have a plan here. First, which bed do you want?

Joey: Well, everybody wants the bottom bunk. Why don't we flip a coin for it?

Billy: Alright. Do you have a coin?

Joey: Yes. Here's a quarter. I flip it, you call it in the air.

Billy: Heads.

Joey: Sorry, it's tails. You lose.

Billy: Oh, well. So, you got the bottom bunk. What about our stereos? It looks like we both brought our stereos. We probably only have room for one.

Joey: Your stereo is better than mine. Do you mind if we use yours?

Billy: No, I don't mind. I just don't know where we can put the speakers in this tiny room.

Joey: We can probably put one on that counter. And we can put the other one on the floor by the bed. Over there.

Billy: Alright. That's a good plan. What about the desks? We have two desks, one by the window and one by the door. Which one do you want?

Joey: Well, the desk by the window is nicer. Don't you think?

Billy: Yes, I agree.

Joey: So, since I got the bottom bunk, why don't you get the desk by the window? That would be fairer.

Billy: Alright.

Communicative Tasks

Work with your partner and take turns to start the conversations.

Task 1

Situation:

A student return his books late, and the librarian charges him late fees.

Tips:

Here are some things the student can say or ask:
I would like to return some books.
I totally forgot they were due.
How much are the late fees?

Here are some things the librarian can say:
These books were due two weeks ago.
You will need to pay late fees on these books.
The fee is 25 cents every day.
It's for each book that is late.

Task 2

Situation:

Two friends are talking about the rule of cleaning the dormitory.

Tips:

Here are some things Student A can say or ask:
I find Steven's dormitory is messy.
My dorm is spotlessly clean, compared with others.
I just swept the floor three days ago.
I bet nobody will care about it.

Here are some things Student B can say or ask:
How can he stand living in such a messy dorm?
Have you even cleaned it since you moved in at the beginning of the semester?
We need to restart the dormitory sanitation inspection system(宿舍卫生检查制度).

Further Development

元音字母的发音（1）

英语的音节可分为开音节和闭音节。开音节分绝对开音节和相对开音节两种。

绝对开音节是指元音字母后面没有辅音字母的音节，在重读绝对开音节中的英语 5 个元音字母即 a, e, i(y), o, u 分别读其字母音。例如：ba-by, se-cret, hi, sky, no, stu-dent, 等等。

相对开音节是指单个元音字母后面加单个辅音字母，再加一个不发音字母 e 构成的重读音节。在重读相对开音节中，元音字母也常读其字母音。例如：name, these, bike, home, ex-cuse 等。相反，以一个或几个辅音字母（r 除外）结尾而中间只有一个元音字母的音节，称为闭音节，例如 map, desk, is 等。

Study the following table to learn about the different pronunciations of each vowel. Then write down more words in the right column to illustrate each pronunciation.

Letter	Sound	Examples	More examples
a	/eɪ/	make, take, lake, face, plane, grape	
	/æ/	active, hand, bank, fan, family	
	/e/	many, any	
	/ɑ:/	pass, last, glass, grass, father	
	/ə/	about, above, cinema	
	/eə/	parent	
	/ɔ/	wash, watch, what, want	
e	/i:/	she, me, he	
	/e/	letter, left, let	
	/ɪ/	pretty, report	
	/ə/	student	

Text B

Two famous Chinese's Early Lives and Their Careers

Mo Yan*

1. The storyteller Mo Yan's unusual life makes his stories **vivid** and lifelike. You do not need to be worried about whether you can understand his minds. When his **mature** writing mixes with unique stories, a spiritual **creation** comes out. Who has **confidence** in refusing this **temptation**? In 2012, Mo was **awarded** the Nobel Prize in Literature*. What's more, he is the first Chinese writer to own this meaningful and priceless **honor**.

2. Mo Yan was born in 1955 in a poor family. His grandpa named him: Guan Moye, meaning being successful in the future. Because of his poor class and ugly face, in his childhood, he was alone all the time. However, his gap of friendship was **crammed** by playing with animals.

3. At that time, Mo's uncle's got a higher salary and he did not worry about livelihood problem. Mo's parents were different. They lived on **ploughs**. Mo's uncle's wife **despised** and looked down on his family. In her heart, he was totally a **freak**.

4. On the contrary, Mo had a great mum. In every speech, Mo Yan always mentioned that his success could not come without his mum's encouragement and education. In his memory, his mum was **humble** to others but strict with him in every detail.

5. His novels are like his **autobiography**. Readers can find his past time and the people who lived in his hometown's personalities.

Ma Yun*

6. Jack Ma or Ma Yun (born October 15, 1964) is a Chinese **entrepreneur**. He is the Executive Chairman of Alibaba Group. He is the first mainland Chinese entrepreneur to appear on the cover of Forbes*.

7. Ma was born in Hangzhou, Zhejiang Province, China. At an young age, Ma rode his bike for 45 minutes each morning to get to a nearby hotel and converse with foreigners to practice and **perfect** his English. Later in his youth, although he failed the entrance exam twice, he attended Hangzhou Teacher's Institute and graduated in 1988 with a bachelor's degree in English. He later became a lecturer in English and International Trade at the Hangzhou Dianzi University.

8. Jack Ma was awarded an honorary doctoral degree by the Hong Kong University of Science and Technology. In 2013, he became Chairman of the Board for the Nature Conservancy's China Program; this was the day after he stepped down from Alibaba as company CEO.

9. Ma reminded everyone that the great fortunes of the world were made by people who saw opportunities that others didn't. As to the future of Alibaba, Ma has said that "our challenge is to help more people to make healthy money, **sustainable** money. That's the **transformation** we are aiming to make."

New Words

vivid[ˈvivid] adj. evoking lifelike images within the mind 生动的；鲜明的
mature[məˈtjʊə] adj. having reached full natural growth or development 成熟的
creation[krɪˈeɪʃən] n. the human act of creating 创造；创作
confidence[ˈkɒnfɪdəns] n. freedom from doubt; belief in yourself and your abilities 自信
temptation[tem(p)ˈteiʃ(ə)n] n. the wish to do or have something which you know you should not do or have 引诱；诱惑物
award[əˈwɔːd] n. a tangible symbol signifying approval or distinction 奖品；奖赏
honor[ˈɒnə(r)] n. a tangible symbol signifying approval or distinction an award for bravery 荣誉
cram[kræm] v. to force a lot of things into a small space, or to do many things in a short period of time 塞满；挤满
plough[plaʊ] n. a farm tool having one or more heavy blades to break the soil and cut a furrow prior to sowing 犁；耕地
despise[diˈspaiz] v. to feel a strong dislike for someone or something because you think they are bad or have no value 鄙视；看不起某人（某事）
freak[friːk] n. a thing, person, animal or event that is extremely unusual or unlikely and not like any other of its type 反常的事；突然的念头；怪异物
humble[ˈhʌmbl] adj. not proud or not believing that you are important 谦逊的；简陋的；（级别或地位）低下的；不大的
autobiography[ɔːtəˌbaiˈɔgrəfi] n. a piece of item or a book about a person's life, written by that person 自传；自传文学
entrepreneur[ˌɔntrəprəˈnəː] n. someone who starts their own business, especially when this involves seeing a new opportunity 企业家；承包人；主办者
executive[igˈzekjutiv] n. someone in a high position, especially in business, who makes decisions and puts them into action 执行者；行政官；经理
perfect[ˈpɜːfɪkt] v. make perfect or complete 完善
sustainable[səˈsteiˌnəbəl] adj. able to continue over a period of time 足可支撑的；养得起的；可以忍受的
transformation[ˌtrænsfəˈmeiʃn] n. a complete change in the appearance or character of something or someone, especially so that they are improved 变化；改造；转变

Useful Expressions

Phrases	Examples
too…to 太……而不能	The box is too heavy for her to carry. 这个箱子太重，她抬不动
due to 因为	Due to your carelessness, it doesn't work now. 因为你的粗心，它现在坏了
look down on 蔑视	We should not look down on manual labor. 我们不应该轻视体力劳动
on the contrary 相反	You think you are clever; on the contrary, I assure that you are very foolish. 你自以为很聪明，相反，我确信你很愚蠢
as to 至于；关于	I have no doubts as to your ability. 关于你的能力我毫不怀疑

 Background Information

1. 莫言（本名管谟业，1955 年 2 月 17 日—），出生于山东省高密市，20 世纪 80 年代中期以乡土作品崛起，充满着"怀乡"以及"怨乡"的复杂情感，被归类为"寻根文学"作家。1987 年《红高粱》获第四届全国中篇小说奖，根据此小说改编并参加编剧的电影《红高粱》获第 38 届柏林电影节金熊奖。2012 年 10 月 11 日莫言以其"用魔幻现实主义将民间故事、历史和现代融为一体"而获得诺贝尔文学奖，是首位获得该奖的中国籍作家。

2. Nobel Prize in Literature: 诺贝尔文学奖。诺贝尔在 1895 年 11 月 27 日写下遗嘱，捐献全部财产 3 122 万余瑞典克朗设立基金，每年把利息作为奖金，授予"一年来对人类做出最大贡献的人"。根据他的遗嘱，瑞典政府于同年建立"诺贝尔基金会"，负责把基金的年利息按五等分授予，文学奖就是其中之一。

3. 马云：1964 年 9 月 10 日出生于浙江省杭州市，阿里巴巴集团、淘宝网、支付宝创始人。2013 年 5 月 10 日，马云卸任阿里巴巴集团 CEO，但兼任阿里巴巴集团董事局主席，是中国 IT 企业的代表性人物。

4. Forbes:《福布斯》，美国福布斯公司商业杂志，每两周发行一次，以金融、工业、投资和营销等主题的原创文章著称。该杂志因其提供的列表和排名而为人熟知，包括最富有美国人列表（福布斯 400）和世界顶级公司排名（福布斯全球 2 000）。

Reading Comprehension

Ⅰ. **Decide whether the following statements are True (T) or False (F).**
(   ) 1. Mo Yan's way seems like having a chat with you. So you need to be nervous or worry about whether you can understand his opinions or minds.
(   ) 2. In 2012, Mo was awarded the Nobel Prize in Literature.
(   ) 3. Mo's grandpa named him: Guan Moye, meaning being healthy in the future.
(   ) 4. Ma Yun attended Hangzhou Teacher's Institute and graduated in 1988 with a bachelor's degree in Business.
(   ) 5. On the day after he stepped down from Alibaba as company CEO In 2013, Ma became Chairman of the Board for the Nature Conservancy's China Program.

Ⅱ. **Choose the best answer to each of the following questions.**
1. You do not need to be nervous or worry about whether you can understand Mo's opinions or minds, because _____ .
   A. his words used in his works are so simple
   B. the stories he told happen to the ordinary common people
   C. his writing style is so vivid
   D. All of the above
2. Mo's birth was a burden to his family because _____ .
   A. his family was too poor to support more kids
   B. he was too naughty
   C. his body was not so strong
   D. he caused too many trouble to his family
3. "Mo's novels are like his autobiography" (first sentence of Para 5) means _____ .
   A. His novels are telling the famous people's story
   B. His novels are bestsellers
   C. His novels are telling the common people's life
   D. His novels are telling his own life
4. Why did Ma Yun ride his bike for 45 minutes each morning to go to a nearby hotel and converse with foreigners? Because he wanted to _____ .
   A. make business with them   B. develop his oral English
   C. train his communication skills   D. make friends with them
5. Ma later became a lecturer in _____ at the Hangzhou Dianzi University.
   A. English Business and trade   B. English International Business
   C. English and International trade   D. International Business English

Grammar

Verbs

动词：表示动作中状态的词叫作动词。

根据在句中的功能，动词可分为四类，分别是：实义动词（Notional Verb）、系动词（Link Verb）、助动词（Auxiliary Verb）、情态动词（Modal Verb）。

1. 实义动词

实义动词根据其后是否带有宾语，可分为两类，分别是：及物动词（Transitive Verb）、不及物动词（Intransitive Verb），缩写形式分别为 vt. 和 vi. 。

说明：同一动词有时可用作及物动词，有时可用作不及物动词。例如：

She can dance and sing. 她能唱歌又能跳舞。（sing 在此用作不及物动词。）

She can sing many English songs. 她能唱好多首英文歌曲。（sing 用作及物动词。）

2. 系动词亦称联系动词（Link Verb）

作为系动词，它本身有词义，但不能单独用作谓语，后边必须跟表语（亦称补语），构成系表结构说明主语的状况、性质、特征等情况。

3. 助动词

协助主要动词构成谓语动词词组的词叫助动词（Auxiliary Verb）。被协助的动词称作主要动词（Main Verb）。助动词自身没有词义，不可单独使用，例如：He doesn't like English. 他不喜欢英语。（doesn't 是助动词，无词义；like 是主要动词，有词义）。

助动词协助主要动词完成以下功用，可以用来：

a. 表示时态。例如：He is singing. 他在唱歌。He has got married. 他已结婚。

b. 表示语态。例如：He was sent to England. 他被派往英国。

c. 构成疑问句。例如：Do you like college life? 你喜欢大学生活吗？Did you study English before you came here? 你来这儿之前学过英语吗？

d. 与否定副词 not 合用，构成否定句。例如：I don't like him. 我不喜欢他。

e. 加强语气。例如：Do come to the party tomorrow evening. 明天晚上一定来参加晚会。He did know that. 他的确知道那件事。

最常用的助动词有：be, have, do, shall, will, should, would.

4. 情态动词

常见的情态动词有：can（could）, may（might）, must, shall（should）, will（would）, dare（dared）, need 等。另外，have to、had better 也当作情态动词使用。情态动词后面必须加动词的原形。

Tense

时态（Tense）是表示行为、动作和状态在各种时间条件下的动词形式。因此，当我们说时态结构的时候，指的是相应时态下的动词形式。英语共有十六种时态，以下列出其中几种。

1. 一般现在时 do/does 或 do not/does not

指经常、反复发生的动作或行为及现在的某种状况。

2. 现在进行时 am/is/are doing 或 am/is/are not doing

表示现阶段或说话时正在进行的动作及行为。

3. 现在完成时 have/has + p. p（过去分词）或 have/has + not + p. p（过去分词）

过去发生或已经完成的动作对现在造成的影响或结果，或从过去已经开始，持续到现在的动作或状态。

4. 一般过去时 did 或 did not

过去某个时间里发生的动作或状态；过去习惯性、经常性的动作、行为。

5. 过去进行时 was/were + doing 或 was/were + not + doing

表示过去某段时间或某一时刻正在发生或进行的行为或动作。

6. 过去完成时 had + p. p（过去分词）或 had + not + p. p（过去分词）

以过去某个时间为标准，在此以前发生的动作或行为，或在过去某动作之前完成的行为，即"过去的过去"。

7. 一般将来时 am/is/are + going to + do 或 will/shall + do am/is/are not going to do 或 will/shall not do

表示将要发生的动作或存在的状态及打算、计划或准备做某事。

8. 过去将来时 was/were + going to + do 或 would/should + do

was/were/not + going to + do 或 would/should + not + do

立足于过去某一时刻，从过去看将来，常用于宾语从句中。

9. 将来完成时 be going to/will/shall + have + p. p（过去分词）

在将来某一时刻之前开始的动作或状态。

10. 现在完成进行时 have/has + been + doing

表示从过去某一时间开始一直延续到现在的动作。这一动作可能刚刚开始，也可能仍在继续，并可能延续到将来。

11. 过去完成进行时 had been doing

就是相对过去的某个时刻来说已经对现在有直接影响并且还在进行的动作。

12. 将来完成进行时 shall/will have been doing

表示某种情况下一直持续到说话人所提及的时间。

Culture

Introduction of American Culture

The United States of America (USA) and the United Kingdom of Great Britain and Northern Ireland (UK) are two major English-speaking countries. Though both speak English, it is a tough job to describe American and British life in general. There are similarities in both, yet differences can be seen not only in terms of the social life within each country, but also in the contrast of the social life between the two countries. In spite of all this, four accounts of both countries are presented here in order to give an overview of American and British social life.

This section will give an overall description of social life in the United States of America in three accounts, the first of which is the diversity of its people. The second is the "nuclear family" which is the mainstream structure of the family both in the USA and the UK. The gap between the poor and the rich is the third, which illustrates the uneven distribution of wealth in American society and one of the main causes of trouble within the USA. The final section looks at violence in the USA. The reporting of violence in the USA is a constant subject in the media all over the world. The accounts listed above are just one perspective to deal with the American social life. The high standard of living in the USA is well-known. There are some other advantages to the American way of life as well.

a. The first account of the USA is the striking diversity of its people. Different people came to the USA from different nations and places at different times. The USA is a country that has more immigrants than any other country in the world.

b. The "nuclear family" is the second account in terms of American social life. In the USA, a family is usually made up of a father, a mother and two children. It is seldom that a family has more than four or five members, or that parents live together with their children who are married.

c. The gap between the poor and the rich is striking. In American society, equality is greatly advocated. However, social equality has never been realized.

d. The fourth is violence. It is reported that in the United States of America a violent case takes place every twenty-seven seconds; and a person is killed ever twenty-four minutes. Indeed, it is a terrible and cruel social phenomenon.

Unit 2

Technology

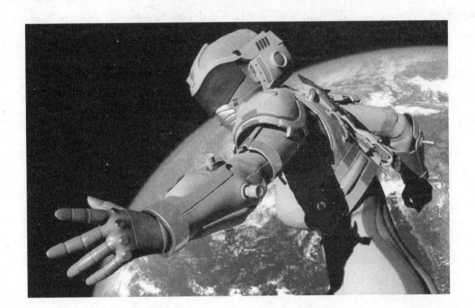

Unit 2 Technology

Warm-up Activities

Ⅰ. Matching

Learn the following words and phrases about different types of design, and match them to the pictures.

1. intelligent robot (   )   2. UAV (unmanned aerial vehicle) (   )
2. charging car (   )   4. VR (virtual reality) headset (   )
5. face identification (   )   6. sharing car (   )

A.    B.

C.    D.

E.    F.

Ⅱ. Reading

Science and technology are the most powerful weapon in humanity's battle against diseases.

人类同疾病较量最有力的武器就是科学技术。

(习近平总书记在北京考察新冠肺炎防控科研攻关工作时的讲话)

weapon　n. 武器
humanity　n. 人类
disease　n. 疾病

Text A

The Book *A Brief History of Time* *

Simon Mitton

1. Stephen Hawking was the most **remarkable** author I had the **privilege** of working with.

2. In 1982, I had **responsibility** for his third **academic** book for the Press, *Superspace And Supergravity*, a **messy** collection on how to **devise** a new theory of **gravity**. While that book was in **production**, I suggested he try something easier: a popular book about the **nature** of the **universe**, **suitable** for the general market. Stephen **mulled** over my suggestion. He already had an **international reputation** as a famous **theoretical physicist** working on **rotating** black holes and theories of gravity. And he had concerns about financial matters: importantly, it was impossible for him to obtain any form of life insurance to protect his family in the event of his death or becoming total dependent on nursing care.

3. At the time, several bestselling physics authors had already published non-technical books on the early Universe and black holes. Stephen decided to write in a more personal way. For a starting point, he took some themes with catchy titles from a course of advanced lectures that he had recently given at Harvard University.

4. In the 1980s, when I pressed him on the market that he **foresaw**, he insisted that it had to be on sale, up front, at all airport bookshops in the UK and the US. Then I read through the typescript. I said: "Steve, it's too technical—every equation will **halve** the market." He eventually removed all except one, $E = mc^2$*. And he decided, fortunately, to place it with a mass market publisher rather than a university press. Bantam published *A Brief History of Time* in March 1988.

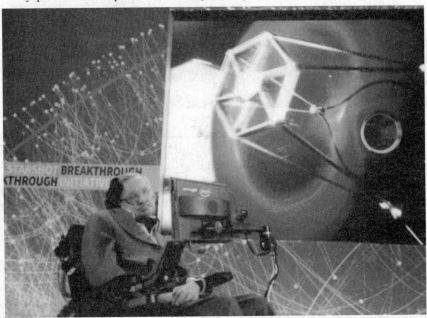

5. Stephen was an inspirational ambassador for the power of science to provide **rational** accounts of the physical laws governing the natural world.

(Dr. Simon Mitton is a historian of science at the University of Cambridge.)

Factfile: Stephen Hawking

6. Born 8 January 1942 in Oxford, England; dead at the age of 76 on 14 March 2018.

7. Earned place at Oxford University to read natural science in 1959, before studying for his Ph. D. at Cambridge.

8. By 1963, was diagnosed with motor neurone disease and given two years to live.

9. Outlined his theory that black holes emit "Hawking radiation" in 1974.

10. Published his book *A Brief History of Time* in 1988, which has sold more than 10 million copies.

11. His life story was the subject of the 2014 film *The Theory of Everything*, starring Eddie Redmayne.

12. The scientist gained **popularity** outside the academic world and appeared in several TV shows including *The Simpsons*, *Red Dwarf* and *The Big Bang Theory*.

New Words

remarkable[rɪˈmɑːkəbl] adj. unusual or special and therefore surprising and worth mentioning 显著的；值得注意的

privilege[ˈprɪvəlɪdʒ] n. an advantage that only one person or group of people has, usually because of their position or because they are rich 特权；优惠；特许

responsibility[rɪsˌpɒnsɪˈbɪlɪtɪ] n. the social force that binds you to the courses of action demanded by that force 责任

academic[ˌækəˈdemɪk] adj. associated with academia or an academy 学术的

messy[ˈmesi] adj. untidy 散乱的；麻烦的

devise[dɪˈvaɪz] v. to invent a plan, system, object, etc., usually cleverly or using imagination 策划；想出

gravity[ˈɡrævəti] n. the force which attracts objects towards one another, especially the force that makes things fall to the ground 重力；引力；地心引力

production[prəˈdʌkʃən] n. the act or process of producing something 产生；排演

nature[ˈneɪtʃə] n. the natural physical world including plants, animals and landscapes etc. 大自然

universe[ˈjuːnɪvɜːs] n. everything that exists anywhere 宇宙

suitable[ˈsuːtəbəl] adj. meant or adapted for an occasion or use 合适的

mull[mʌl] v. reflect deeply on a subject 深思熟虑

international[ˌɪntəˈnæʃənəl] adj. concerning to all or at least two nations 国际（上）的

reputation[repjuˈteɪʃn] n. the opinion that people in general have about someone or something, or how much respect or admiration someone or something receives 名誉；声望；信誉

theoretical[ˌθiːəˈretɪkəl] adj. concerned primarily with theories or hypotheses rather than practical considerations 理论的；假设的

physicist[ˈfɪzɪsɪst] n. a scientist trained in physics 物理学家

rotate[rəʊˈteɪt] v. turn on or around an axis or a center （使）旋转

catchy[ˈkætʃi] adj. pleasing and easy to remember 易记住的；吸引人的

foresee[fɔːˈsiː] v. (foresaw, foreseen) to know about something before it happens 预见；预知

halve[hɑːv] v. to reduce something by half or divide something into two equal pieces 分成两半，平分；减少到一半

rational[ˈræʃnəl] adj. showing clear thought or reason 合理的；理性的；能推理的

popularity[ˌpɒpjʊˈlærɪtɪ] n. the quality of being widely admired or accepted or sought after 受大众欢迎；流行

Useful Expressions

Phrases	Examples
have responsibility for 对……负责	One was thrown into this world from the moment, has responsibility for all his or her actions. 人从被投进这个世界的那一刻起，就要对自己的一切行为负责
be suitable for 适合	I have small doubt whether he is suitable for the job. 他是否适合这份工作我有点怀疑
mull over 仔细考虑	I sat there and tried to mull things over in my mind. 我坐在那儿，尽量把事情仔细考虑一下
have a reputation as 有……的称呼	Toxic spiders have a reputation as "deadly killers". 毒蜘蛛拥有"致命杀手"的称号
have concerns about. 担心	The U. S. has been a close ally of Israel, both countries have concerns about Iran's nuclear program. 美国一直是以色列的亲密盟友，两个国家都担心伊朗有核项目

 Background Information

1. *A Brief History of Time*: 《时间简史》，1988 年出版，作者斯蒂芬·霍金。作者尽可能地将当时高深的前沿物理知识用通俗的语言详尽地讲述给读者，将读者引进物理的世界。该书主要讲述了宇宙的起源、黑洞、狭义相对论的时空观等，同时作者也对物理学前沿的大一统理论以及 M 理论做出了讲解。

2. $E = mc^2$，这是爱因斯坦一生众多理论中最经典的公式。20 世纪爱因斯坦推导出了狭义相对论，他指出，物质的质量和它的能量成正比，可用以下公式表示：$E = mc^2$. 公式中 E 为能量；m 为质量；光速 $c = 299\ 792.50 \pm 0.10$ km/s（一般取 300 000 km/s）. 这个公式说明物质可以转变为辐射能，辐射能也可以转变为物质。这一现象并不意味着物质会被消灭，而是物质的静质量转变成另外一种运动形式。由于当时科学的局限，这条定律只在微观世界得到验证，后来又在核试验中得到验证。所以 20 世纪以后，这一定律已经发展成为质量守恒定律和能量守恒定律，合称质能守恒定律。

Reading Comprehension

Ⅰ. **Decide whether the following statements are True (T) or False (F).**

(　　) 1. It wasn't possible for him to obtain any form of life insurance to protect his family in the event of his death or becoming total dependent on nursing care.

(　　) 2. Stephen mulled over my suggestion of publishing a popular book partly because of financial matters.

(　　) 3. Stephen Hawking was the first scientist to publish non-technical books on the early Universe and black holes.

(　　) 4. For a starting point, Stephen took some themes from a course of advanced lectures that he had recently given at Cambridge University.

(　　) 5. In *A Brief History of Time*, Stephen Hawking removed all equations.

(　　) 6. Cambridge University Press published *A Brief History of Time* in March 1988.

(　　) 7. By 1963, Stephen Hawking was diagnosed with motor neurone disease and given two years to live.

Ⅱ. **Complete the answers to the following questions.**

1. When was Stephen Hawking born and dead?(Para. 6)
   He was born on _____ and dead on _____.

2. In which university did he have learning experience? (Para. 7)
   He read natural science in 1959 at _____ before studying for his Ph. D. at _____.

3. What disease was he diagnosed with? (Para. 8)
   He was diagnosed with _____.

4. Which film was based on his life story? (Para. 11)
   His life story was the subject of the 2014 film _____, starring Eddie Redmayne.

5. Outside the academic world, in which area did the scientist gain his popularity?(Para. 12)
   The scientist gained popularity outside the academic world and appeared in _____.

Unit 2 Technology

 Vocabulary and Structure

Words and Phrases to Drill

remarkable	reputation	catchy	devise	messy
privilege	gravity	foresee	rational	halve
mull over	have a reputation	be suitable for	have responsibility	have concerns about

I. Choose the appropriate explanation from Column B for each of the words in Column A.

A	B
_____ 1. remarkable	a. (especially of a tune or song) pleasing and easy to remember
_____ 2. privilege	b. the force which attracts objects towards one another, especially the force that makes things fall to the ground
_____ 3. messy	c. to reduce something by half or divide something into two equal pieces
_____ 4. devise	d. unusual or special and therefore surprising and worth mentioning
_____ 5. gravity	e. to invent a plan, system, object, etc., usually cleverly or using imagination
_____ 6. reputation	f. to know about something before it happens
_____ 7. catchy	g. an advantage that only one person or group of people has, usually because of their position or because they are rich
_____ 8. foresee	h. showing clear thought or reason
_____ 9. halve	i. untidy
_____ 10. rational	j. the opinion that people in general have about someone or something, or how much respect or admiration someone or something receives, based on past behavior or character

II. Fill in the blanks with the correct forms of the words in Column A of the above table. Change the form if necessary.

1. We need a new slogan. The old one's not _____ enough.
2. We will _____ a way of escaping from this prison.
3. We are very anxious to keep up the _____ of the firm.
4. Working underneath the car is always a _____ job.
5. She has made _____ headway in her writing skills.
6. An apple falls down because of _____.
7. No one can _____ what will happen in the future.
8. Of course, no country has the _____ of fishing in our coastal water.
9. Let's _____ the project between our two teams.
10. It was a _____ plan and bound to succeed.

Ⅲ. **Compare each pair of words and choose the correct one to fill in each blank.**

1. remarkable   remark
   a. These cars are _____ for the quietness of their engines.
   b. He got angry with me because of my _____ .
2. mess   messy
   a. Don't _____ up my homework.
   b. She found herself in a _____ spot.
3. catch   catchy
   a. The poems were so _____ that they became popular as soon as they were published.
   b. She failed to _____ the early bus.
4. half   halve
   a. I'll _____ expenses with you.
   b. _____ of six is three.
5. ration   rational
   a. I have my own _____ of sugar, and I must not deprive you of yours.
   b. The reasoning seems _____ .

Ⅳ. **Add the prefix "un-" to the following words in brackets. Then complete the sentences with the words formed.**

> **Tips:** 前缀 un-加在形容词、动词前面，表否定意义，但不改变词性，如 un＋happy→unhappy（不开心的），un＋lock→unlock（未开锁）。

Sample: It's considered <u>unlucky</u> to walk under a ladder. (luck)
1. This bookcase is too _____ to hold so many books. (stable)
2. He seemed _____ whether to go or stay. (decide)
3. His eyes were hard and _____ . (smile)
4. Food in that restaurant is _____ priced. (reason)
5. What is said cannot be easily _____ . (say)

Ⅴ. **Choose the best phrase to complete each sentence.**

1. Bremen have a reputation _____ a team who charge forward in numbers and score plenty of goals.
   A. in   B. to   C. as   D. for
2. Then which method is suitable _____ our corporation?
   A. to   B. for   C. of   D. as
3. You even can mull _____ these questions for a day!
   A. over   B. upon   C. about   D. above
4. If women have concerns _____ their weight, they should be helped with a weight-loss plan.
   A. over   B. upon   C. about   D. above
5. I hope my future husband is: open-minded, humorous, mature; have responsibility _____

family and career; he must care for his wife.

    A. in   B. to   C. as   D. for

Ⅵ. **Complete the following sentences by translating the Chinese given in brackets into English.**

1. I'd read a few lines to myself, _____(揣摩将它们译为英语).
2. By this time next year, who will _____(有解决这一问题的责任)?
3. None of these people _____(关注交通法规).
4. I already _____(有个坏名声) and don't want to make it worse.
5. Past experiences have shown that this kind of strict management method may not _____ _____(适合中国人的温和性格).

Ⅶ. **Translate the following sentences into Chinese.**

1. He already had an international reputation as a famous theoretical physicist working on rotating black holes and theories of gravity. (Para. 2)

_____

2. …it was impossible for him to obtain any form of life insurance to protect his family in the event of his death or becoming total dependent on nursing care. (Para. 2)

_____

3. …he took some themes with catchy titles from a course of advanced lectures that he had recently given at Harvard University. (Para. 3)

_____

4. In the 1980s, when I pressed him on the market that he foresaw, he insisted that it had to be on sale, up front, at all airport bookshops in the UK and the US. (Para. 4)

_____

Ⅷ. **Combine sentence beginnings in Column A with the endings in Column B to form complete sentences.**

> 句意的连贯：要写出清晰流畅的英文语句，需要把句中各部分巧妙地连接在一起，这样才可使语句自然，并能层层展开主题，完整地表达中心含义。过渡词（Transitional Words）是连接这些部分的纽带，代词、连词、上下文的近义词等可作过渡词。
>
> Sample: Though he is young + he is good at dealing the interpersonal relationship.

Column A

1. Of the two paintings, the former may be more important…

2. His life changed greatly…

3. Today, we'll discuss…

Column B

A. …just because he lost his job.

B. …what is left behind in the last meeting.

C. …than the latter in terms of its artistic value.

IX. Rewrite the following sentences using the structure "While + v. ing".

> While, 引导时间状语从句，意为"当"。当主句主语和从句主语一致时，可省略主语和谓语；While 后的动作和主句主语是主动的逻辑关系时，while 后加现在分词 doing.
>
> Sample: Sam had seen his ex-wife while taking his savings to the post office.
>
> 此句中，Sam 和 take 之间是主动的逻辑关系，所以用现在分词 taking.

1. She lost her purse while she was walking in the street.

2. Kevin met an old friend while he was running.

3. She hurt her ankle while she was laying tennis.

4. I like to sing while I'm taking a bath.

5. The children read a very interesting story while they were waiting at the doctor's.

Dialogue Samples

Listen and read the samples carefully, and then complete the communicative tasks that follow.

Dialogue 1　Asking the way to the ATM

Parker: Peter, where's the closest ATM?
Peter: It's not far. Do you see that Yellow building over there?
Parker: The big one or the little one?
Peter: The big one.
Parker: Yes.
Peter: It's right next to it, on the right.
Parker: Do you know if there's a convenience store around here?
Peter: I don't think there's one around here. The closest one is on 3rd street, but that's probably closed now.
Parker: I really need to get some things before I leave.
Peter: Well, you could go down to 22nd street. There are lot of stores down there that are open 24 hours a day.
Parker: Can I take the subway to get there?
Peter: Yes, but that'll probably take about half an hour. You should just take a cab.
Parker: Won't that be expensive?
Peter: No, from here I think it's only about 5 dollars.

Dialogue 2　Asking the way to the bookstore

Aaron: Excuse me, does this bus go to the new bookstore?
Mark: No, you'll have to get off at the bank, and take No. 50.
Aaron: Thank you. How much is the fare to that stop?
Mark: One dollar.
Aaron: How many stops are there?
Mark: Two stops after this one.
Aaron: Could you please tell me when we get there?
Mark: Sure.
Aaron: By the way, do I need a transfer again after No. 50?
Mark: No, No. 50 will take you right there.

Communicative Tasks

Work with your partner and take turns to start the conversations.

Task 1

Situation:

Ask the way to the zoo.

Tips:

Here are some things the person asking the way can say or ask:
Is this where I catch the bus for the zoo?
I don't want to walk that long.
I don't care that money.

Here are some things the person showing the way can say:
You can take the No. 36 bus from here, but then you have to walk about 30 minutes.
If you go to the bus stop in the next block, you can take bus 301 which will let you right off in front of the zoo. But the ticket costs 1 RMB more.

Task 2

Situation:

The best way downtown.

Tips:

Here are some things the person asking the way can say or ask:
What's the best way downtown?
Is that expensive?
I am in no particularly hurry.
That's not so bad.

Here are some things the person showing the way can say:
It depends.
If you are in a hurry, you should take a taxi.
It will cost you more than one hundred RMB.
Take a bus then. It will only cost you 5 dollars.

Further Development

元音字母的发音（2）

Study the following table to learn about the different pronunciations of each vowel. Then write down more words in the right column to illustrate each pronunciation.

Letter	Sound	Examples	More examples
i	[ai]	high, library, ice, size, night	
	[i]	sit, pick, chicken, piano, city	
o	[ɔ]	hot, pot, lot, office	
	[əu]	cold, note, okay, old, home	
	[ʌ]	love, other, mother, honey, company	
	[u:]	do, who, whose	
	[ə]	today, tomorrow, together	
u	[ju:]	university, cute, use, excuse	
	[u]	put	
	[ʌ]	but, duck, bus, cut, umbrella	

Practice the following tongue twisters.

1. Can you can a can as a canner can can a can?
你能够像罐头工人一样罐装罐头吗？

2. All I want is a proper cup of coffee made in a proper copper coffee pot.
我只想要一杯用真正铜制的咖啡壶煮的正宗咖啡。

3. A big black bug bit a big black bear.
大黑虫咬大黑熊。

4. Fresh fried fish, fish fresh fried, fried fish fresh, fish fried fresh.
鲜炸鱼，鱼鲜炸，炸鱼鲜，鱼炸鲜。

5. If you notice this notice, you will notice that the notice is not worth noticing.
你如果看完这则通知，就知道这则通知根本不值得一看。

Text B

Virtual Reality Making It Possible to Travel in Time

1. When Daniel and Ilana tied the knot in Guatemala City earlier this year, the couple wanted to create a modern-day time **capsule** that would allow them to **relive** the day.

2. "It became clear we needed something that could truly **capture** everything about the day," said Daniel, who **declined** to share the couple's last name.

3. In fact, the **newlyweds** have re-experienced their wedding several times by watching it back in **virtual** reality*. The couple hired YouVisit to capture 360-degree **footage** and turn it into something that virtually **transports** them back to that day.

4. "My wife, who has watched the video many times already, cries every time," Daniel said. "No matter how much we see it, there's always something we hadn't noticed before. These are things that would have gone unnoticed because we were so wrapped up in the moment, but it feels like a whole new day every time we step into the virtual environment."

5. A small team from the **professional** VR filming service attended the wedding and set up cameras at specific spots throughout the grounds. YouVisit then **compiled** the footage and **released** it online, so the couple could share it with anyone with access to a desktop computer, mobile phone or VR headset.

6. Technology has always played a key role in their relationship. When Daniel spotted Ilana on Tinder(a social website) nearly two years ago—and she didn't return his "swipe right". He **ultimately** got her phone number and asked her out.

7. "The ability to capture personal moments in VR is a trend that has been growing **exponentially**, particularly as 360 cameras are becoming mainstream," You Visit cofounder Abi Mandelbaum told CNN* Money. "As a fully **immersive** medium, VR has the ability to completely shift how we tell stories, both on a company level through business marketing but also a personal and social level."

8. YouVisit has produced more than 1 000 **interactive** VR experiences. While filming a custom VR experience is costly, the company offers free access to its platform called Experience Builder, which allows users to create their own VR experiences by **uploading** 360-degree videos and photos.

9. The overall process for developing Daniel and Ilana's wedding VR experience, from **conceptualizing** to final editing, took about 2 to 3 months. The couple has since shown it to friends and family members who weren't able to make it to the **destination** wedding. The pair also hopes to show it to their children one day. "The takeaway for us was not so much to be **leveraging** innovative technology, but to be able to capture this magical day in Guatemala and to go back and visit whenever we want."

New Words

capsule[ˈkæpsjuːl] n. a small container with medicine inside which you swallow 太空舱；胶囊
relive[riːˈliv] v. to remember clearly an experience that happened in the past 再体验
capture[ˈkæptʃə] v. capture as if by hunting, snaring, or trapping 拍摄
decline[diˈklain] n. to gradually become less, worse, or lower 衰微；跌落；下降
newlyweds[nˈjuːliˌwedz] n. the new couples of marriage 新婚夫妇
virtual[ˈvɜːtʃuəl] adj. almost a particular thing or quality 虚拟的
footage[ˈfʊtidʒ] n. film that has been shot 以尺计算长度；尺数；影片的镜头
transport[trænsˈpɔːt] v. move something or somebody around; usually over long distances 传输
professional[prəˈfeʃənl] adj. related to work that needs special training or education 专业的
compile[kəmˈpail] v. to collect information from different places and arrange it in a book 编辑
release[rɪˈliːs] v. grant freedom to; free from confinement 公开；释放
ultimately[ˈʌltɪmɪtlɪ] adv. as the end result of a succession or process 最后地
exponentially[ˌekspəˈnenʃəli] adv. in an exponential manner 成倍地；指数地；幂地
immersive[ɪˈmɜːsɪv] adj. seemingly to be in certain situation oneself 使人身临其境的
interactive[ˌɪntərˈæktɪv] adj. capable of acting on or influencing each other 互相作用的
upload[ʌpˈləʊd] v. transfer a file or program to a central computer from a smaller computer or a computer at a remote location 上传（或上载）数据
conceptualize[kənˈseptjʊəlaɪz] v. have the idea for 概念化
destination[destɪˈneɪʃən] n. written directions for finding some location; written on letters or packages that are to be delivered to that location 目的地
leverage[ˈliːvərɪdʒ] n. the mechanical advantage gained by being in a position 优势

Useful Expressions

Expressions	Examples
tie the knot 喜结连理	Fred and Betty finally decided to tie the knot. 福瑞德和贝蒂终于决定要缔结连理了
wrap up 包起来	Diana is wrapping up the family presents. 黛安娜正在将家人的礼物包起来
with access to 联系	I am currently out of the office with limited access to the e-mail. 由于收到邮件受限，我最近和办公室断绝联系了
set up 建立	Leah has set up her second art studio since her graduation. 自从毕业后，丽已经创建了她第二家艺术工作室了
track down 追寻	She had spent years trying to track down her parents. 她已经花了好多年时间试图追寻父母的下落

 Background Information

1. 虚拟现实技术是仿真技术的一个重要方向，是仿真技术与计算机图形学、人机接口技术、多媒体技术、传感技术、网络技术等多种技术的集合，是一门富有挑战性的交叉技术前沿学科和研究领域。虚拟现实技术（Virtual Reality）主要包括模拟环境、感知、自然技能和传感设备等方面。

2. CNN 是美国有线电视新闻网（Cable News Network）的英文缩写，由特纳广播公司（TBS）的特德·特纳于1980年6月创办，通过卫星向有线电视网和卫星电视用户提供全天候的新闻节目，总部设在美国佐治亚州的亚特兰大。

Reading Comprehension

Ⅰ. **Decide whether the following statements are True (T) or False (F).**

(   ) 1. When Daniel and Ilana got married in Guatemala City earlier this year, the couple wanted to create a modern-day time capsule that would allow them to relive the day.

(   ) 2. Daniel agreed to public the couple's last name.

(   ) 3. In fact, the newlyweds have re-experienced their wedding several times by visiting back in Guatemala City.

(   ) 4. The couple had watched the video many times already, and almost every time they found there's something they hadn't noticed before.

(   ) 5. These are things that would have gone unnoticed because the people on spot were so wrapped up in the moment.

Ⅱ. **Choose the best answer to each of the following questions.**

1. When Daniel and Ilana tied the knot in Guatemala City earlier this year, the couple wanted to create a modern-day time capsule that would allow them to _____ .
   A. reexperience the wedding day
   B. lead a life of that day
   C. make a life on that day
   D. report the wedding day

2. The couple hired YouVisit to capture _____ .
   A. the day in picture
   B. the experience of the day with the technology of VR
   C. the important time with the VR headset
   D. the golden time with one 360-degree footage camera

3. YouVisit then compiled the footage and released it online, so the couple could share it with anyone by using _____ .
   A. a desktop computer
   B. mobile phone
   C. VR headset
   D. all of the above

4. Which one of the following does NOT play a role in the development of their relationship?
   A. internet
   B. modern-day time technology
   C. reality meeting
   D. blind-dating

5. The capturing in virtual reality can show the wedding to the _____ to enjoy. Which one is NOT the answer?
   A. the strangers who are not interested in the incident
   B. the people on the spot of the wedding to relive the experience
   C. themselves and their children
   D. friends and family members who weren't able to take part in the wedding

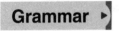

Passive Voice

一、语态概述

英语的语态是通过动词形式的变化表现出来的。英语中有两种语态：主动语态和被动语态。

主动语态表示主语是动作的执行者。

例如：Many people speak Chinese. (谓语 speak 的动作是由主语 many people 来执行的。)

被动语态表示主语是动作的承受者，即行为动作的对象。

例如：Chinese is spoken by many people. (主语 English 是动词 speak 的承受者。)

二、被动语态的构成

被动语态由"助动词 be + 及物动词的过去分词"构成。人称、数和时态的变化是通过 be 的变化表现出来的。

三、被动语态的用法

(1) 不知道或没有必要说明动作的执行者是谁。

例如：Some new computers were stolen last night. 一些新电脑在昨晚被盗了。(不知道电脑是谁偷的)

This bridge was founded in 1981. 这座桥竣工于 1981 年。

(2) 强调动作的承受者，而不强调动作的执行者。

例如：The glass was broken by Mike. 玻璃杯是迈克打破的。

四、主动语态变被动语态的方法

(1) 把主动语态的宾语变为被动语态的主语。

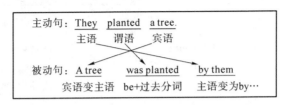

(2) 把谓语变成被动结构（be + 过去分词）。

根据被动语态句子里主语的人称和数，以及原来主动语态句子中动词的时态来决定 be 的形式。

(3) 把主动语态中的主语放在介词 by 之后作宾语，将主格改为宾格。例如：

All the people laughed at him.　　The bikes are made by them in the factory.

He cut down a tree.　　A tree was cut down by him.

五、含有情态动词的被动语态

含有情态动词的主动句变成被动句时,由"情态动词 + be + 过去分词"构成,原来带 to 的情态动词变成被动语态后"to"仍要保留。

被动语态由"助动词 be + 及物动词的过去分词"构成。被动语态的时态变化只改变 be 的形式,过去分词部分不变。疑问式和否定式的变化也如此。

(1) 被动语态的时态较常见的有八种,现以动词 clean 为例列表说明。

形态	现在	过去	将来
一般	am / is / are cleaned	was / were cleaned	will / Shall be cleaned
进行	am / is / are being cleaned	was / were being cleaned	
完成	have / has been cleaned	had been cleaned	will / shall have been cleaned

(2) 被动语态的句式变化。

以一般现在时和动词 invite 为例,列表说明被动语态的句式变化。

肯定句	否定句		
I am invited. He/She/It is invited. We/You/They are invited	I am not invited. He/She/It is not invited. We/You/They are not invited		
疑问句	简略回答		
	肯定回答	否定回答	
Am I invited? Is {he/she/it} invited?	Yes, you are Yes, {he/she/it} is.	No, you aren't. No, {he/she/it} isn't.	
Are you invited? Are {we/they} invited	Yes, {I am. / we are.} Yes, {we/you / they} are.	No, {I am not. / we aren't.} No, {we/you / they} aren't.	

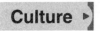

Uncle Sam

Uncle Sam is a nickname and popular symbol of the United States of America, which denotes a tall cartoon figure with white hair and chin whiskers, wearing a tall hat, a swallow-tailed coat with stars, a vest and striped trousers. His appearance is derived from two earlier symbolic figures in American folklore-Brother Jonathan and Yankee Doodle.

The origin of the term Uncle Sam, though disputed, is usually associated with a businessman from Troy, New York, Samuel Wilson, known affectionately as "Uncle Sam" Wilson. The barrels of beef that he supplied the army during the War of 1812 were stamped "U. S. " to indicate government property. That identification is said to have led to the widespread use of the nickname Uncle Sam for the United States, and a resolution passed by Congress in 1961 recognized Wilson as the namesake of the national symbol.

Uncle Sam and his predecessor Brother Jonathan were used interchangeably to represent the United States by American cartoonists from the early 1830s to 1861. Cartoonists such as Sir John Tenniel and John Leech of the British humor magazine Punch helped evolve the modern figure by drawing both Brother Jonathan and Uncle Sam as lean, whiskered gentlemen wearing top hats and striped pants. Probably the first U. S. political cartoonist to crystallize the figure of Uncle Sam was Thomas Nast, beginning in the early 1870s. By 1900, through the efforts of Nast, Joseph Keppler, and others, Uncle Sam was firmly entrenched as the symbol for the U. S. One of the most familiar treatments in the 20th century was shown in James Montgomery Flagg's World War I recruiting poster, also used in World War II, for which the caption read, "I Want You."

Unit 3

Calligraphy and Painting

Warm-up Activities

I. Matching

Learn the following words and phrases about different Chinese cultures, and match them to the pictures.

1. Beijing embroidery (   )   2. paper cuts (   )   3. porcelain (   )
4. shadow puppetry (   )   5. blown candy (   )   6. clay sculpture art (   )

A.

B.

C.

D.

E.

F.

II. Reading

cultural confidence 文化自信
rejuvenate   v. 复兴
prosperous   adj. 繁荣的

Chinese nation will not be able to rejuvenate itself without strong cultural confidence and a rich and prosperous culture.

没有高度的文化自信，没有文化的繁荣兴盛，就没有中华民族伟大复兴。

Unit 3 Calligraphy and Painting

Text A

Calligraphy

1. Calligraphy is something every special for Chinese. It is not only an important part of traditional Chinese culture but also a way of life for people of all stripes. Chinese characters **evolved** from pictures and signs, and the Chinese art of calligraphy developed naturally from this special writing system. By using the brush to write Chinese characters, calligraphers can express their **aesthetic** ideas, thoughts and feelings, personalities and temperatures in a point or line, so Chinese calligraphy is also called the art of lines.

2. Like oil painting and **sculpture** in the West, calligraphy is as much an artistic form as a spiritual **anchor** for many Chinese throughout history. Rarely do any things influence culture in such a **profound** way. Calligraphy has played a **critical** role in Chinese culture and history for thousands of years.

3. Calligraphy was well-respected, or even **worshiped** in history. It was a steppingstone to become the **elite** class and a prerequisite for admiration among **peers**. In essence, calligraphy is also the cultural **identity** and the collection of aesthetic philosophy.

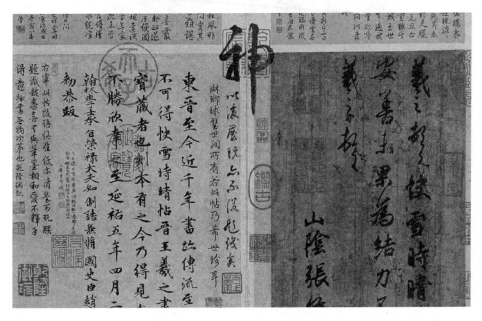

4. During Jin Dynasty (AD 265—420), calligraphy became an expression of **superiority** among **noble** families. The competitions were so intense that young children were ordered to receive extensive training in calligraphy. Wang Xizhi* was among those raised in noble families. Along with his son, Wang Xianzhi, the Wangs were considered the greatest calligraphers in Chinese history whose achievements were **insuperable** for late generations. Therefore, Jin Dynasty is the peak of calligraphic works in Chinese history.

5. In the past, children were trained at an early age to practice writing. People were often judged by their handwriting. It was believed that the force used in writing **betrayed**(表露) one's disposition (性情) and that the written characters revealed the calligrapher's understanding of life and arts. Practicing calligraphy could help a person to achieve relaxation and **repel** outside disturbances. So it was also regarded as a way to keep mind and body fit and healthy. Even in daily lives, people with calligraphic skills were highly respected and in high demand for letters, contracts, Buddhist scriptures, as well as **decorations** for weddings and **funerals**.

6. Chinese calligraphy is an Oriental art. Like chopsticks, calligraphy was once entirely Chinese, but as Chinese culture spread to Korea, Japan and Singapore, calligraphy became a **unique** feature of the Oriental art.

7. Calligraphy is even widely accepted by the West; as once Picasso* said, "Had I been born Chinese, I would have been a calligrapher, not a painter." Many calligraphic **elements** are being **adopted** by modern western art.

Unit 3 Calligraphy and Painting

 New Words

evolve[iˈvɒlv] v. to develop gradually, especially from a simple to a more complicated form 使进化；使发展

aesthetic[iːsˈθetɪk] adj. of or relating to art or beauty 美学的；审美的

sculpture[ˈskʌlptʃə] n. a piece of art that is made by carving or molding clay stone, metal, ect. 雕刻；雕塑

anchor[ˈæŋkə] n. a heavy device that is attached to a boat or ship by a rope or chain and that is thrown into the water to hold the boat or ship in place 锚；锚状物

profound[prəˈfaʊnd] adj. having or showing great knowledge or understanding 深度的；深远的；知识渊博的

critical[ˈkrɪtɪk(ə) l] adj. marked by a tendency to find and call attention to errors and flaws 批评的；挑剔的

worship[ˈwɔːʃɪp] v. love unquestioningly and uncritically or to excess; venerate as an idol 崇拜

peer[pɪə] n. a person who is of equal standing with another in a group 同等人；同龄人

elite[eɪˈliːt]] adj. selected as the best 精英的；精华的

identity[aɪˈdentɪtɪ] n. the distinct personality of an individual regarded as a persisting entity 身份；同一性

superiority[suːˌpɪərɪˈɒrɪtɪ; sjuː-] n. the quality of being superior 优越，优势；优越性

noble[ˈnəʊb(ə) l] adj. of or belonging to or constituting the hereditary aristocracy especially as derived from feudal times 高尚的；贵族的

insuperable[ɪnˈsuːpərəbl] adj. impossible to surmount 难以超越的；难以克服的

betray[bɪˈtreɪ] v. reveal unintentionally 露出……迹象

repel[rɪˈpel] v. cause to move back by force or influence 击退；抵制

decoration[dekəˈreɪʃ(ə) n] n. something used to beautify 装饰；装潢，装饰品

funeral[ˈfjuːn(ə) r(ə) l] n. a ceremony at which a dead person is buried or cremated 葬礼

unique[juːˈniːk] adj. radically distinctive and without equal 独特的；稀罕的

element[ˈelɪm(ə) nt] n. an abstract part of something 元素；要素

adopt[əˈdɒpt] v. choose and follow; as of theories, ideas, policies, strategies or plans 采取；接受

Useful Expressions

Phrases	Examples
all stripes 所有的类型	These days, banker-bashing is a popular sport for politicians of all stripes. 如今，攻击银行家已成为各类政治家的一项时尚运动
at an early age 在早年	They learned to take public transportation at an early age. 他们在早期学会乘坐公共交通工具
in essence 本质上；其实	In essence, learning cultures is important in learning foreign languages. 其实，学习文化在学习外语中很重要
judge by 评判	We should be judged by the quality of our products. 我们的价值应该以我们产品的质量来衡量
in demand 非常需要；受欢迎	Being in demand can be rather wearing. 受欢迎也可能是件累人的事

Background Information

1. Wang Xizhi: 王羲之。王羲之（公元303—361），东晋最杰出的书法家。其兼善隶、草、楷、行各体，精研体势，心摹手追，广采众长，备精诸体，冶于一炉，摆脱了汉魏笔风，自成一家，影响深远。其书法作品风格平和自然，笔势委婉含蓄，遒美健秀。李志敏评价："王羲之的书法既表现以老庄哲学为基础的简淡玄远，又表现以儒家的中庸之道为基础的冲和。"王羲之的代表作《兰亭序》被誉为"天下第一行书"。在书法史上，他与其子王献之合称为"二王"。

2. Picasso: 巴勃罗·毕加索（1881年10月25日—1973年4月8日），西班牙画家、雕塑家。毕加索是现代艺术的创始人，是西方现代派绘画的主要代表。毕加索是当代西方最有创造性和影响最深远的艺术家，是20世纪最伟大的艺术天才。毕加索的艺术生涯几乎贯穿其一生，作品风格丰富多样，后人用"毕加索永远是年轻的"的说法形容毕加索多变的艺术形式。

Unit 3　Calligraphy and Painting

 Reading Comprehension

I. Decide whether the following statements are True (T) or False (F).

(　　) 1. Chinese calligraphy is also called the art of pictures.
(　　) 2. Calligraphy became an expression of superiority among noble families during Tang Dynasty.
(　　) 3. Practicing calligraphy could help a person to achieve relaxation and repel outside disturbances.
(　　) 4. Jin Dynasty is the peak of calligraphic works in Chinese history.
(　　) 5. In daily lives, calligraphic skills are not so important, people are indifferent to it.
(　　) 6. Calligraphy is a form of art that is unique to China.
(　　) 7. Many calligraphic elements are being adopted by modern western art.

II. Complete the answers to the following questions.

1. Where did Chinese character evolve from? (Para. 1)
   Chinese characters evolved from _____ and _____.
2. What kind of family was Wang Xizhi raised? (Para. 4)
   Wang Xizhi was among those raised in _____.
3. When is the pinnacle of calligraphic works in Chinese history? (Para. 4)
   _____ is the peak of calligraphic works in Chinese history.
4. What were children trained to do in the past at an early age? (Para. 5)
   In the past, children were trained at an early age to _____.

Vocabulary and Structure

Words and Phrases to Drill

evolve	element	profound	betray	repel
decoration	adopt	unique	funeral	elite
judge by	at an early age	in demand	all stripes	in essence

I. Choose the appropriate explanation from Column B for each of the words in Column A.

A	B
_____ 1. evolve	a. something used to beautify
_____ 2. repel	b. choose and follow; as of theories, ideas, policies, strategies or plans
_____ 3. decoration	c. reveal unintentionally
_____ 4. element	d. having or showing great knowledge or understanding
_____ 5. adopt	e. to develop gradually
_____ 6. betray	f. radically distinctive and without equal
_____ 7. unique	g. a ceremony at which a dead person is buried or cremated
_____ 8. profound	h. cause to move back by force or influence
_____ 9. funeral	i. selected as the best
_____ 10. elite	j. an abstract part of something

II. Fill in the blanks with the correct forms of the words in Column A of the above table.

1. This hotel is _____; it's for VIPs only.
2. This book contains a very _____ discussion of universe.
3. Even today, the human race continues to _____.
4. There are many pretty _____ on the Christmas gift.
5. My girl friend _____ me. She fell in love with someone else.
6. The Great Wall is _____ in China.
7. Like poles _____, unlike poles attract.
8. That country is free to _____ policies to bolster its economy.
9. Laughing and joking are improper at a _____.
10. Water contains the _____ of hydrogen and oxygen.

III. Compare each pair of words and choose the correct one to fill in each blank. Change the form if necessary.

1. evolve   evolution
    a. Birds are widely believed to have _____ from dinosaurs.
    b. That is the _____ of basketball.
2. critical   critic
    a. We had better call in a specialist at this _____ moment.
    b. As a strict food _____, I think the pizza is just so so.

3. superior   superiority
   a. A few years ago it was virtually impossible to find _____ quality coffee in local shops.
   b. She was prepossessed with the notion of her own _____ .
4. adopt   adoption
   a. _____ is a good option because it helps out many kids.
   b. She _____ her son when he was very young.

IV. **Add the prefix "in-/il-/ir-/im" to the following words in brackets. Then complete the sentences with the words formed.**

> **Tips:** 前缀 in-和 un-加在形容词前面，表否定意义，但不改变词性，如 un + forgettable→unforgettable（难忘的）、in + correct→incorrect（不正确的）、un + true→untrue（不真实的）等。但应注意：以字母 m、l 和 r 开头的形容词在变成否定意思时，应分别加前缀 im-、il-和 ir-，如 im + possible→impossible（不可能的）、il + legal→illegal（非法的）、ir + responsible→irresponsible（不负责任的）等。

Sample: He was told that the doors had been installed <u>incorrectly</u>. (correct)
1. The black car drove away and _____ . (appear)
2. It's _____ to stare at a girl. (polite)
3. Every year we have fundraisers to raise money for _____ people. (fortunate)
4. Her _____ to concentrate could cause an accident. (ability)
5. She was taken to a hospital suffering from an _____ heartbeat. (regular)

V. **Choose the best phrase to complete each sentence.**
1. The children must be taught _____ that this is South Africa's game.
   A. in an early time   B. at a early time   C. in an early age   D. at an early age
2. The two things are the same in outward form but different _____ .
   A. in essence   B. at essence   C. on essence   D. for essence
3. The Bible says that we are going to be _____ our actions, because our actions show what is in our heart.
   A. judged from   B. judged by   C. judged in   D. judged into
4. Cold drinks are _____ in the summer.
   A. by demand   B. at demand   C. in demand   D. under demand
5. There are scholars of _____ who support his theory.
   A. kinds   B. all stripes   C. stripes   D. kind of

VI. **Complete the following sentences by translating the Chinese given in brackets into English.**
1. We have to teach them to be aggressive _____ (在年纪小的时候).
2. A mind is just a bundle of thoughts and _____ (在本质上它和你是谁没有关系).
3. These proposals should be voted by readers and _____ (由专家来评选).
4. The company if highly responsive to _____ (需求变化).
5. We strive to make our world comfortable _____ (各种各样的人).

VII. Translate the following sentences into Chinese.

1. Rarely do any things influence culture in such a profound way. (Para. 2)

2. Calligraphy was well-respected, or even worshiped in history. (Para. 3)

3. Therefore, Jin Dynasty is the peak of calligraphic works in Chinese history. (Para. 4)

4. Practicing calligraphy could help a person to achieve relaxation and repel outside disturbances. (Para. 5)

VIII. Combine the following sentences using the structure "not only...but also..."

> "not only...but also..."结构用于连接两个并列的词、短语或句子，表示"不但……而且……"。
> Sample: He likes football.   His friends like football.
> Not only he but also his friends like football.

1. He works on weekdays.   He also works on Sundays.

2. He writes plays.   He also acts in his own plays.

3. She sings well.   She writes music too.

4. The parents enjoy the movie.   The children enjoy the movie too.

5. She likes watch football match.   Her friends like to watch football match.

IX. Combine the following sentences using the structure "not so much...as..."

> "not so much...as..."是一个用于表示比较关系的短语，意为"与其说……倒不如说是……"
> Sample: Others are not very interested in who.   Others are interested in how.
> Others are interested not so much in who as in how.

1. I am not so skillful at singing.   I am skillful at dancing.

2. I am not very fond of the book.   I am fond of the writer.

3. He is a hard actor rather than a genius.

4. Success lies in hard work rather than in luck.

5. My mother is not a scientist.   My mother is a musician.

Unit 3   Calligraphy and Painting

 Dialogue Samples

Listen and read the samples carefully, and then complete the communicative tasks that follow.

Dialogue 1   Ordering Meals

Waiter: What can I do for you, sir?

Customer: What do you have this morning?

Waiter: Fruit juice, cakes and everything.

Customer: I'd like to have a glass of orange juice, please.

Waiter: And an egg?

Customer: Bacon and eggs with buttered toast. I like my bacon very crisp.

Waiter: How do you want your eggs?

Customer: Fried, please.

Waiter: Anything else, sir?

Customer: No, that's enough. Thank you.

Dialogue 2   Talking about food

Foreigner: I'd like to try some real Chinese cuisine. What would you recommend, waiter?

Waiter: Well, it depends. There are eight famous Chinese cuisines: like Sichuan cuisine, and Human cuisine.

Foreigner: I've heard they are both spicy hot. Are there any special Beijing dishes?

Waiter: There's the Beijing Roast duck.

Foreigner: I've heard a lot about it. I'd like to try it. Where can I find it?

Waiter: You can find it in most restaurants, but the best place is Quanjude Restaurant.

Foreign: Is it near here?

Waiter: A taxi will take you there in 15 minutes, if the traffic is not too bad.

Foreigner: Thank you.

Waiter: You're welcome.

Communicative Tasks

Work with your partner and take turns to start the conversations.

Task 1

Situation:

A Chinese student meets John, an American student in school library, they go to restaurant together.

Tips:

Here are some things the Chinese student can say or ask:

Let's eat out for a change.

Do you want to try some local food /local specialties?

What kind of food do you like best?

Here are some things the American student can say:

What do you recommend?

Can I have the same dish like that?

I have to avoid food containing fat/salt/sugar.

Do you have vegetarian dishes?

May I see the wine list?

Task 2

Situation:

A couple waiting to be seated in a crowded restaurant.

Tips:

Here are some things the waiter can say or ask:

Do you have a reservation?

Sorry, the restaurant is full now. You have to wait for half an hour.

We'll try to arrange it but I can't guarantee.

Here are some things the couple can say:

Do you have a table available now?

May I reserve a table for two?

By the way, can I have a table by the window?

And just some vegetables and some boiled potatoes please.

Unit 3 Calligraphy and Painting

 Further Development

辅音字母的发音

英语字母中 a, e, i, o, u 是元音字母。元音字母，也称为母音字母，是指语言里起着发声作用的字母。辅音字母和元音字母相对，所有非元音字母，就是辅音字母。元音发音时不受发音器官的阻碍，辅音发音时受发音器官的阻碍。在英语单词中，像元音字母一样，辅音字母的发音也有一定的规律可循，掌握这些规律对迅速掌握单词有事半功倍的效果。下面简单总结一下辅音字母的发音规律。

Study the following table to learn about the different pronunciations of each consonant. Then write down more words in the right column to illustrate each pronunciation.

Letter	Sound	Examples	More examples
b	[b]	but, basket, bad, job	
c	[k]	cake, catch, care, cup	
	[s]	city, cite, rice	
d	[d]	bird, dog, advertise, student	
f	[f]	five, fox, fog, future	
g	[g]	good, mug, glad, go	
h	[h]	house, hot, hate, how	
k	[k]	kite, book, milk, kick	
l	[l]	latter, like, bottle, luck	
m	[m]	mouse, mine, mushroom, much	
n	[n]	nut, note, nice, enough	
p	[p]	put, pull, proper, pig	

Text B

Chinese Ancient Painting

1. Ancient Chinese paintings* can be **traced** back to as early as 5 000 to 6 000 years ago, when people began to use minerals to draw simple pictures on rocks and produce designs and decorations on the surface of potteries and later bronze containers. However, only a few of the works have **survived** over time. The earliest drawings that have been **preserved** till today were produced on paper and silk, which were burial articles with a history of over 2 000 years.

2. As far as the subject is concerned, Chinese paintings fall into several **categories**, such as figure paintings, landscapes, and flower-and-bird paintings. European paintings, introduced into China in 17th century, were called "Western paintings". As the **representative** of Eastern paintings, Chinese paintings greatly differ from the Western counterpart in terms of contents, forms, and styles.

3. In terms of drawing skills, Chinese paintings can be categorized into two styles: colored paintings and water-ink paintings, with the former **dominant** before the 12th century by professional or **craftsman** painters, and the latter in and after the 12th century by **literati** painters. However, there is no absolute line between the two schools. No matter which school they belonged to, painters could and did **compromise** a little and learn from each other, giving rise to a mixed style including elements from both.

4. Traditional Chinese paintings perfectly integrate poetry, calligraphy, painting, and seal engraving, all of which are necessary **components**. As Chinese is an **ideographic** language system, which naturally generated an artistic form of calligraphy closely connected with painting.

5. Chinese painters, in particular literati painters, would **unconsciously** draw with the styles of

calligraphy. Writing poems became an established way to express their feelings during the process of drawing. In the end, according to the tradition of Chinese literati, red seals with their names **engraved** were used to sign their works, a tradition that continues to this day.

6. Actually, Chinese paintings clearly reveal that Chinese think in a **holistic** way. In other words, before drawing, painters must have an **overall** planning concerning the content of poems, the style of calligraphy, and the place where the works should be signed. The **criterion** of "Painting in poetry and poetry in painting" for excellent works was originally set by Sushi* (1036—1101), the well-known painter and litterateur in the Northern Song Dynasty (960—1127). Other painters later held this idea in high **esteem**.

7. An obvious distinction between Chinese and European paintings lies in the fact that a piece of blank space is always reserved in Chinese paintings for clouds over mountains, fog haunting above rivers, light circles reflected from the sun or the moon, or nothing at all. Some argue that the "blankness" in Chinese paintings is the most appropriate vehicle to **convey** the uncertainty and **ambiguity** featured in Chinese poems.

New Words

trace[treɪs] v. follow, discover, or ascertain the course of development of something 追踪；查探
survive[səˈvaɪv] v. continue to live; endure or last 幸存；生还；比……活得长
preserve[prɪˈzɜːv] v. keep or maintain in unaltered condition; cause to remain or last 保存；保护
category[ˈkætɪɡ(ə)rɪ] n. a collection of things sharing a common attribute 种类；分类
representative[reprɪˈzentətɪv] n. a person who represents others 代表
dominant[ˈdɒmɪnənt] adj. exercising influence or control 显性的；占优势的；支配的，统治的
literati[ˌlɪtəˈrɑːtɪ] n. the literary intelligentsia 文人；文学界
craftsman[ˈkrɑːf(t)smən] n. a professional whose work is consistently of high quality 工匠
compromise[ˈkɒmprəmaɪz] n. a middle way between two extremes 妥协，和解；折中
component[kəmˈpəʊnənt] n. an abstract part of something 成分；组件
ideographic[ˌɪdɪəʊˈɡræfɪk] adj. of or relating to or consisting of ideograms 表意的；表意字构成的
unconsciously[ʌnˈkɒnʃəslɪ] adv. without awareness 不知不觉；无意识地
engrave[ɪnˈɡreɪv; en-] v. carve, cut, or etch into a material or surface 雕刻；铭记
holistic[həʊˈlɪstɪk; hɒ-] adj. emphasizing the organic or functional relation between parts and the whole 整体的；全盘的
criterion[kraɪˈtɪərɪən] n. a basis for comparison; a reference point against which other things can be evaluated (批评判断的) 标准；准则；规范；准据
overall[ˈəʊvərɔːl] adj. including everything 全部的；全体的
esteem[ɪˈstiːm; e-] n. the condition of being honored 尊重；尊敬
convey[kənˈveɪ] v. make known; pass on, of information 传达；运输；让与
ambiguity[æmbɪˈɡjuːɪtɪ] n. unclearness by virtue of having more than one meaning 含糊；不明确

Useful Expressions

Phrases	Examples
trace back 追溯	Tea houses in Hangzhou trace back to the Southern Song Dynasty (1127—1279). 杭州的茶馆历史可以追溯到南宋时期（1127—1279）
differ from 与……不同	How and why does this differ from the advice from the WHO? 这项研究如何以及为什么与世界卫生组织的建议不同
in terms of 依据；按照	It can not be measured in terms of money. 这是不能用金钱衡量的
give rise to 使发生；引起	Many things will give rise to success. 很多因素都能带来成功
lie in 在于……	The Rocky Mountains lie in the west part of America. 落基山脉位于美国西部

Background Information

1. Chinese Painting: 中国画，简称"国画"，是我国传统造型艺术之一。从美术史的角度讲，民国前的绘画作品都统称为古画。国画在古代无确定名称，一般称为丹青，在世界美术领域中自成体系。中国画在内容和艺术创作上，体现了古人对自然、社会及与之相关联的政治、哲学、宗教、道德、文艺等方面的认识。主要是用毛笔、软笔或手指，用国画颜色和墨在帛或宣纸上作画的一种中国传统的绘画形式，是琴、棋、书、画四艺之一。

2. Sushi: 苏轼（1037年1月8日—1101年8月24日），字子瞻，又字和仲，号铁冠道人、东坡居士，世称苏东坡、苏仙 。汉族，眉州眉山（今属四川省眉山市）人，祖籍河北栾城，北宋文学家、书法家、画家。

　　苏轼是北宋中期的文坛领袖，在诗、词、散文、书、画等方面取得了很高的成就。其文纵横恣肆；其诗题材广阔，清新豪健，善用夸张、比喻，独具风格，与黄庭坚并称"苏黄"；其词开豪放一派，与辛弃疾同是"豪放派"代表，并称"苏辛"；其散文著述宏富，豪放自如，与欧阳修并称"欧苏"，为"唐宋八大家"之一。苏轼亦善书，为"宋四家"之一；工于画，尤擅墨竹、怪石、枯木等；有《东坡七集》《东坡易传》《东坡乐府》等传世。

Reading Comprehension

Ⅰ. **Decide whether the following statements are True (T) or False (F).**

(   ) 1. In ancient Chinese paintings, people began to use pigment to draw simple pictures.

(   ) 2. Chinese paintings greatly differ from the Western counterpart in terms of contents, forms and styles.

(   ) 3. In terms of drawing skills, Chinese paintings can be categorized into two styles: figure paintings and landscapes.

(   ) 4. An obvious distinction between Chinese and European paintings lies in the fact that a piece of blank space is always reserved in Chinese paintings.

Ⅱ. **Choose the best answer to each of the following questions.**

1. Where did people draw simple pictures and produce drawings of amazing designs and decorations in ancient times?
   A. rocks, potteries and bronze containers
   B. the fur of animals
   C. wall
   D. paper

2. We can learn from Paragraph 3 that _____.
   A. The two categories of drawing skills are completely separated from each other
   B. The two categories of drawing skills are contrary to each other
   C. The two categories of drawing skills affected each other
   D. The two categories of drawing skills are nearly the same

3. What are the necessary components in traditional Chinese paintings?
   A. poetry
   B. calligraphy
   C. painting and seal engraving
   D. above all

4. It can be inferred from Paragraph 5 that _____.
   A. poems are the essential parts when drawing pictures
   B. painters still like to use red seals with their names engraved to sign their works today
   C. red seals with names of painters are not used in Chinese paintings
   D. painters don't like anything in their paintings

5. What is the function of "blankness" in Chinese paintings?
   A. to convey uncertainty and ambiguity
   B. to sign the name of the painter
   C. to add a poem to the painting
   D. to do nothing

Grammar

Non-finite Verbs

非谓语动词，又叫非限定动词。非谓语动词是指在句子中不是谓语的动词，主要包括不定式、动名词和分词（现在分词和过去分词），即动词的非谓语形式。非谓语动词除了不能独立作谓语外，可以承担句子的其他成分。

1. 非谓语动词时态和语态的基本形式

非谓语动词类型	不定式	动名词	分词	
			现在分词	过去分词
句中语法成分	主语、宾语、定语、表语、状语、补语	主语、宾语、定语、表语	表语、定语、状语、补语	表语、定语、状语、补语
一般式（主/补动）	to do/ to be done	doing/being done	doing/being done	done
进行式	to be doing			
完成式（主/被动）	to have done/ to have been done	having done/ having been done	having done/ having been done	
完成进行式	to have been doing			

2. 动词不定式

动词不定式：(to) + do, 具有名词、形容词、副词的特征。

（1）作主语。

动词不定式短语作主语时，常用 it 作形式主语，真正的主语不定式置于句后。

It is very hard to finish the work in ten minutes. 十分钟之内完成这项工作是很难的。

（2）作表语。

Her job is to clean the hall. 她的工作是打扫大厅。

（3）作宾语。

常与不定式做宾语连用的动词有：want, hope, wish, offer, fail, plan, learn, pretend, refuse, manage, help, agree, promise, prefer. 如果不定式（宾语）后面有宾语补足语，则用 it 作形式宾语，真正的宾语（不定式）后置，放在宾语补足语后面。例如：Marx found it important to study the situation in Russia. 马克思发现研究俄国的情况是很重要的。

（4）作宾语补足语。

在复合宾语中，动词不定式可充当宾语补足语，如下动词常跟这种复合宾语：want, wish, ask, tell, order, beg, permit, help, advise, persuade, allow, etc.

He asked me to help him. 他让我帮他。

（5）作定语。

动词不定式作定语，放在所修饰的名词或代词后。

I have a meeting to attend. 我有一个会议要出席。

（6）作状语。

They were very sad to hear the news. 他们听到这条新闻非常伤心。

3. 动名词

动名词既具有动词的一些特征，又具有名词的句法功能。

一般式（谓语动词同时发生）	doing	being done
完成式（谓语动词发生之前）	having done	having been done

（1）作主语。

Reading aloud is very helpful. 朗读是很有好处的。

（2）作表语。

In the ant city, the queen's job is laying eggs. 在蚂蚁王国，蚁后的工作是产卵。

（3）作宾语。

They haven't finished building the dam. 他们还没有建好大坝。

We have to prevent the air from being polluted. 我们必须阻止空气被污染。

注意动名词既可作动词宾语也可作介词宾语，如上面两个例句。此外，动名词作宾语时，若跟有宾语补足语，则常用形式宾语 it，例如：

We found it no good making fun of others. 我们发现取笑他人不好。

（4）作定语。

He can't walk without a walking-stick. 他没有拐杖不能走路。

4. 分词

（1）分词的种类及功能。

分词是动词的又一种非谓语形式，主要有两种，即现在分词和过去分词。这两种分词在句中都能充当表语、定语、状语和补语，主要是在意思上有主动和被动之分，现在分词一般有主动意思，过去分词一般有被动意思，有时表示的时间也不相同。

表语：His speech was encouraging. 他的话鼓舞人心。（主动）

We were encouraged by his speech. 我们被他的话所鼓舞。（被动）

定语：The story is interesting. 这个故事有趣。（主动）

Interested members will meet at two. 有兴趣的成员两点钟集合。（被动）

状语：Taking a dictionary, she began to prepare her lessons.（主动）

拿了本字典，她开始预习功课。

Taken separately, the problems are not difficult to solve.（被动）

分开解决，这些问题不难解决。

补语：I heard someone crying in the room. 我听见有人在房间里哭。（主动）

I heard the song sung by many people. 我听见这首歌被很多人唱过。（被动）

（2）分词的时态和语态。

	主动形式	被动形式
一般式	doing	Being done
完成式	having done	having been done

① 一般式所表示的动作往往和谓语动词同时发生，或前后相邻；完成式表示该动作发生在谓语动词之前，强调谓语动词的时间和原因。

② 分词的否定式由 not 加分词构成。

例如：Not being seen by anyone, he escaped. 没有被人看见，他溜走了。

③ 独立主格结构。

分词做状语时，如果分词短语的逻辑主语与句子主语不一致，分词短语前需要带逻辑主语，构成独立主格结构。

例如：Weather permitting; we'll have the picnic tomorrow. 如果天气允许，我们明天野餐。

分词的独立主格前也可加上 with 或 without，表示谓语动作的原因、条件或伴随的动作等。

例如：The day was bright, with a fresh breeze blowing. 随着一缕清新的微风吹来，天亮了。

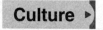

The American Spirit of "Do-It-Yourself"

Every nation has its own inimitable character. The one value that nearly every American would agree upon is individual freedom. It is the cornerstone of American values. American views themselves as highly individualistic in their thoughts and actions. They have been trained since very early in their lives to consider themselves as separate individuals who are responsible for their own situations in life and their own destinies.

There is however a price to be paid for this individual freedom: self-reliance or do-it-yourself. Over three hundred years ago, when the Europeans first came to settle in the New World, they were very poor and in front of them was a great wilderness. They had to cut down the trees in order to make farms. They had to dig and develop mines so as to have something to keep warm or to cook with. They had to build houses to live in, have shops to buy and sell goods, and public buildings for social activities. All they did was done by their own hands. Since then, manual labor has been highly valued.

It is curious that a man may be proud of the position which he obtained by his own efforts and even though it is not necessary any ore to depend on manual labor or a living, he still takes great delight in what he can do with his own hands. The American history made the American spirit of do-it-yourself come into being.

The young make their own decisions while parents are only willing to give some suggestions or advice. The whole society also calls people to do it themselves. "DIY" may be reflected in many aspects of American life. For example, the hostess never minds taking trouble, but takes great delight and pride in preparing special dishes and food carefully when a guest is invited.

Unit 4

World Heritage Sites

Warm-up Activities

I. Matching

Learn the following words and phrases about different heritage sites, and match them to the pictures.

1. Stonehenge, Britain (　　)
2. Mount Fuji, Japan (　　)
3. Pizza Cathedral, Italy (　　)
4. Forbidden city, China (　　)
5. Athen Acropolis(　　)
6. Angkor Wat, Cambodia (　　)

A.

B.

C.

D.

E.

F.

II. Reading

Cultural heritage is often expressed as either intangible or tangible cultural heritage, including customs, places, objects, artistic expressions and values.

文化遗产通常表现为非物质文化遗产或有形文化遗产，包括风俗习惯、场所、物品、艺术表现形式和价值观念。

heritage　n. 遗产
intangible　adj. 无形的

Text A

World Cultural Heritage in China

1. **Heritage** is our legacy from the past, what we live with today, and what we pass on to future generations. Our cultural and natural heritages are both **irreplaceable** sources of life and inspiration. What makes the concept of World Heritage exceptional is its universal application. World Heritage sites belong to all the peoples of the world, regardless of the **territory** on which they are located.

2. Up to December 2013, among the over 800 World Heritage Sites listed by UNESCO*, China has 45 listed, only second to Italy. Among them, 31 are cultural heritages, 10 natural heritages, and 4 dual heritages (cultural and natural mixed). These sites are the most essential part of China's valuable and rich tourism resources. Here are some **iconic** places on the list.

The Great Wall

3. The Great Wall was continuously built from the 3rd century BC to the 17th century AD on the northern border of the country as the great military **defense** project of **successive** Chinese Empires, with a total length of more than 20 000 kilometers. The Great Wall begins in the east at Shanhaiguan in Hebei province and ends at Jiayuguan in Gansu province to the west. The main body consists of walls, horse-tracks, watch-towers, shelters, and includes fortresses and passes along the Wall.

4. The Great Wall **reflects** collision and exchanges between agricultural civilizations and **nomadic** civilizations in ancient China. It is an **outstanding** example of the superb military architecture, technology and art of ancient China. It **embodies** unparalleled significance as the national symbol for safeguarding the security of the country and its people.

The Summer Palace

5. The Summer Palace in Beijing—first built in 1750, largely destroyed in the war of 1860 and restored on its **original** foundations in 1886—is a **masterpiece** of Chinese landscape garden design. The natural landscape of hills and open water is combined with **artificial** features such as pavilions, palaces, temples and bridges to form a harmonious aesthetic value.

6. The Summer Palace in Beijing **integrates** numerous traditional halls and pavilions into the Imperial Garden **conceived** by the Qing emperor Qianlong* between 1750 and 1764 as the Garden of Clear Ripples.

7. The Summer Palace combined political and administrative, residential, spiritual, and **recreational** functions within a landscape of lakes and mountains, in accordance with the Chinese **philosophy** of balancing the works of man with nature. Destroyed during the Second Opium War* of the 1850s, it was **reconstructed** by Emperor Guangxu for use by Empress Dowager Cixi and renamed the Summer Palace.

8. As the **culmination** of several hundred years of Imperial garden design, the Summer Palace has had a major influence on **subsequent** oriental garden art and culture.

New Words

heritage[ˈherɪtɪdʒ] n. any attribute or immaterial possession that is inherited from ancestors 遗产；传统；继承物；继承权

irreplaceable[ɪrɪˈpleɪsəb(ə)l] adj. impossible to replace 不能替代的；不能调换的

territory[ˈterɪt(ə)rɪ] n. a region marked off for administrative or other purposes 领土；领域

iconic[aɪˈkɒnɪk] adj. relating to or having the characteristics on an icon 图标的；形象的

defense[dɪˈfens] n. military action or resources protecting a country against potential enemies 防卫，防护；防御措施；防守

successive[səkˈsesɪv] adj. in regular succession without gaps 连续的；继承的；依次的；接替的

reflect[rɪˈflekt] v. manifest or bring back 反映；反射，照出；表达；显示；反省

nomadic[nəʊˈmædɪk] adj. (of groups of people) tending to travel and change settlements frequently 游牧的；流浪的；游动的

outstanding[aʊtˈstændɪŋ] adj. distinguished from others in excellence 杰出的；显著的

embody[ɪmˈbɒdɪ; em-] v. represent in bodily form 体现，使具体化；具体表达

original[əˈrɪdʒɪn(ə)l; ɒ-] adj. preceding all others in time or being as first made or performed 原始的；最初的；独创的；新颖的

masterpiece[ˈmɑːstəpiːs] n. the most outstanding work of a creative artist or craftsman n. 杰作；绝无仅有的人

artificial[ɑːtɪˈfɪʃ(ə)l] adj. contrived by art rather than nature 人造的；仿造的；虚伪的

integrate[ˈɪntɪgreɪt] v. make into a whole or make part of a whole 使……完整；使……成整体

conceive[kənˈsiːv] v. have the idea for 怀孕；构思；以为；持有

recreational[rekrɪˈeɪʃənl] adj. of or relating to recreation 娱乐的，消遣的；休养的

philosophy[fɪˈlɒsəfɪ] n. a belief (or system of beliefs) accepted as authoritative by some group or school 哲学；哲理；人生观

reconstruct[riːkənˈstrʌkt] v. build again 重建；改造

culmination[kʌlmɪˈneɪʃ(ə)n] n. a final climactic stage 顶点；高潮

subsequent[ˈsʌbsɪkw(ə)nt] adj. following in time or order 后来的；随后的

Useful Expressions

Phrases	Examples
belong to 属于	These Games belong to you. They are your Games. 这场盛事属于你们，这是你们的比赛
consist of 由……构成	So what should a real interview consist of? 那么，一场真正的面试包括什么呢
combine with 与……相结合	Cholesterol has to combine with certain proteins. 胆固醇必须和特定的蛋白质结合
integrate into 成为一体；融入	Some countries want to integrate into this organization. 一些国家想加入这个组织
in accordance with 依照；与……一致	We should make decisions in accordance with specific conditions. 我们应当根据具体情况做出决定

 Background Information

1. UNESCO: 联合国教育、科学及文化组织，简称"联合国教科文组织（United Nations Educational, Scientific and Cultural Organization, UNESCO)"，于1946年11月4日正式成立，是联合国（UN）旗下专门机构之一。

2. Qianlong: 乾隆（Emperor qianlong）是清代高宗年号，前后一共六十年，起止时间为公元1736年至1796年。在这期间的重要事件有平定大小和卓叛乱、巩固多民族国家的发展、大兴文字冤狱、《四库全书》的编撰等。

3. The Second Opium War: 第二次鸦片战争是英、法在俄、美支持下联合发动的侵华战争；是英国与法国为了进一步打开中国市场，扩大在华侵略利益、趁中国太平天国运动之际，以亚罗号事件及马神甫事件为借口，联手进攻清朝政府的战争。第二次鸦片战争迫使清政府先后签订《天津条约》和《北京条约》、中俄《瑷珲条约》等和约，列强侵略更加深入。中国因此而丧失了东北及西北共150多万平方千米的领土，战争结束后清政府集中力量镇压太平天国，维持统治。

Unit 4　World Heritage Sites

 Reading Comprehension

Ⅰ. **Decide whether the following statements are True (T) or False (F).**
(　) 1. World heritage sites belong to the people of the place on which they are located.
(　) 2. The world heritage sites in China are valuable and rich tourism resources.
(　) 3. The Great Wall was built as the great military defense project of successive Empires.
(　) 4. The Great Wall only consists of walls with a total length of less than 20 000 kilometers.
(　) 5. The Summer Palace was largely destroyed in 1860 during the First Opium War.
(　) 6. The design of the Summer Palace is in accordance with the Chinese philosophy of balancing the works of man with nature.
(　) 7. The Summer Palace was never reconstructed after being destroyed during the war.

Ⅱ. **Complete the answers to the following questions.**
1. What is heritage? (Para. 1)
   Heritage is our _____ from the past, what we live with today, and what we pass on to _____.
2. What does main body of the Great Wall consist of? (Para. 3)
   It consists of walls, _____, watch-towers, _____ and includes fortresses and passes along the war.
3. What happened to the Summer Palace during the Second Opium War? (Para. 5)
   It was _____ in the war of 1860 and _____ on its original foundations in 1886.
4. What is the status of the Summer Palace in history? (Para. 8)
   As the culmination of Imperial garden design, it has had a major influence on _____ _____.

Vocabulary and Structure

Words and Phrases to Drill

irreplaceable	artificial	conceive	reconstruct	integrate
reflect	subsequent	territory	original	outstanding
consist of	integrate into	in accordance with	belong to	combine with

I. Choose the appropriate explanation from Column B for each of the words in Column A.

A	B
_____ 1. irreplaceable	a. build again
_____ 2. integrate	b. a region marked off for administrative or other purposes
_____ 3. reconstruct	c. following in time or order
_____ 4. conceive	d. preceding all others in time or being as first made or performed
_____ 5. territory	e. impossible to replace
_____ 6. subsequent	f. contrived by art rather than nature
_____ 7. outstanding	g. have the idea for
_____ 8. original	h. distinguished from others in excellence
_____ 9. artificial	i. manifest or bring back
_____ 10. reflect	j. make into a whole or make part of a whole

II. Fill in the blanks with the correct forms of the words in Column A of the above table.

1. The _____ of the city is underway.
2. So, first impressions can shape _____ impressions not just when dealing with people.
3. Not all the immigrants want to _____ into the community.
4. She was despised because she was of humble _____ .
5. As I said yesterday, this is also a moment of _____ and respect.
6. You play an _____ role in promoting China-Africa mutual understanding.
7. How about this _____ leather purse?
8. There are other small _____ and islands that have colonial relationship to countries.
9. The boy who won the scholarship was a quite _____ student.
10. Scientists may have discovered why drinking coffee makes it harder for women to _____ .

III. Compare each pair of words and choose the correct one to fill in each blank. Change the form if necessary.

1. reflect   reflection
   a. What is _____?
   b. What he said did not _____ back the views of the people.
2. heritage   inherit
   a. All of our cultural _____ which is useful should be inherited, but in a critical way.
   b. I have the ambition to _____ some property.

3. origin   original
   a. The plan of the work is _____ with the author.
   b. Well, you have to put something at the _____ .
4. conceive   conception
   a. You'd better _____ the new project.
   b. They have a _____ of what the Bible is.

IV. **Add the suffix "-ment" to the following words in brackets. Then complete the sentences with the words formed.**

> **Tips:** 后缀 "-ment" 接在动词后面，表示状态或状况，行为的过程或结果，例如：develop + ment→ development（发展）、agree + ment→ agreement（同意）等。

Sample: Both of them were happy with their <u>agreement.</u> (agree)
1. I don't want to have a _____ with you, it is nonsense. (argue)
2. I made an _____ with my doctor last Friday. (appoint)
3. I notice that the _____ misses out the price of the product. (advertise)
4. The Renaissance was an epoch of unparalleled cultural _____ . (achieve)
5. Television has displaced film as our country's most popular form of _____ . (entertain)

V. **Choose the best phrase to complete each sentence.**
1. To put it simply, no one knows whom the islands _____ but everybody wants them.
   A. belong for   B. belong in   C. belong to   D. belong with
2. A balanced breakfast _____ fruit, grains, and milk.
   A. consists of   B. made of   C. is consisted of D. is make of
3. Tourism must _____ the culture as to build a characteristic city.
   A. put up with   B. combine with   C. work with   D. stand with
4. The ways of combating stress can be _____ our daily lives.
   A. integrate on   B. integrated on   C. integrate in   D. integrated in
5. She was dismissed _____ the company's usual procedures.
   A. in accordance with   B. in accordance to
   C. in accordance by   D. in accordance on

VI. **Complete the following sentences by translating the Chinese given in brackets into English.**
1. _____ (他们属于上一代人), more self-denying generation.
2. This hamburger _____ (由面包、芝士、牛肉饼和蔬菜组成).
3. _____ (氢气和氧气结合) to form water.
4. Not all the countries want to _____ (加入这个组织).
5. One's opinion tends to differ _____ (不同的立场).

VII. **Translate the following sentences into Chinese.**
1. What makes the concept of World Heritage exceptional is its universal application. (Para. 1)
   _____

2. These sites are the most essential part of China's valuable and rich tourism resources. (Para. 2)

3. The natural landscape of hills and open water is combined with artificial features. (Para. 5)

4. The Summer Palace has had a major influence on subsequent oriental garden art and culture. (Para. 8)

VIII. Rewrite the following sentences into two different patterns of exclamatory sentences.

> 英语感叹句的表现形式主要有两种：
> （1） What + 形容词 + 名词（+ 主语 + 谓语）！
> （2） How + 形容词（副词）（+ 主语 + 谓语）！
> Sample: She is a beautiful girl.　　What a beautiful girl she is!
> 　　　　He runs quickly.　　　　How quickly he runs!

1. It is a vivid film.

2. You asked a complicated question.

3. We have a responsible teacher.

4. It might be a good idea to ask Mum for help.

5. It is a lovely Teddy Bear.

IX. Translate the following Chinese sentences into English using the structure "see…as…".

> "see…as…"表示"将……看作……"
> Sample: The Chinese people see the dragon as a symbol of power, fortune, and wisdom.

1. 人们将鸽子看作是和平的象征。

2. 人们认为钻石代表着爱情和长久。

3. 人们把龙看作是中国的象征。

4. 美国人很喜欢熊猫，并把熊猫看作是中美关系的纽带。

5. 西方人把狗看作是他们的朋友。

Dialogue Samples

Listen and read the samples carefully, and then complete the communicative tasks that follow.

Dialogue 1 Leaving a message

John: May I speak to Mr. Smith?

Stuart: Sorry, he is out. You've just missed him.

John: Will he come back soon?

Stuart: He's out on his lunch break right now. Would you like to leave a message?

John: Yes, when he comes back, can you have him call me at 024-4578321?

Stuart: Again, please?

John: Call me at 024-4578321, this is John.

Stuart: OK.

John: Thank you.

Stuart: It's my pleasure.

Dialogue 2 Calling for inviting

Wayne: Hello! Who is speaking?

Bruce: Hello! This is Bruce. I want to speak to Wayne.

Wayne: Speaking.

Bruce: Hi, Wayne. I'm just calling to invite you to a dinner party tomorrow evening.

Wayne: Really? When and where?

Bruce: 7:30 pm, at Longding Chinese restaurant. I'll be at your place at 7:00 to pick you up if you need a ride.

Wayne: Thank you. I need a ride. I'll be waiting for you then.

Bruce: See you tomorrow at 7:00. Make sure you dress a little formally. I've heard the restaurant is kind of upscale.

Wayne: Thank you. See you then.

Bruce: See you.

Communicative Tasks

Work with your partner and take turns to start the conversation.

Task 1

Situation:

Lily is a worker in acompany; she is answering the phone calling from a customer.

Tips:

Here are some things Lily can say or ask:

Who is calling please?

Who in particular would you like to talk?

He's been expecting your call.

Would you mind calling back later?

Here are some things the customer can say:

Is this ABC company?

May I speak to…?

I'm sorry for calling you so early.

I hope I'm not disturbing you.

It is urgent.

I need to talk to Mr. Bill immediately.

I'm calling you back.

Is this the finance department?

Task 2

Situation:

Bob is talking to Smith about the shoe exhibition holding next month.

Tips:

Here are some things that Bob can say or ask:

I'd like to make an appointment for our manager.

He is looking forward to seeing you.

I will call you tomorrow and we can talk about it then.

Here are some things Smith can say:

Which day is convenient?

What kind of hotel do you want to live?

We'll book the airplane tickets in advance.

I'll make a note of it.

By the way, I will email you the product introduction.

Do you have any other requirements?

Hope to see you soon.

Further Development

辅音字母的发音

Study the following table to learn about the different pronunciations of each consonant. Then write down more words in the right column to illustrate each pronunciation.

Letter	Sound	Examples	More examples
q(+ u)	[kw]	queen, quiet, queue, question	
r	[r]	red, rock, right, reach	
s	[s]	sit, seen, sick, search	
	[z]	rise, raise, towards	
t	[t]	tend, teach, ticket, to	
v	[v]	very, vacant, vacation	
w	[w]	watch, walk, work, want	
x	[ks]	six, sex, exercise	
	[z]	Xerox, xylography	
	[gz]	example, exactly	
y	[i]	physics, baby, kitty	
	[aI]	bye, eye	
	[j]	yoke, you, yesterday	
z	[z]	zigzag, aero, zipper	

Text B

Mount Taishan

1. Mount Taishan with exceptional historic, cultural, aesthetic and scientific value is the leader of the "Five Sacred Mountain"* in China although they each have their own attraction. It has always been a source of inspiration for Chinese artists and **scholars** and **symbolizes** ancient Chinese **civilizations** and beliefs.

2. Mount Taishan is **situated** in the centre of Shandong province, lying across the cities of Tai'an, Jinan and Zibo. The mountain was once called Mount Daishan, Mount Daizong or Mount Taiyue and was renamed Mount Taishan in the Spring and Autumn Period* (770BC—476BC). Its main peak, the Jade Emperor Summit* (玉皇顶), which lies in the north of Tai'an city, is about 1 532.7 meters high, is an **ideal** place to watch the sunrise and sunset.

3. Mount Taishan is considered as an important cradle of oriental East Asian culture since the earliest times. The first thing for an emperor to do on **ascending** to the throne was to climb Mount Taishan and pray to heaven and earth or their **ancestors.** It was said that 72 emperors of different dynasties made pilgrimages here. These special ceremonies and **sacrifices** earned the mountain **widespread** fame. In addition, many poets and literary scholars also visited the mountain to gain inspiration. Mountain Tai also played an important role in the development of Buddhism and Taoism.

4. Besides historic **relics**, this mountain boasts unique natural scenery too. The lofty peaks, deep valleys, **spectacular** waterfalls, enchanting rocks and the centuries-old pines and cypresses will undoubtedly encourage you **linger** with no thought of leaving. The four wonders here are Sunrises from the East, the Sunset Glow, the Sea of Clouds and the Golden Belt along the Yellow River. It would be a great pity to miss the four wonders.

5. A cable car was built before the property was inscribed as World Heritage, but most visitors reach the **summit** area by climbing the 6 660 steps. It takes about four hours at an average to reach the peak.

6. Due to its long-standing status as a **sacred** place, Mount Taishan has been preserved with little **alteration**. All the architectural elements, paintings, sculptures, stone inscriptions and ancient trees are integrated into the **landscape** of Mount Taishan. The philosophical, aesthetical and scientific ideas about the **harmonious** development of Heaven, Earth and man can be seen here. It is the symbol of **spiritual** culture of China.

7. Mount Taishan **epitomizes** splendid Chinese culture and was listed in the World Natural and Cultural Heritage List of UNESCO in 1987.

New Words

exceptional[ɪkˈsepʃ(ə)n(ə)l; ek-] adj. far beyond what is usual in magnitude or degree 异常的；例外的

scholar[ˈskɒlə] n. a learned person 学者

symbolize[ˈsɪmbəlaɪz] v. express indirectly by an image, form, or model; be a symbol 象征；用符号表现

civilization[ˈsɪvɪlaɪˈzeɪʃən] n. a society in an advanced state of social development 文明；文化

situate[ˈsɪtʃʊeɪt] v. determine or indicate the place, site, or limits of, as if by an instrument or by a survey 使位于；使处于

ideal[aɪˈdɪəl; aɪˈdiːəl] adj. the idea of something that is perfect; something that one hopes to attain 理想的；完美的；想象的；不切实际的

ascend[əˈsend] v. travel up 攀登；上升

ancestor[ˈænsestə] n. someone from whom you are descended 始祖；祖先

sacrifice[ˈsækrɪfaɪs] n. the act of killing (an animal or person) in order to propitiate a deity 供奉

widespread[ˈwʌɪdsprɛd] adj. widely circulated or diffused 普遍的，广泛的；分布广的

relic[ˈrɛlɪk] n. an antiquity that has survived from the distant past 遗迹；遗骸；纪念物

spectacular[spekˈtækjʊlə] adj. sensational in appearance or thrilling in effect 壮观的；惊人的

linger[ˈlɪŋɡə] v. remain present although waning or gradually dying 消磨；缓慢度过

summit[ˈsʌmɪt] n. the highest level or degree attainable; the highest stage of development 顶点

sacred[ˈseɪkrɪd] adj. concerned with religion or religious purposes 神的；神圣的

alteration[ɔːltəˈreɪʃ(ə)n; ˈɒl-] n. the act of making something different 修改，改变；变更

landscape[ˈlændskeɪp] n. an expanse of scenery that can be seen in a single view 风景；风景画

harmonious[hɑːˈməʊnɪəs] adj. musically pleasing 和谐的；和睦的

spiritual[ˈspɪrɪtʃʊəl; -tjʊəl] adj. concerned with or affecting the spirit or soul 精神的；心灵的

epitomize[ɪˈpɪtəmaɪz; e-] v. embody the essential characteristics of or be a typical example of 摘要；概括；成为……的缩影

Useful Expressions

Phrases	Examples
ascend to 追溯；升至	Their inquiries ascend to the antiquity. 他们的研究上溯古代
earn a fame 获得名声	This is a great opportunity to earn fame and fortune! 这是获得名誉与财富的最好机会
play a role in 在……起作用	Genes play a role in how your body balances calories and energy. 基因在你的身体平衡热量和能量中扮演很重要的角色
at average 平均的	He will race at average speeds approaching 200 mph. 他将以接近每小时 200 英里的平均车速参赛
the symbol of 象征	Pandas have been a symbol of U. S. -China partnership for decades. 熊猫在过去数十年来一直是美中伙伴关系的象征

 Background Information

1. Five Sacred Mountain: 五岳，是中国五大名山的总称。即东岳泰山（位于山东）、西岳华山（位于陕西）、北岳恒山（位于山西）、中岳嵩山（位于河南）、南岳衡山（位于湖南），其中泰山居首。它们是封建帝王仰天功之巍巍而封禅祭祀的地方，更是封建帝王受命于天、定鼎中原的象征。五岳景色各有特点，受到许多游客的青睐，许多文人作家也留下了大量诗文作品。

2. Spring and Autumn Period: 春秋时期是中国历史东周前半期历史阶段。自公元前770年至公元前476年（一说公元前453年，另一说公元前403年）。这段历史时期，史称"春秋时期"。鲁国史官把当时各国的重大事件，按年、季、月、日记录下来，一年分春、夏、秋、冬四季记录，简括起来就把这部编年史命名为《春秋》。

春秋时期开始于公元前770年（周平王元年）周平王东迁东周开始的一年，止于公元前476年（周敬王四十四年），战国前夕，总共295年。

3. Jade Emperor Summit: 玉皇顶，是泰山主峰之巅，因峰顶有玉皇庙而得名。玉皇顶旧称太平顶，又名天柱峰，始建年代无考，明成化年间重修。神龛上匾额题"柴望遗风"，说明远古帝王曾于此燔柴祭天，望祀山川诸神。

Reading Comprehension

Ⅰ. **Decide whether the following statements are True (T) or False (F).**
(   ) 1. Mount Taishan is the leader of the Five Sacred Mountain in China.
(   ) 2. Mount Taishan has nothing to do with the development of Buddhism and Taoism.
(   ) 3. The only way to get the Jade Emperor Summit is using a cable car since it is too high.
(   ) 4. Mount Taishan has been changed a lot through the years of history.
(   ) 5. Sunrises from the East, the Sunset Glow, the Sea of Clouds and the Golden Belt along the Yellow River are four wonders of Mount Taishan.

Ⅱ. **Choose the best answer to each of the following questions.**
1. Where is Mount Taishan?
   A. It is in Hunan Province   B. It is in Shandong Province
   C. It is in Henan Province   D. It is in Shanxi Province
2. Why Mount Taishan is considered as an important cradle of oriental East Asian culture?
   A. Many emperors in ancient times climbed it to pray after ascending the throne
   B. Mount Tai has unique natural scenery
   C. It was the birthplace of many emperors in ancient times
   D. It is the leader of the Five Sacred Mountain
3. Which of the following is not the four wonder in Mount Taishan?
   A. Sunrises from the east   B. Sunset Glow
   C. Sea of Clouds   D. Sculptures
4. It can be inferred from Paragraph 6 that _____ .
   A. Mount Taishan has been altered a lot in the long history
   B. The agricultural elements, paintings, sculptures, stone inscriptions and ancient trees are separated from each other
   C. Ideas about harmonious development of Heaven, Earth and man are integrated together
   D. It don't play a key role in the spiritual culture of China
5. When was Mount Taishan listed in the World Natural and Cultural Heritage?
   A. 1984   B. 1986   C. 1987   D. 1990

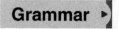

Subjunctive Mood

虚拟语气用来表示假想,而不表示客观存在的事实,所说的是一个条件,不一定是事实,或与事实相反。虚拟语气通过谓语动词的特殊形式来表示。

1. 条件句中虚拟语气的形式

从句中提出一种与客观现实不相符或根本不可能存在的条件,主句会产生的一种不可能获得的结果。条件句中的虚拟语气根据不同的时间有三种不同的形式。

时间	主句谓语形式	从句谓语形式
将来	would / should / might / could + 动词原形	动词过去式(be 用 were)/were to + 动词原形
现在	would / should / might / could + 动词原形	动词过去式(be 用 were)
过去	would / should / might / could have + 动词过去分词	had + 动词过去分词

如:

If he were to come, I would tell you about it. 如果他要来的话,我就会通知你们一声。

If he were free, he would help us. 要是他有空的话,他会帮助我们的。

If I had got there earlier, I would have joined the group. 如果我早点到,我就会加入团队了。

2. 非真实条件从句的特殊用法

(1) 如果条件从句与主句不在同一时间,则叫错综条件句。

If he had taken care of himself at that time, he would not be sick now. (从句指过去,主句指将来)

如果他那时能好好照顾自己,现在就不会生病了。

(2) 如果条件从句没有明确表示出来,则叫含蓄条件句。

Without your help, I couldn't have finished the book. 如果没有你的帮助,我不可能写完这本书。

3. 虚拟语气在其他从句中的应用

(1) 虚拟语气在宾语从句中的应用。

① 在表示建议、命令、请求等意义的动词引导的宾语从句中,要用"should + 动词原形"来表示虚拟语气,should 可以省略。常用动词为:suggest, insist, propose, demand, order, advise, command, recommend, decide, intend, request, require 等。

The doctor suggested that he not go there. 医生建议他不要去那里。

② wish 引导的宾语从句可用虚拟语气,表示与事实相反的愿望,意为"但愿"。

从句的谓语动词可用过去式,表示现在的愿望(与现在事实相反);还可用"could/would/might + 动词原形",用来表示将来的愿望;也可用"had + 过去分词",表示与过去事实相反的愿望，无能为力。

（2）虚拟语气在主语从句中的应用。

常在 it is (was) + 形容词/过去分词 + that 引导的主语从句句型中用虚拟语气。从句的谓语动词要用虚拟式"should + 动词原形"，should 通常可以省略。这类形容词常见的有：essential, important, advisable, desirable, necessary, crucial 等。常见的过去分词有：desired, required, requested, demanded, suggested 等。

It is required that all the teachers (should) attend the meeting. 要求所有老师都必须参加会议。

（3）虚拟语气在表语从句和同位语从句中的应用。

在表示建议、命令、请求等意义的名词的同位语和表语从句中，谓语动词也要用虚拟语气，动词用"should + 动词原形"，should 通常可以省略。

He made the suggestion that all the teachers (should) help the poor girl.
他的建议是所有的老师都来帮助这个可怜的女孩。

4. 虚拟语气在其他句型中的应用

（1）as if / as though 引导的状语从句中。

as if / as though 引导的状语从句中，谓语动词要用虚拟语气，其动词形式和 wish 引导的宾语从句中谓语动词变化一致。

The old man treats the boy as if he were his own son. 这位老人像对待儿子一样对待这个孩子。

（2）would rather, would sooner 等句型中。

would rather, would sooner 等句型中，后面所跟的从句要用虚拟语气，表示宁愿别人做某事或不做某事，如果与现在或将来事实相反，从句谓语动词需用过去时；如果表示与过去的事实相反，从句谓语动词则需用过去完成时。

I would rather you hadn't called me yesterday. 我宁愿你昨天没有给我打过电话。

（3）It is time that... 句型中。

在 It is high/about/time 后的 that 从句中，要用虚拟语气，从句谓语动词常用过去时，句意是"该是……的时候了"。

It is time that we had a good rest. 我们该好好休息一下了。

（4）if only 引导的感叹句中。

在 if only 引导的感叹句中，要用虚拟语气，意为"要是……就好了，但愿……"。其动词形式和 wish 引导的宾语从句谓语动词变化一致。

Culture ▶

Thanksgiving

Thanksgiving is a holiday in the United States and Canada when people give thanks. It is celebrated every year on the fourth Thursday of November in the United States.

The day for Thanksgiving was not fixed until the time of the Civil War. On October 3rd, 1863, Lincoln issued the first National Thanksgiving Proclamation. Since then it has been the custom for the President of the United States of America to proclaim manually the fourth Thursday of November as Thanksgiving Day. American immigrants brought the customs and practices of the American Thanksgiving to Canada, beginning on April 5, 1872.

Thanksgiving Day is traditionally day for families and friends to get together for a special meal. The meal often includes a turkey, whether roasted, basked or deep-fried, stuffing, mashed potatoes, cranberry sauce, and pumpkin pie. Thanksgiving Day is a time for many people to give thanks for what they have. Volunteering is common Thanksgiving Day activity, and communities often hold food drives and host free dinners for the less fortunate.

Today, the American people have four days for this holiday, although the first Thanksgiving lasted three days. More people in the USA celebrate Thanksgiving than Christmas. Americans eat 46 million turkeys each Thanksgiving.

Unit 5

Animated Film and Oil Painting

Unit 5 Animated Film and Oil Painting

Warm-up Activities

Ⅰ. **Matching**

Learn the following words and phrases about different types of design, and match them to the pictures.

1. watercolor painting (　　)　　2. sketch (　　)　　3. gouache (　　)
4. oil painting (　　)　　5. pochade (　　)　　6. print painting (　　)

A. 　　B. 　　C.

D. 　　E. 　　F.

Ⅱ. **Reading**

pursuit　n. 追求
eternal　adj. 永恒的
literature and art 文艺

The pursuit of truth, goodness and beauty is the eternal value of literature and art. The highest realm of art is to discover the beauty of nature, life and soul.

追求真善美是文艺的永恒价值。艺术的最高境界就是让人们发现自然的美、生活的美、心灵的美。

(习近平总书记在全国文艺工作座谈会上的讲话)

Text A

Loving Vincent
—the world's first fully oil painted animated feature film

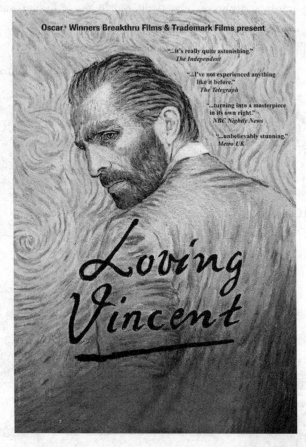

1. *Loving Vincent* has won many audiences' hearts since its first run in Britain October 13, 2017. The film was written and directed by Dorota Kobiela and Hugh Welchman. Based on the 800 letters of Van Gogh before his death, it is an experimental **animated biographical** film about the life of great painter Vincent van Gogh*, and in particular, the **circumstances** of his death. The film is in memory of the 125th anniversary of Van Gogh's birth.

2. It is the world's first fully oil painted animated feature film. Each of the film's 65 000 frames is an oil painting on canvas, using the same **technique** as Van Gogh, created by 125 painters worldwide in more than six years. Many of the scenes are based on more than 100 paintings by Van Gogh and each second **displays** 12 pictures.

3. The director chose **classically** trained painters rather than traditional animators. Welchman said he wanted to avoid animators with "personalized styles" and preferred people who "were very pure oil painters".

4. Production for the film began with a live-action **cast** filming against a green screen. After filming, editors combined Van Gogh paintings into scene backgrounds, and finally cut the film together as usual. However, once the actual film was complete, they shot each **individual** frame onto a blank canvas, and artists painted over each image. It took four years to finish the entire process, from the actual filming to **completion** of the paintings. Even Welchman himself **admitted**, "We have **definitely** without a doubt invented the slowest form of film-making ever devised in 120 years. "

5. The flagship *Loving Vincent* **Exhibition** opened in Noordbrabants Museum on October 2017. This exhibition **contained** more than 100 oil paintings from the film *Loving Vincent*, 10% of the paintings remaining after the filming process.

6. The exhibition showed how the film-makers re-imagined the paintings of Vincent van Gogh into the **medium** of film, using the very technology, oil-painting, that Vincent himself used. Be **overwhelmed** by the countless number of paintings made as you walk through the rooms. Find out about Vincent's life as a painter, and also the life of the film, how it developed from an idea into the world's first fully painted feature film.

7. On December 9, 2017, *Loving Vincent* won Best Animated Feature Film Award at the 30th European Film Awards in Berlin. It also received Best Animated Feature **nominations** at both the Academy Awards* and Golden Globes. Till March 22, 2018, the film has grossed more than $30.5 million worldwide on a **budget** of $5.5 million.

New Words

animated[ˈænɪmeɪtɪd] adj. (of pictures, drawings, etc. in a film) made to look as if they are moving(指电影的画面、图画等) 栩栩如生的；(似) 能活动的

biographical[ˌbaɪəˈɡræfɪkl] adj. of or relating to or being biography 传记的

circumstances[ˈsɜːkəmstənsɪz] n. the conditions that affect a situation, action, event etc. 环境；情况

anniversary[ˌænɪˈvɜːs(ə)rɪ] n. the date on which an event occurred in some previous year (or the celebration of it) 纪念日

technique[tekˈniːk] n. a practical method or art applied to some particular task 技术

display[dɪˈspleɪ] v. to put sth. in a place where people can see it easily; to show sth. to people 陈列；展示

classically[ˈklæsɪklɪ] adv. Something that is classically designed is traditional, and beautiful in a simple way 传统地；古典地

cast[kɑːst] n. the actors in a play 演员表

individual[ˌɪndɪˈvɪdʒuəl] adj. being or characteristic of a single thing or person 个人；个体

completion[kəmˈpliːʃn] n. a concluding action 结束；完工

admit[ədˈmɪt] v. declare to be true or admit the existence or reality or truth of 承认

definitely[ˈdefɪnətli] adv. without question and beyond doubt 毫无疑问地

exhibition[ˌeksɪˈbɪʃn] n. a collection of things (goods or works of art etc.) for public display 陈列；展览

contain[kənˈteɪn] v. include or contain; have as a component 包含；由……组成

medium[ˈmiːdiəm] n. a means or instrumentality for storing or communicating information 媒介、媒体

overwhelm[ˌəʊvəˈwelm] v. overcome by superior force 压倒；淹没；压垮；覆盖

nomination[ˌnɒmɪˈneɪʃn] n. the act of officially naming a candidate 提名

gross[ɡrəʊs] v. earn before taxes, expenses, etc. 总共收入；共计赚得

budget[ˈbʌdʒɪt] n. a sum of money allocated for a particular purpose 预算

Unit 5　Animated Film and Oil Painting

 Useful Expressions

Phrases	Examples
in particular 尤其是	Unemployment has hit unskilled workers in particular. 失业尤其冲击到了无技能的工人
in memory of 纪念	He founded the charity in memory of his late wife. 他兴办那个慈善机构以纪念他已故的妻子
rather than 而不是	She had started to devote her energies to teaching rather than performing. 她已经开始将精力从表演转移到教学中
as usual 像往常一样	She was getting breakfast as usual. 她像往常一样在准备早餐
without a doubt 毫无疑问	Without a doubt will improve the techniques used by many designers around the world. 毫无疑问，这些内容将提升世界各地设计师的应用技巧

 Background Information

1. Vincent van Gogh: 文森特·威廉·梵·高（1853—1890），荷兰后印象派画家，后印象主义的先驱，深深地影响了20世纪艺术，尤其是野兽派与表现主义。在他去世之后，他的作品《星夜》《向日葵》与《麦田乌鸦》等，已跻身全球最著名、最珍贵的艺术作品的行列。文森特的作品目前主要收纳在阿姆斯特丹的梵高美术馆，以及奥特洛的国立克罗-米勒美术馆。

2. Academy Awards: 奥斯卡金像奖，正式名称是美国电影艺术与科学学院奖，简称学院奖，为世界著名电影奖项。奥斯卡金像奖是美国一项表彰电影业成就的年度奖项，旨在鼓励优秀电影的创作与发展，囊括了各种电影类型，有20多个不同的奖项，是全世界最具影响力的电影奖项。

Reading Comprehension

I. Decide whether the following statements are True (T) or False (F).

(   ) 1. *Loving Vincent* is a biographical film about the life of Van Gogh.

(   ) 2. The film is made up of about 100 oil paintings.

(   ) 3. The director preferred the traditional animators.

(   ) 4. The process of completing the film is a very tough work.

(   ) 5. The speed of taking this form of film-making is 120 years slower than that of the traditional one.

(   ) 6. The flagship *Loving Vincent Exhibition* displayed more than 100 oil paintings by Van Gogh.

(   ) 7. *Loving Vincent* received Best Animated Feature nominations at the Academy Awards.

II. Complete the answers to the following questions.

1. What's theme of this animated biographical film? (para. 1)

   It about the life of Van Gogh and _____.

2. Why did the director prefer the classically trained painters? (para. 3)

   Because he wanted to avoid _____.

3. What is the beginning of production of the film? (para. 4)

   The film began with _____.

4. How much money did the film make till March 22, 2018? (para. 7)

   Till March 22, 2018, the film has grossed _____ worldwide.

Unit 5 Animated Film and Oil Painting

 Vocabulary and Structure

Words and Phrases to Drill

animated	circumstances	anniversary	technique	display
individual	admit	definitely	exhibition	budget
in particular	in memory of	rather than	as usual	without a doubt

I. Choose the appropriate explanation from Column B for each of the words in Column A.

A	B
_____ 1. animated	a. to put sth. in a place where people can see it easily
_____ 2. circumstances	b. declare to be true or admit the existence or reality or truth of
_____ 3. anniversary	c. the date on which an event occurred in some previous year
_____ 4. technique	d. (of pictures, drawings, etc.) made to look as if they are moving
_____ 5. display	e. a collection of things (goods or works of art etc.) for public display
_____ 6. individual	f. the conditions that affect a situation, action, event etc.
_____ 7. admit	g. a sum of money allocated for a particular purpose
_____ 8. definitely	h. being or characteristic of a single thing or person
_____ 9. exhibition	i. without question and beyond doubt
_____ 10. budget	j. a practical method or art applied to some particular task

II. Fill in the blanks with the correct forms of the words in Column A of the above table.
1. He won the third _____ gold medal at the Olympics Games.
2. Weightlifting is a test of skill and _____, rather than brute strength.
3. Can you give me a _____ answer by tomorrow?
4. He bought his wife a diamond ring on their fifth wedding _____.
5. Those treasure will be officially _____ in that museum next week.
6. In these _____, a password recovery procedure must be followed.
7. Disney pioneered in making full-length _____ feature films.
8. All restaurants must _____ their prices outside.
9. In Holland, the government sets a yearly _____ for health care.
10. By her own _____, she was responsible for the accident.

III. Compare each pair of words and choose the correct one to fill in each blank. Change the form if necessary.
1. animate   animated
   a. The best _____ short, "Peter & the Wolf", was British and Polish.
   b. How long does it take to _____ a shot?
2. technique   technology
   a. They need to learn modern management _____.
   b. Science and _____ have made major changes to the way we live.

99

3. admit   admission
   a. I have to _____ that I have bad handwriting.
   b. Were you just trying to trap her into making some _____?
4. definitely   definite
   a. A great team-leader always has _____ views about most things.
   b. She thought that acting is _____ a young person's profession in many ways.

IV. **Add the suffix "-sion, -tion" to the following words in brackets. Then complete the sentences with the words formed.**

> **Tips:** -ion 附在动词后面构成名词。如 instruct (v.) + ion → instruction (n.).

Sample: You should make a reasonable decision on this important matter. (decide)
1. In average, the _____ system in Paris carries 950 000 passengers a day. (transport)
2. He came along very well after the _____. (operate)
3. A _____ of talent, hard work took her to the top. (combine)
4. These poems have helped inspire the _____ of children. (image)
5. We had a serious _____ about the fund. (discuss)

V. **Choose the best phrase to complete each sentence.**
1. I think a lot of people, women _____, steer clear of these sensitive issues.
   A. in particular   B. in particularly   C. on particular   D. on particularly
2. They will build a monument _____ the national hero.
   A. in memory   B. in memorize of   C. in memory of   D. in memorize
3. These successful firms are biased towards growth _____ profits.
   A. would rather   B. rather than   C. would like   D. other than
4. In the hotel, the old men were drinking away _____.
   A. as usual as   B. as usually   C. as usual   D. as usually as
5. _____, she's the strongest candidate we've interviewed for the post.
   A. Without hesitation   B. Without a doubt
   C. Without thinking   D. Without caring

VI. **Complete the following sentences by translating the Chinese given in brackets into English.**
1. He made some remarks _____ (不针对任何人) and said goodbye.
2. The monumental pillar was built _____ (为了纪念那些为国牺牲的人).
3. They wait for the group to decide _____ (而不是做出个人的决定).
4. Although he is getting along in years, _____ (他能像往常一样努力工作).
5. _____ (毫无疑问), this makes League of legends the most popular game on the planet.

Unit 5 Animated Film and Oil Painting

VII. Translate the following sentences into Chinese.

1. It is an experimental animated biographical film about the life of Vincent Van Gogh. (para. 1)
   _____

2. It is the world's first fully oil painted animated feature film. (para. 2)
   _____

3. The director chose classically trained painters rather than traditional animators. (para. 3)
   _____

4. Till March 22, 2018, the film has grossed more than ＄30.5 million worldwide. (para. 7)
   _____

VIII. Combine the following sentences using "even though".

> even though 引导让步状语从句,表示"虽然,尽管",可置于句首或句中。
> Sample: I'm so introverted. I like making friends.
>   Even though I'm so introverted, I like making friends.
> Or: I like making friends, even though I'm so introverted.

1. The task is difficult. We'll manage to finish it in time.
   _____

2. It was snowing heavily. Several boys went out.
   _____

3. I am 18 years old. I cannot live separately from parents.
   _____

4. I went to gym everyday. I am still gaining weight.
   _____

5. She was getting angry. Her mind was clear.
   _____

IX. Complete the following sentences by translating the Chinese given in brackets into English using "where".

> where 在定语从句中作地点状语,不可省略,先行词一般是表示地点的名词。
> Sample: The bookshop where I bought this book(我买这本书的书店) is not far from here.

1. This is _____(我两年前住的房子).
2. That is _____(我父亲工作的大楼).
3. A tall building was put up at _____(以前曾是沙漠的地方).
4. It was _____(我过去工作过的工厂).
5. We are going to _____(我出生的那个小村庄).

Dialogue Samples

Listen and read the samples carefully, and then complete the communicative tasks that follow.

Dialogue 1 Booking a room

Clerk: Royal Holiday Hotel, Reservations. Can I help you?

Customer: I'd like to reserve a standard room during Labor Day. How much does it cost, please?

Clerk: It's ＄190 a day including meals but excluding service charges. How long will you stay, Sir?

Customer: Probably more than a week, from May 1st to the morning of May 9th.

Clerk: Very good. May I have your name, please?

Customer: Yes, it's Simon, S-I-M-O-N.

Clerk: Thanks. One moment…Now that's all settled, Sir. Thank you for reserving with us, and we look forward to seeing you.

Dialogue 2 Checking in

Clerk: Welcome to Royal Holiday Hotel. How can I help you, Sir?

Customer: I have a reservation in the name of Simon.

Clerk: Give me one second…It's Simon? Yes, we have it in our records, your room number is 205. Here is your room card.

Customer: Thank you. Where is the dining room? What time do they serve breakfast?

Clerk: It's opposite the lobby. The breakfast is from 6:30 to 9:00 AM.

Customer: Thank you. It's a nice place here.

Clerk: I hope you will enjoy your stay.

Dialogue 3 Checking out

Customer: I'd like to check out, please. My name is Simon, room 205.

Clerk: Did you enjoy your stay here, Sir?

Customer: Yes, I enjoyed it very much. Everything was perfect.

Clerk: How would you like to pay, Sir?

Customer: Can I pay by card?

Clerk: Sure. It's ＄1 710 dollars in total…Could you sign here, please?

Customer: Thanks. Have a nice day!

Unit 5   Animated Film and Oil Painting

 Communicative Tasks

Work with your partner and take turns to start the conversations.

Task 1

Situation:

James intends to reserve a single room from a hotel. He is going to ask receptionist about some details.

Tips:

> **Here are some things the person who wants to reserve a room can say or ask:**
>
> I'd like to reserve a room.
>
> Probably more than a week, from May 1st to the morning of May 9th.
>
> How much does it cost, please?

> **Here are some things the receptionist can say:**
>
> Sorry, there're no vacancies during that period of time.
>
> How long will you stay, Sir?
>
> Thank you for reserving with us, and we look forward to seeing you.

Task 2

Situation:

After ten days stay, James will leave for other city, he is going to check out.

Tips:

> **Here are some things the customer can say or ask:**
>
> I'd like to check out, please.
>
> Could you tell me how to get to the railway station nearby?
>
> Can I pay by card?

> **Here are some things the receptionist can say:**
>
> Did you enjoy your stay here, Sir?
>
> How would you like to pay?
>
> Could you sign here, please?
>
> Have a wonderful journey, sir!

Further Development

不发音的元音字母

1. 以元音 e 结尾

绝大多数情况下，在以 e 结尾的多音节单词中 e 不发音。但以 ee 结尾的单词除外，如 see[siː], employee[ɪmˈplɔIiː] 等。

① 在一些以 e 结尾的单词中，e 的作用是使前一个元音从短元音变为长元音，或从单元音变为双元音，但 e 不发音。如 win[wɪn]-wine[waɪn]，cub[kʌb]-cube[kjuːb]，hop[hɒp]-hope[həʊp]。

② 另外一些以 e 结尾的单词，如：

以 ke 结尾：cake, bike, take, make.

以 ce 结尾：face, voice, office, practice.

以 se 结尾：sense, please, house, course.

以 me 结尾：home, some, come, game.

以 le 结尾：battle, little, apple, trouble.

以 ve 结尾：drive, active, believe, brave.

2. 一些来自法语的词的词尾 -que 或 gue

其中 -ue 不发音，如 tongue [tʌŋ], dialogue [ˈdaɪəlɒg], catalogue [ˈkætəlɒg], technique [tekˈniːk].

3. 元音字母 e, i, o 在轻读音节中

且其前后都是辅音时不发音，如 travel [ˈtrævl], garden [ˈgɑːdn], evil [ˈiːvl], business [ˈbɪznəs].

Text B

Is she really smiling?

1. Is the Mona Lisa in Leonardo da Vinci's masterpiece smiling at us when we look at her? For years, viewers of the painting have been divided into two groups: those who see a little smile and those who don't. But now **Spanish researchers** may have solved the **mystery** of the Mona Lisa, reports the U. K.'s *The Daily Telegraph**.

2. According to them, it's not a matter of the painting but the viewer. It's a question of how the eyes and the brain work. Different areas of the eye are responsible for picking up different information about light and dark colors, background and **foreground**. Different **channels** through the brain are in charge of the information conveying. In short, whether one think Mona Lisa is smiling or not depends upon which cells in the eye catch the **image** first and how information from the image moves through the brain.

3. Luis Martinez Otero, a Spanish scientist, **insisted**, "Sometimes one channel wins over the other, and you see the smile. Sometimes others take over, and you don't see the smile."

4. So, whether Leonardo da Vinci had intended to **confuse** viewers? This Spanish scientist thought so. "He (Leonardo da Vinci) wrote in one of his notebooks that he was trying to paint vivid and dynamic **expressions**."

5. This great Italian master painted the work between 1503 and 1506, shortly before his passing away. While the identity of the Mona Lisa has been **debated** for centuries, the **speculation** about it has **ranged** from Lisa del Gherardini, the wife of a wealthy Florentine businessman, to Da Vinci's mother. Some scholars have insisted that in this work Da Vinci may have painted himself as a woman, they **compared** this masterpiece and the **self-portrait** of Da Vinci and then came to this conclusion.

6. Today it may be the most famous painting in the world. However it only became well-known in the middle of the 19th century, when Europeans began to really regard highly the works of the Renaissance* painters.

7. The mystery of the Mona Lisa has always attracted the attention of many art **historians** and other researchers. It is also the theme of a famous popular song named "Mona Lisa" sung by Nat King Cole, an American jazz pianist and **vocalist**. In the song, "the lady with the **mystic** smile" is asked, "Are you real, Mona Lisa? Or just a cold and lonely, lovely work of art?"

Unit 5　Animated Film and Oil Painting

 New Words

Spanish[ˈspænɪʃ] adj. from or connected with Spain 西班牙的

researcher[rɪˈsɜːtʃə(r)] n. a scientist who devotes himself to doing research 研究者

mystery[ˈmɪstri] n. something that baffles understanding and cannot be explained 秘密，谜；神秘，神秘的事物；推理小说，推理剧

foreground[ˈfɔːɡraʊnd] n. the part of a view, picture, etc. that is nearest to you when you look at it 前景；突出的地方，最显著的位置

channel[ˈtʃænl] n. official routes of communication 渠道；通道；频道；海峡

image[ˈɪmɪdʒ] n. a visual representation (of an object or scene or person or abstraction) produced on a surface 图像

insist[ɪnˈsɪst] v. to demand that sth. happens or that sb. agrees to do sth. 坚持；强调；坚决要求；坚决认为

confuse[kənˈfjuːz] v. make unclear, indistinct, or blurred 使困窘；使混乱；使困惑；使更难于理解；使糊涂

expression[ɪkˈspreʃn] n. the feelings expressed on a person's face 表现，表达；表情，脸色

debate[dɪˈbeɪt] n. an argument or discussion expressing different opinions 辩论；争论；讨论 v. have an argument about something 辩论；仔细考虑；盘算

speculation[ˌspekjuˈleɪʃn] n. the act of forming opinions about what has happened or what might happen without knowing all the facts 投机活动；思考；推断

range[reɪndʒ] v. to vary between two particular amounts, sizes, etc., including others between them (在一定的范围内) 变化；变动

compared[kəmˈpeəd] adj. consider or describe as similar, equal, or analogous 比较的；对照的

self-portrait[ˌselfˈpɔːtrɪt, -ˌtreɪt, -ˈpəʊr-] n. a painting, etc. that you do of yourself 自画像

historian[hɪsˈtɔːrɪənz] n. a person who is an authority on history and who studies it and writes about it 历史学家；史学工作者

vocalist[ˈvəʊkəlɪst] n. a singer, especially in a pop or jazz band 歌手；声乐家

mystic[ˈmɪstɪk] adj. having an import not apparent to the senses nor obvious to the intelligence 神秘的

Useful Expressions

Phrases	Examples
be responsible for 为……负责	You'll be responsible for receiving and talking with all visitors. 来访者由你负责接谈
depend upon 依赖；依靠	You may depend upon my not mentioning it. 你放心好了，我不会说出去的
intend to 打算做	I really intended to pen this letter to you early this morning. 我真的打算今天一大早给你写这封信的
came to a conclusion 得出结论	I quickly came to a conclusion that I liked making other people happy. 我很快得出了一个结论，那就是我很喜欢让别人幸福
attract the attention 引起注意	I shouted to attract the attention of the children. 我大声喊着引起孩子们的注意

 Background Information

1. *The Daily Telegraph*:《每日电讯报》是一份英国大开型报章，由斯雷上校创立，创刊于1855年，由电讯报业公司出版。它是英国四家全国性"高级"日报中销量最大的一家。第一版于1855年6月29日公布，当时报纸长为四页，售价两便士。该报排版紧凑，内容广泛，但其消息比其他全国性大报简洁明了。

2. Renaissance: 文艺复兴是指发生在14世纪到16世纪的一场欧洲思想文化运动。最先在意大利各城市兴起，以后扩展到西欧各国，是西欧近代三大思想解放运动之一。文艺复兴以人文主义精神为核心，期间代表人物为但丁、达·芬奇、莎士比亚等。文艺复兴运动推动了世界文化的发展，促进了人民的觉醒，为资本主义的发展做了必要的思想文化准备，为资产阶级革命做了思想动员和准备。

Reading Comprehension

I. Decide whether the following statements are True (T) or False (F).

(　　) 1. When we look at Mona Lisa, she is smiling at us.

(　　) 2. Different channels through the brain are in charge of the information conveying.

(　　) 3. The scholars have confirmed that in this work Da Vinci may have painted himself as a woman.

(　　) 4. Europeans began to regard highly the works of the Renaissance painters in the middle of the 19th century.

(　　) 5. The mystery of the Mona Lisa has always attracted the attention of many art historians.

II. Choose the best answer to each of the following questions.

1. According to the researchers, which factor decide whether we can see the smile?
   A. The painting and the painter
   B. The light and color
   C. The background and foreground
   D. The eyes and brain

2. The word "confuse" in Paragraph 4 most probably means ＿＿＿＿＿ .
   A. compose　　　B. puzzle　　　C. quiet　　　D. trick

3. Which one of the following is NOT one of the speculations about the identity of the Mona Lisa?
   A. The wife of a wealthy Florentine businessman　　B. One of Da Vinci's girlfriends
   C. Da Vinci's mother
   D. The female image of Da Vinci himself

4. According to the author, which statement is right?
   A. There is not an affirmative conclusion about the identity of the Mona Lisa
   B. The Mona Lisa became well-known since its appearance
   C. Europeans began to regard highly the works of the Renaissance painters in the early 19th century
   D. The Mona Lisa is a self-portrait of Da Vinci

5. Why did Nat King Cole sing the song named "Mona Lisa"?
   A. Because he didn't believe that she was real
   B. Because he thought that she was lovely
   C. Because he thought that she was cold and lonely
   D. Because he was attracted by her mystery

Practical Writing

Note for Leave

便条是一种简短、明了的书信。只需写明时间、地点、事件、原因等必要因素即可。

请假条采用书信格式，写明日期、称呼、落款，并说明理由。日期应写在右上角的位置，称呼在左上角并低于日期一行的位置，落款在右下角的位置。

Sample 1

你叫李华，由于得了重感冒和发烧，今天上午的两节英语课不能去上。医生说需卧床休息一天，兹附上证明一张。只要身体一康复就立即回校上课。

请就此事给王老师写一张请假条。5 月 30 日。

May 30

Dear Ms. Wang,

  I am terribly sorry that I shall be unable to attend this morning's two periods of English class due to a bad cold and high fever. Enclosed is a certificate from the doctor who said I must stay in bed for the whole day. I will go back to school as soon as I recover.

Yours respectfully,
LiHua

Sample 2

说明：假设你是公司职员王建，给经理 Mr. Johnson 写一张请假条。

时间：8 月 24 日，星期四。

1. 咳嗽特别厉害，想去医院看病。
2. 因本周大部分工作已经完成，故星期五请假一天。
3. 看完病后，会给经理打电话。
4. 对由此造成的不便表示歉意。
5. 希望能得到经理的批准。

August 24, Thursday

Dear Mr. Johnson,

  I feel very sorry that I have a very bad cough and would like to go to the hospital for treatment. As I have finished most of the work of this week, and tomorrow is Friday, I'm afraid I will be off for the whole day. After I get the treatment, I'll surely call you. I feel extremely sorry for the inconvenience I bring about. I sincerely hope you would approve my request for leave.

Yours respectfully,
Wang Jian

Notice

通知的写法包括如下内容：

1. 标题：多以 NOTICE 或 ANNOUNCEMENT 为标题。

2. 日期：和书信式的日期位置一样，位于右上角。

3. 称呼：和书信式的称呼位置一样，位于左上角并低于日期一行的位置。如果以第三人称来写，可以无称呼语。

4. 正文：简明扼要。写明具体时间、地点、内容、要求、对象、相关事宜。

5. 落款：发出通知的人或单位名称，一般在右下角位置。

常用句型：

1. This is to announce that…

现通知……。

2. All the students are requested to attend the meeting in the main hall on…, at….

要求全体学生在大礼堂，……（周几），……（几点）参加会议。

3. It's decided that a meeting will be held to discuss…

兹定召开会议讨论……。

Sample 1

英语系将举办关于美式英语和英式英语比较的英语讲座. 请根据以下内容写一个通知。

1. 主讲人是著名的英语教授 Mr. Alexander.

2. 时间和地点：4月23日星期六晚7点至9点，学术报告厅。

3. 有兴趣的同学均可参加，也可邀请外校的朋友参加。

4. 要求不能迟到。报告完毕还可以和 Mr. Alexander 照相。

5. 发布通知的时间是4月20日。

NOTICE

April 20th

There will be an English lecture on the differences between American English and British English by a famous English professor, Mr. Alexander. It will be given in the Lecture Hall from 7:00 to 9:00 on Saturday evening, April 23rd. Those who are interested in it are warmly welcome, you may also invite your friends of other schools to attend it.

Be sure not to be late. After the lecture, you may have a picture taken with Mr. Alexander.

The English Department Office

Sample 2

学生会打算举办一次英语写作比赛，根据以下内容写一份书面通知。

1. 举办写作比赛的目的是提高学生的英语写作水平。

2. 比赛形式为：上机考试。

3. 时间和地点：11月25日上午8点，图书馆五楼计算机中心。

4. 请参加比赛的同学于 11 月 23 日前到学生会报名。
5. 欢迎大家积极参与并按时做好准备,预祝成功!
6. 通知发布日期:11 月 20 日。

NOTICE

November 20th

We are going to have an English writing contest for students so as to improve our written English. The form of contest is typing the words on the computers. It will be held in the computer center on the 5th floor in library at 8 A. M. November 25th. Those who want to take part in the contest are supposed to come to sign up at the office of the Student Union before November 23rd. All the students are warmly welcome, please try your best and get ready in time.

Wish you success!

The Student Union

Culture

The self-made man

In many countries, one's social position is determined by that of his or her family or neighborhood, or the district or the whole town. But the United States is different from those countries. In the USA a man can succeed by his own efforts rather than by outside conditions. The self-made man is used to describe individuals whose success lay within themselves rather than related to family or other conditions. Americans believe that there is no class system as an obstacle will stop one from becoming somebody in any professions, they have great admiration for the self-made man who fights his way to the top of society by nurturing qualities, such as perseverance, hard work, and ingenuity, as opposed to achieving these goals through inherited fortune, family connections, or other privileges.

The story of the self-made man begins with Benjamin Franklin, one of the Founding Fathers of the United States, who has been described as the greatest exemplar of the self-made man. Though he was hardly the first man to rise from poverty to prominence, no one in America's short history had started out so low and ended up so high. He was the tenth son of a Boston candle-maker, and finally became a world-famous scientist, an influential diplomat, and a wealthy man of business.

Another famous example is Abraham Lincoln who was born in a poor family, his mom died when he was very young, he had to live with his father in a very shabby house with only three walls. Even so, Abraham Lincoln had a strong will and worked very hard, he accomplished most of his study by himself because he had no chance to go to school. Meanwhile, little Lincoln did many kinds of work to earn money and support family. As he grew up, he studied law, he became an outstanding speaker and a good student of political philosophy. He eventually became the president of the United States through many years of struggle.

Nowadays, values and ways to success may be somewhat different from those at the time of Abraham Lincoln, however, the American spirit of gaining success by one's own efforts are still widely admired in the United States.

Unit 6

What is Good Design?

Warm-up Activities

I. Matching

Learn the following words and phrases about different types of design, and match them to the pictures.

1. interior design ( ) 2. industrial design ( ) 3. graphic design ( )
4. brand design ( ) 5. furniture design ( ) 6. landscape design ( )

A.

B.

C.

D.

E.

F.

II. Reading

Innovation is the soul of a nation's progress, the inexhaustible power of a country's prosperity.

创新是一个民族进步的灵魂，是一个国家兴旺发达的不竭动力。

innovation　n. 创新
progress　　n. 进步
prosperity　n. 繁荣兴旺

Text A

Ten Principles for Good Design

1. Dieter Rams began studies in **architecture** and **interior** design at Wiesbaden School of Art in 1947. In 1955, he was recruited to Braun* as an **industrial** designer. In addition, in 1961, he became the Chief Design Officer at Braun until 1995.

2. Rams and his staff designed many famous products for Braun including the SK-4 record player and the high-quality D-series (D45, D46) of 35 mm film slide **projectors**. He is also known for designing a **furniture** collection for Vitsoe in the 1960s including the 606 Universal Shelving System and 620 Chair Program.

3. By producing **electronic** devices that were remarkable in their simple aesthetic and user friendliness, Rams made Braun a household name in the 1950s. His design style is "Less, but better". After making his **significant contribution**, he asked himself an important question: is my design good one? As good design cannot be measured in a way, so he put forward the ten most important **principles** which were also called the "Ten commandments"*.

4.
A. Good Design is **Innovative**.

The possibilities for innovation are not **exhausted**. Technological development is always offering new opportunities for innovative design.

B. Good Design is Useful.

A product is bought to be used. Good design **emphasizes** the functional usefulness of a product.

C. Good Design is Aesthetic.

The aesthetic quality of a product is essential to its usefulness because products we use every day affect our well-being.

D. Good Design is Understandable.

It makes the product's structure clear. Better still, it can make the product talk. At best, it **is self-explanatory**.

E. Good Design is Modest.

Products fulfilling a purpose are like tools, their design should therefore leave room for the user's self-expression.

F. Good Design is Honest.

It does not attempt to confuse the consumer with presenting more useful than it really is.

G. Good Design is Long-lasting.

Unlike fashionable design, it lasts many years—even in today's throwaway society.

H. Good Design is Detail-**oriented**.

Care and **accuracy** in the design process show respect towards the user. Remember, good and timeless design aims for **excellence** in every detail.

I. Good Design is Environmentally-friendly.

Design makes an important contribution to the **environment** protection. It reduces physical and visual pollution throughout the lifecycle of the product.

J. Good Design is Simple.

It focuses on the **essential** aspects, back to purity, back to **simplicity**. Less, but better.

Unit 6　What is Good Design?

New Words

architecture[ˈɑːkɪtektʃə(r)] n. the art of planning, designing, and constructing buildings 建筑学

interior[ɪnˈtɪəriə(r)] adj. the inside part of sth. 内部的；内地的，国内的

industrial[ɪnˈdʌstriəl] adj. connected with industry 工业的；产业的

projector[prəˈdʒektə] n. a machine that projects films or slides onto a screen or wall 电影放映机；幻灯机

furniture[ˈfɜːnɪtʃə(r)] n. objects that can be moved, such as tables, chairs and beds, that are put into a house or an office to make it suitable for living or working in 家具

electronic[ɪˌlekˈtrɒnɪk] adj. of or relating to electronics 电子的

significant[sɪɡˈnɪfɪkənt] adj. large or important enough to have an effect or to be noticed 重要的；有意义的

contribution[ˌkɒntrɪˈbjuːʃn] n. the part played by a person in bringing about a result 贡献；捐赠

principle[ˈprɪnsəpl] n. a general belief that you have about the way to behave 原则；原理

innovative[ˈɪnəveɪtɪv] adj. being or producing something like nothing done or experienced or created before 创新的；革新的

exhausted[ɪɡˈzɔːstɪd] adj. very tired 精疲力竭的；耗尽的，用完的

emphasize[ˈemfəsaɪz] v. to give special importance to sth. 强调；着重

self-explanatory [ˌselfɪkˈsplænətrɪ] adj. easy to understand and not needing any more explanation 不解自明的；明显的

oriented[ˈɔːrɪəntɪd] adj. to direct sb./sth. towards sth. 导向的，定向的；以……为方向的

accuracy[ˈækjʊrəsi] n. the state of being exact or correct 精确（性）；准确（性）

excellence[ˈeksələns] n. the quality of being extremely good 优点；优秀，卓越；美德

environment[ɪnˈvaɪrənmənt] n. the conditions that affect the behaviour and development of sb./sth.; the physical conditions that sb./sth. exists in 环境

essential[ɪˈsenʃl] a. absolutely necessary, of the greatest importance 必要的；重要的

simplicity[sɪmˈplɪsəti] n. the quality of being easy to understand or use 简单，朴素；质朴

Useful Expressions

Phrases	Examples
in addition 另外；除此之外	You need money and time; in addition, you need diligence. 你需要钱和时间，此外还需要努力
put forward 提出	The students have put forward a series of questions. 学生们提出了一系列问题
attempt to 尝试；企图	The authorities have said they will attempt to maintain essential services. 当局已表示他们将努力维持公共基础服务
be essential to 对……是必要的	Creative thinking is essential to a designer. 创新性思维对一个设计师来说是必要的
focus on 致力于	It took efforts to focus on preparing his classes or correcting his students' work. 备课和批改学生的作业花费了他很多精力

 Background Information

1. Braun: 德国博朗公司。德国博朗公司成立之初便设定了一个宗旨：产品外型完全根据其预定功能设计，杜绝肤浅、花哨和与产品功能无关的时髦元素，追求明快、简洁与平衡的线条。由此保证了德国博朗产品在世界各地一经推出就广受喜爱。博朗的设计宗旨延伸至今，已成为独特的博朗设计理念 Braun Design，可归纳为创新、品质、实用、美观、简洁、细节、经典、环保。

2. Picasso: 十诫，有时写作十戒。据《圣经》记载，上帝借由以色列的先知和众部族首领摩西向以色列民族颁布了十条规定，它是以色列人一切立法的基础，也是西方文明核心的道德观。此文将迪特·拉姆斯的十个设计原则比喻成"摩西十诫"，是设计界所认可的设计准则。

Reading Comprehension

I. **Decide whether the following statements are True (T) or False (F).**

( ) 1. In 1955, Dieter Rams became the Chief Design Officer at Braun until 1995.
( ) 2. Rams is known for designing a furniture collection and electronic gadgets.
( ) 3. Rams put forward the ten most important principles for good design.
( ) 4. The possibilities for innovation are limited.
( ) 5. Good design makes the viewers or the users understand it easily.
( ) 6. The unfashionable design would be threw away.
( ) 7. Good design contributes the environment protection to some extent.

II. **Complete the answers to the following questions.**

1. What were the features of Braun's remarkable electronic gadgets? (para. 3)
   They were remarkable in their _____.
5. How did Dieter Rams explain his design style? (para. 3)
   His design style is _____.
6. Why are the possibilities for innovation not exhausted? (para. 4)
   _____ is always offering new opportunities for innovative design.
7. What are the "Ten Commandments" in design? (para. 4)
   Innovative, useful, aesthetic, understandable, modest, _____ simple.

Vocabulary and Structure

Words and Phrases to Drill

architecture	electronic	significant	contribution	principle
innovative	emphasize	accuracy	environment	essential
in addition	put forward	attempt to	be essential to	focus on

I. Choose the appropriate explanation from Column B for each of the words in Column A.

A	B
_____ 1. architecture	a. a general belief that you have about the way you should behave
_____ 2. electronic	b. the conditions that affect the behaviour and development of sb./sth.; the physical conditions that sb./sth. exists in
_____ 3. significant	c. absolutely necessary, of the greatest importance
_____ 4. contribution	d. large or important enough to have an effect or to be noticed
_____ 5. principle	e. of or relating to electronics
_____ 6. innovative	f. to give special importance to sth.
_____ 7. emphasize	g. the part played by a person in bringing about a result
_____ 8. accuracy	h. the state of being exact or correct
_____ 9. environment	i. the art of planning, designing, and constructing buildings
_____ 10. essential	j. being or producing something like nothing done or experienced or created before

II. Fill in the blanks with the correct forms of the words in Column A of the above table.

1. They commissioned an _____ to design the new library.
2. The two things are the same in outward form but different in _____.
3. This technical _____ will save us much time and labour.
4. Our college _____ on teaching and scientific research.
5. _____ mail has become an extremely important and popular means of communication.
6. We should live by our own _____.
7. Marks were given for _____ spelling and punctuation.
8. What is the _____ of life? Is there any criterion to measure?
9. We need a peaceful international _____.
10. The Chinese people should make a greater _____ to mankind.

III. Compare each pair of words and choose the correct one to fill in each blank. Change the form if necessary.

1. electronic   electric

   a. _____ computers are now in common use all over the world.

   b. An _____ heater consumes too much electricity.

Unit 6 What is Good Design?

2. innovative   innovation

   a. They need new technology and _____ .

   b. If you search various designs, you will find _____ use of color by designers in their work.

3. essential   essence

   a. She cannot pin down the _____ of true beauty.

   b. Simplifying the choices and factors in your life is _____ .

4. significant   significance

   a. We made some _____ progress through great efforts.

   b. On no account can we ignore the _____ of education.

Ⅳ. **Add the suffix "-er, -or, -ee" to the following words in brackets. Then complete the sentences with the words formed.**

> **Tips:** 后缀-ee 附于动词后，表示动作的受动者。与之相应，动作的施动者则由后缀-er/-or 表示。如：employ(v.) + er→employer(n. 雇主)；employ(v.) + e→employee(n. 雇员)。

Sample: When I was a little girl, my dream is to be a <u>painter</u> in the future. (paint)

1. My first job was as a graduate _____ in a big company. (train)
2. He sold newspaper to earn his own living when he was a _____ . (teenage)
3. He is not the interviewer, but the _____ . (interview)
4. Confucius was the greatest _____ in Chinese history. (educate)
5. President Ronald Reagan used to be an _____ . (act)

Ⅴ. **Choose the best phrase to complete each sentence.**

1. _____ to my weekly wage, I got a lot of tips.

   A. In additional   B. In addition   C. Except   D. Besides

2. The theory _____ by these scientists is quite reasonable.

   A. put forward   B. put about   C. put off   D. put up

3. These books _____ explain why that is, and what should be done about it.

   A. attend to   B. tempt to   C. attempt at   D. attempt to

4. Being yourself may _____ your long-term happiness.

   A. be essence to   B. be essential to   C. essence to   D. essential to

5. _____ one task until it's done, then move to the next.

   A. Focus on   B. Focus at   C. Focus in   D. Focus from

Ⅵ. **Complete the following sentences by translating the Chinese given in brackets into English.**

1. She is beautiful and wealthy, _____(此外，还非常努力)。
2. _____ (我认为我提出了一些很好的想法), but none of them were accepted.

3. _____ (他试图掌控公司), but at last he failed.
4. _____ (阅读对……是必不可少的) students' growth and success.
5. _____ (学生们应该集中注意力在考试上) and resist the temptation.

VII. Translate the following sentences into Chinese.

1. As good design cannot be measured in a way, so he put forward the ten most important principles. (para. 3)

2. Technological development is always offering new opportunities for innovative design. (para. 4)

3. Good design emphasizes the functional usefulness of a product. (para. 4)

4. Remember, good and timeless design aims for excellence in every detail. (para. 4)

VIII. Combine the following sentences using the conjunction "yet".

> yet 用作并列连词时，表转折，意思为"然而，但是，却"。
> Sample: Jimmy worked very hard.   Jimmy failed the exam.
> Jimmy worked very hard, yet he failed the exam.

1. Linda said she was my best friend.   Linda didn't help me.

2. We have made some progress.   We still have a lot of work to do.

3. I thought I would be late.   I arrived there on time.

4. The test was rather easy.   Most students haven't passed it.

5. The house was old.   The house was in good condition.

IX. Complete the following sentences by translating the Chinese given in brackets into English using "if".

> if 引导的条件状语从句，如果从句用一般现在时，主句则用一般将来时。
> Sample: If you are very lucky, <u>you will get the job</u> (你将会得到这份工作).

1. If it rains tomorrow, _____ (我就不去爬山).
2. If Johnny is late again, _____ (老师会很生气).
3. If it doesn't rain tomorrow, _____ (他们就去露营).
4. _____ (如果你去那个聚会), you'll have a great time.
5. _____ (如果她起来晚了), she won't catch the early bus.

Dialogue Samples

Listen and read the samples carefully, and then complete the communicative tasks that follow.

Dialogue 1 Asking and stating the symptoms

Clark: Hey! You look pale. Are you okay?

Kent: I feel terrible. I think I'm sick.

Clark: My goodness! Do you have any other symptoms?

Kent: Well, I don't have any appetite and sometimes I feel nauseous.

Clark: Did you eat something unusual?

Kent: Oh, I can't remember it, my head is pounding.

Clark: You must have a bad cold, you need a doctor.

Kent: I don't think that will be necessary.

Clark: Are you taking any medicine regularly?

Kent: No.

Clark: You should go see a doctor, take some pills and have a good rest.

Kent: OK, thank you very much.

Dialogue 2 Giving Diagnosis and treatment

Doctor: What's the matter with you?

Patient: Oh, I broke my leg.

Doctor: Sounds terrible, how do you feel now?

Patient: It hurts now!

Doctor: Well, your leg is broken, I think you should be treated right away.

Patient: Should I be hospitalized?

Doctor: Certainly, you need an operation and some shots.

Patient: I hate shots, Can I take the medicine orally?

Doctor: I'll prescribe some pain-killers. Take 1 tablet when you feel bad. Don't take more than 3 tablets a day. Stay in bed, have a good rest. I will arrange for your operation.

Patient: How long will it take?

Doctor: Maybe a few hours it depends on how serious the break is.

Patient: Thank you.

Doctor: Don't mention it. I'm only doing my job.

Communicative Tasks

Work with your partner and take turns to start the conversations.

Task 1

Situation:

Eric feels bad, and he wonders if he should go to see the doctor. John is a friend of him, he expresses some opinions.

Tips:

Here are some things the person who feels bad can say or ask:

I have a headache.

Do you think it is necessary to go to the hospital to see the doctor?

I don't like taking the medicine.

Here are some things his friend can say:

The medicine will make you feel better.

You should go to see a doctor.

The injection may bring down your temperature.

You should drink some water and have a good rest.

Task 2

Situation:

One has a high fever with headache and a sore throat. The doctor gives him some diagnosis and treatment.

Tips:

Here are some things the patient can say or ask:

I feel very bad.

I hate injections, Can I take the medicine orally?

Should I be hospitalized?

Here are some things the doctor can say:

What are your symptoms?

Let me check / take your temperature.

I'll give you an injection.

I'll prescribe some pain-killers, they will relieve your headache.

Further Development

不发音的辅音字母

（1）字母 b 在字母 t 之前，如 debt[det]。
（2）字母 b 在字母 m 之后，如 comb[kəʊm]。
（3）字母 c 在字母 s 之后，如 muscle[ˈmʌsl]。
（4）字母 d 在词尾 -dge 中，如 bridge[brɪdʒ]。
（5）字母 g 在字母 n 之前，如 sign[sain]。
（6）字母 gh 在 t 之前，如 fight[fait]。
（7）字母 h 在 r 之后，如 rhythm[ˈrɪðəm]。
（8）字母 h 在词首 ex- 之后，如 exhibition[ˌeksɪˈbɪʃn]。
（9）字母 h 在词首 gh 中，如 ghost[gəʊst]。
（10）字母 k 在字母 n 之前，如 knee[niː]。
（11）字母 l 在 -alf, -alk, -alm, -ould 中，如 could[kud]。
（12）字母 n 在词尾 -mn 中，如 autumn[ˈɔːtəm]。
（13）字母 t 在词尾 -sten, -stlet 和 -ften 中，如 listen[ˈlisn]。
（14）字母 w 在字母 r 之前，如 write[raɪt]。

Text B

The logo designs for 24 solar terms shine at the UN headquarters

1. In Feb 2018, a collection of logo designs based on the 24 **solar** terms* of the traditional Chinese solar **calendar** was displayed at the UN* **headquarters** in New York.

2. It was **created** by a Chinese lady named Shao Luyun, who was born in the 1980s. She **specializes** in research related to **graphic** design, **illustration** art, and folk **handicrafts**, now she is a teacher in the Department of **Visual** Communication and Design at Huzhou University.

3. Solar Terms is a calendar of 24 periods and **climate** to govern **agricultural** arrangements in ancient China. "In the field of illustration art, traditional festivals, solar terms and seasons are popular elements, which are often used to create artworks," Shao introduced.

4. During Beijing Design Week in September 2017, a logo design competition based on the 24 solar terms attracted much attention. Shao was invited by its organizers to take part in the contest and represent professional designers.

5. Inspired by a large number of **publications** and artworks, she added some elements such as raindrops and swallows in her designs. "I learned many interesting things about folk customs during the process, and I took about more than two months to finish the whole design collection." Shao added.

6. Shao's artwork stood out among the over 500 artworks, and was awarded after being reviewed by experts in various fields, including art, folk customs, and **literature**. After that, she was invited to **promote** the 24 solar terms at the UN headquarters as an "international cultural exchange **ambassador**" at the end of 2017.

7. On Feb 1, her award-winning artwork made its international **debut** in New York. "After explaining my design concept, many visitors took out their phones and cameras to take photos. UN **staff** talked a lot about traditional Chinese culture with us," She recalled.

8. This is the first time the 24 solar terms have been promoted at the UN headquarters since

they were selected as the UNESCO's intangible cultural heritage of **humanity** * in 2016.

9. Shao was also pleased that a **promotional** event on traditional Chinese culture for youth was held at the Brooklyn City Hall on Feb 2, allowing local students to learn more about Chinese painting, seal-cutting and paper-cutting. During this event, she taught foreign children paper-cutting.

10. Shao hopes that her 24 solar terms logo design and her teaching will inspire more young people to take part in promoting traditional Chinese culture.

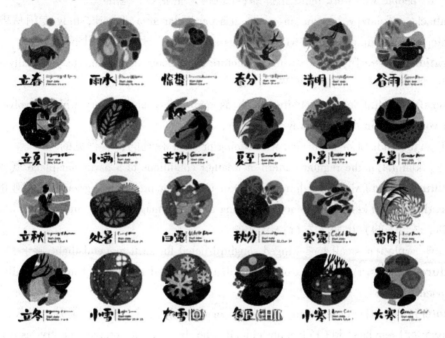

New Words

solar[ˈsəʊlə(r)] adj. of or connected with the sun 太阳的；日光的

calendar[ˈkælɪndə(r)] n. a list or register of events 日历

headquarters[ˌhedˈkwɔːtəz] n. a place from which an organization or a military operation is controlled; the people who work there 指挥部；（机构，企业等）总部

specialize[ˈspeʃəlaɪz] v. become an expert in a particular area of work, study 专门从事

graphic[ˈɡræfɪk] adj. connected with drawings and design 图解的；用图表示的

illustration[ˌɪləˈstreɪʃn] n. a drawing or picture in a book, magazine, etc. especially one that explains sth. 插图；说明；例证；图解

handicraft[ˈhændiˌkrɑːft] n. activities such as embroidery and pottery which involve making things with your hands in a skillful way 手工艺品；手工艺

visual[ˈvɪʒuəl] adj. of or connected with seeing or sight 视觉的；看得见的

climate[ˈklaɪmət] n. the regular pattern of weather conditions of a particular place 气候

agricultural[ˌæɡrɪˈkʌltʃərəl] adj. relating to or used in or promoting agriculture 农业的

publication[ˌpʌblɪˈkeɪʃn] n. the act of printing a book, a magazine, etc. and making it available to the public (书刊等的) 出版，发行；出版物

swallow[ˈswɒləʊ] n. small long-winged songbird noted for swift graceful flight 燕子

literature[ˈlɪtrətʃə(r)] n. pieces of writing that are valued as works of art, especially novels, plays and poems 文学

promote[prəˈməʊt] v. to help sth. to happen or develop 促进，推进；提升，助长；促销

ambassador[æmˈbæsədə(r)] n. an official who lives in a foreign country as the senior representative of his or her own country 大使；使节

debut[ˈdeɪbjuː] n. the first public appearance of a performer or sports player 初次露面；初次表演；首次出场；处女秀

staff[stɑːf] n. all the workers employed in an organization considered as a group 全体职工

humanity[hjuːˈmænəti] n. people in general; the quality of being kind to people and animals by making sure that they do not suffer more than is necessary (统称) 人；人类，人道，仁慈

promotional[prəˈməʊʃənl] adj. promotional material, events, or ideas are designed to increase the sales of a product or service 推销的；推广的；宣传的

Useful Expressions

Phrases	Examples
specialize in 专门从事于	Many students specialize in engineering. 许多学生专攻工程学
relate to 与……相关	All these questions relate to art. 这些问题都跟艺术有关
in the field of 在……的领域中	Disney was a pioneer in the field of animation. 迪士尼是动画领域的开拓者
make its debut 首次露面	A new mobile phone will soon make its debut in China. 一种新型的手机不久将投入中国市场
take part in 参与	They all dressed up to take part in the New Year's party. 他们都盛装打扮，去参加新年晚会

Background Information

1. 24 solar terms: 24 节气。24 节气是中国农历中的 24 个特定节令。通过观察太阳周年运动，把太阳周年运动轨迹等分，每一等份为一个节气，始于立春，终于大寒，周而复始。二十四节气由中国古代先秦时期开始订立、到汉代完全确立，是古代中国劳动人民长期的经验积累和智慧的结晶，准确反映了季节的变化并用于指导农事活动。

2. UN: 联合国。联合国（United Nations）是一个世界性、综合性的政府间国际组织。联合国在第二次世界大战后成立，由主权国家组成，致力于促进各国在国际法、国际安全、经济发展、社会进步、人权及实现世界和平方面的合作，总部设立在美国纽约。

3. the UNESCO's intangible cultural heritage of humanity: 联合国教科文组织非物质文化遗产。联合国教科文组织（United Nations Educational, Scientific, and Cultural Organization）成立于 1946 年，其宗旨是促进教育、科学及文化方面的国际合作，以利于各国人民之间的相互了解，维护世界和平。非物质文化遗产：非物质文化包括所有传统和民间文化的表达形式，如习俗、语言、舞蹈、音乐、宗教仪式、节日、传统医学和药典、烹调艺术、口传文化传统及所有与物质文化相关的特殊技能。截至 2019 年 11 月底，我国入选联合国教科文组织世界非物质类文化遗产名录项目总数已达 40 项，成为世界上入选"非遗"项目最多的国家。

Reading Comprehension

Ⅰ. **Decide whether the following statements are True (T) or False (F).**

(   ) 1. The designer of the 24 solar terms is working at the UN headquarters.

(   ) 2. Solar Terms is a calendar of 24 periods and climate to govern industrial arrangements in ancient China.

(   ) 3. Shao's design inspiration came from a large number of publications and artworks.

(   ) 4. Shao was invited to be an "international cultural exchange ambassador" because of her outstanding performance in Beijing Design Week.

(   ) 5. The 24 solar terms are the UNESCO's intangible cultural heritage of humanity.

Ⅱ. **Choose the best answer to each of the following questions.**

1. Which kind of field doesn't Shao specialize in?

    A. product design   B. graphic design   C. illustration art   D. folk handicrafts

2. Which one of the following is NOT true?

    A. Traditional festivals, solar energy and seasons are popular in the field of illustration art

    B. There was a logo design competition in Beijing Design Week in September 2017

    C. Shao won the competition and was invited to be an cultural exchange ambassador

    D. Shao added some natural elements in her designs

3. Why was Shao invited to be an cultural exchange ambassador?

    A. She specializes in Chinese traditional culture

    B. She was born in China and worked in UN

    C. She made an outstanding performance in Beijing Design Week

    D. She had promoted the 24 solar terms times and times again

4. It can be inferred from Paragraph7—8 that _____.

    A. Shao knew little about traditional Chinese culture

    B. The 24 solar terms have been promoted at the UN headquarters

    C. The 24 solar terms is the UNESCO's intangible cultural heritage

    D. Shao likes taking photos with the visitors

5. What is not included into the promotional event held at the Brooklyn City Hall on Feb 2?

    A. Chinese painting   B. Chinese literature

    C. seal-cutting   D. paper-cutting

Practical Writing

Letter of Invitation

邀请信明了、热情，表达诚挚的邀请，需说明邀请的原因和活动的时间、地点、内容。采用书信格式。常用句型：

1. We would be very honored if you could come….

如蒙光临，不胜荣幸。

2. Please accept our warm welcome and sincere invitation.

请接受我们热情的欢迎、诚挚的邀请。

3. I would like to take the opportunity to invite you to….

借此机会，我想邀请您……。

4. I'm looking forward to seeing you then, please let us know if you're available.

期待您届时光临，如果您能成行请告知。

Sample 1

邀请人：王楠

被邀请人：Tony

内容：

王楠夫妇为了庆祝结婚50周年纪念日，特举行聚会，希望Tony和妻子一起参加。定于4月6日（下周一）下午5点在Hilton酒店举行。

Dear Tony,

We're planning a tea party to celebrate our fiftieth wedding anniversary and of course we want you and your wife to come. It's at five o'clock, next Monday, April 6th, at the Hilton Hotel.

I do hope you can make it. We are both looking forward with great pleasure to seeing you and your wife.

Sincerely yours,
Wang Nan

Sample 2

根据下列提示，以Eric的名义写一封邀请信。

Eric邀请朋友Richard和George于12月8日星期五晚上八点到家里参加他20周岁生日的聚会，已准备好蛋糕、水果和可口可乐，让朋友们带来一些气球，不用带礼物。如果有空前来参加，请告知。

写信日期：11月30日。

November 30

Dear Richard and George,

I hope you'll join us at an informal party at my home on Friday, December 8, at 8 p. m. to celebrate my birthday of 20 years old.

I'll provide cake, fruits and Coca cola; I'm asking my friends to bring some balloons. No gifts, please.

I'm looking forward to seeing you then, please let us know if you're available.

Sincerely,
Eric

Letter of Thanks

感谢信一般包含三部分。开头要明确地对对方提供的帮助或赠送的礼品表示谢意；主体部分则需列举对方提供的帮助，说明该帮助所起的作用，或表达对所受礼品的喜爱等；结尾部分需再次表达诚挚的谢意并问候对方。采用书信格式，常用句型：

1. Many thanks for your….
非常感谢您……。
2. Please accept my sincere appreciation for your….
请接受我对您……的真诚谢意。
3. I'm grateful to you for….
真心感谢您……。
4. I sincerely appreciate what you have done.
我真诚地感谢您所做的一切。

Sample 1

上周，Richard 到张丽的大学，得到了张丽的热情接待，参观了校园里很多地方，张丽很有耐心地回答她的问题，让她的参观十分有趣。希望将来还有机会再见面。

请以 Richard 的名义给张丽写封感谢信。

写信时间是 5 月 7 日。

May 7th

Dear Zhangli,

I want to thank you very much for your kindness to me personally on my visit to your university last week. I am very grateful for the time you spent taking me to many places in the campus, answering my questions and for the trouble you have taken to make my stay in your university as interesting as possible.

I hope to meet you again one day.

Thank you again. See you soon.

Sincerely yours,
Richard

Unit 6　What is Good Design?

Sample 2

请你以 David 的名义在 9 月 27 日给中国朋友卢先生写一封感谢信，信中的内容须包括：
1. 上个月在中国期间，David 受到卢先生的热情欢迎和帮助。
2. 在中国的所见所闻给 David 留下了深刻的印象，特别是中国的快速发展让 David 感到鼓舞。

September 27th

Dear Mr. Lu,

I would like to thank you very much for your warm welcome and your assistance throughout my stay in China last month.

What I had seen and heard in your country left a deep impression on me. I felt encouraged about the developments in China. I think there can be nothing more important than that.

All the very best for you and thank you again for your hospitality.

Yours sincerely,
David

Culture ▶

Halloween

In Britain and the United States, people celebrate Halloween annually on October 31. Halloween is also known as the eve of All Saints' Day, which originated hundreds of years before Christ as the Druid festival of Samhain, Lord of the Dead and Prince of Darkness, who collected all the souls of the dead during the year. At that time, in this ancient Celtic festival, people would light bonfires and wear costumes to ward off roaming ghosts.

In modern times, Halloween activities include trick-or-treating, attending costume parties, carving pumpkins into jack-o'-lanterns with lighting candles, playing pranks, visiting haunted attractions, telling scary stories, and watching horror films.

Symbols of Halloween are various, such as black cats, bats, spiders, ghosts, skeletons, witches, pumpkins, haunted houses, cobwebs, etc. . Many houses are decorated these symbols to fit the Halloween theme.

Halloween celebrations include costume parties where people dress up as ghosts, witches, monsters, devils and other figures or characters from some horror films. While many children also dress up and play a game named "trick or treat" which means knocking on the doors of their neighbors' houses and yelling "trick or treat", most people give out some candies or chocolates as treats to them while others request a trick or a small joke.

There are several games traditionally associated with Halloween. Some have become more widespread and continue to be popular today. One common game is apple bobbing in which apples float in a tub or a large basin of water and the participants must use only their teeth to remove an apple from the basin. A variant of dunking involves kneeling on a chair, holding a fork between the teeth and trying to drive the fork into an apple.

Up until the 19th century, the Halloween bonfires were also used in parts of Scotland and Wales. When the fire died down, a ring of stones would be laid in the ashes, one for each person. In the morning, if any stone was mislaid it was said that the person it represented would not live out the year.

Telling ghost stories and watching horror films are common fixtures of Halloween parties. New horror films, episodes of television series and Halloween-themed specials (usually aimed at children) are often released several days before Halloween to take advantage of the holiday.

附录 I 词汇表

A

academic [ˌækəˈdemɪk] adj. 学术的 U2A
accuracy [ˈækjʊrəsi] n. 精确（性）U6A
admit [ədˈmɪt] v. 承认 U5A
adopt [əˈdɒpt] v. 采取；接受 U3A
adorable [əˈdɔː,rəbəl] adj. 迷人的 U1A
aesthetic [iːsˈθetɪk] adj. 美学的 U3A
agricultural [ˌægrɪˈkʌltʃərəl] adj. 农业的 U6B
alteration [ɔːltəˈreɪʃ(ə)n; ˈɒl-] n. 修改；改变 U4B
ambassador [æmˈbæsədə(r)] n. 大使 U6B
ambiguity [ˌæmbɪˈgjuːɪtɪ] n. 含糊；不明确 U3B
analyze [ˈænəˌlaɪz] v. 分析 U1A
ancestor [ˈænsestə] n. 始祖；祖先 U4B
anchor [ˈæŋkə] n. 锚；锚状物 U3A
animated [ˈænɪmeɪtɪd] adj. (指电影的画面、图画等)栩栩如生的 U5A
anniversary [ˌænɪˈvɜːs(ə)rɪ] n. 纪念日 U5A
architecture [ˈɑːkɪtektʃə(r)] n. 建筑学 U6A
artificial [ˌɑːtɪˈfɪʃ(ə)l] adj. 人造的；仿造的 U4A
ascend [əˈsend] v. 攀登，上升 U4B
attempt [əˈtempt] n. 尝试 U1A
attentive [əˈtentɪv] adj. 周到的 U1A
autobiography [ˌɔːtəˌbaɪˈɒgrəfi] n. 自传 U1B
award [əˈwɔːd] n. 奖品，奖赏 U1B

B

betray [bɪˈtreɪ] v. 露出……迹象 U3A
biographical [ˌbaɪəˈgræfɪkl] adj. 传记的 U5A
blossom [ˈblɒsəm] v. 开花 U1A
budget [ˈbʌdʒɪt] n. 预算 U5A

C

calendar[ˈkælɪndə(r)] n. 日历 U6B
capsule[ˈkæpsjuːl] n. 太空舱；胶囊 U2B
capture[ˈkæptʃə] v. 拍摄 U2B
cast[kɑːst] n. 演员表 U5A
catchy[ˈkætʃi] adj. 易记住的；吸引人的 U2A
category[ˈkætɪɡ(ə)rɪ] n. 种类；分类 U3B
channel[ˈtʃænl] n. 渠道；通道；频道；海峡 U5B
circumstances[ˈsɜːkəmstənsɪz] n. 环境；情况 U5A
civilization[ˌsɪvɪlaɪˈzeɪʃən] n. 文明；文化 U4B
classically[ˈklæsɪklɪ] adv. 传统地；古典地 U5A
climate[ˈklaɪmət] n. 气候 U6B
commencement[kəˈmensmənt] n. (美) 毕业典礼 U1A
compared[kəmˈpeəd] adj. 比较的 U5B
compile[kəmˈpaɪl] v. 编辑 U2B
completion[kəmˈpliːʃn] n. 结束；完工 U5A
component[kəmˈpəʊnənt] n. 成分；组件 U3B
compromise[ˈkɒmprəmaɪz] n. 妥协；和解 U3B
conceive[kənˈsiːv] v. 怀孕；构思 U4A
conceptualize[kənˈseptjʊəlaɪz] v. 概念化 U2B
confidence[ˈkɒnfɪdəns] n. 自信 U1B
confuse[kənˈfjuːz] v. 使混乱；使困惑 U5B
contain[kənˈteɪn] v. 包含；由……组成 U5A
contribution[ˌkɒntrɪˈbjuːʃn] n. 贡献；捐赠 U6A
convey[kənˈveɪ] v. 传达 U3B
craftsman[ˈkrɑːf(t)smən] n. 工匠 U3B
cram[kræm] v. 塞满；挤满 U1B
create[krɪˈeɪt] v. 创造 U1A
creation[krɪˈeɪʃən] n. 创造；创作 U1B
criterion[kraɪˈtɪərɪən] n. 标准；准则 U3B
critical[ˈkrɪtɪk(ə)l] adj. 批评的；挑剔的 U3A
culmination[ˌkʌlmɪˈneɪʃ(ə)n] n. 顶点；高潮 U4A

D

debate[dɪˈbeɪt] n. 辩论；争论 U5B
debut[ˈdeɪbjuː] n. 初次露面 U6B
decline[diˈklaɪn] n. 衰微；跌落；下降 U2B

decoration[ˌdekəˈreɪʃ(ə)n] n. 装饰；装潢 U3A
defense[dɪˈfens] n. 防卫；防护 U4A
definitely[ˈdefɪnətli] adv. 毫无疑问地 U5A
despise[diˈspaɪz] v. 鄙视；看不起某人（某事）U1B
destination[ˌdestɪˈneɪʃən] n. 目的地 U2B
devise[diˈvaɪz] v. 策划；想出 U2A
display[dɪˈspleɪ] v. 陈列；展示 U5A
dominant[ˈdɒmɪnənt] adj. 显性的；占优势的 U3B
dot[dɒt] n. 小点 U1A

E

education[ˌedʒʊˈkeɪʃən] n. 教育 U1A
electronic[ɪˌlekˈtrɒnɪk] adj. 电子的 U6A
element[ˈelɪm(ə)nt] n. 元素；要素 U3A
elite[eɪˈliːt] adj. 精英的 U3A
embody[ɪmˈbɒdɪ; em-] v. 体现；使具体化 U4A
empathetic[ˌempəˈθetɪk] adj. 移情作用的；感情移入的 U1A
emphasize[ˈemfəsaɪz] v. 强调；着重 U6A
engrave[ɪnˈɡreɪv; en-] v. 雕刻；铭记 U3B
entrepreneur[ˌɒntrəprəˈnɜː] n. 企业家；主办者 U1B
environment[ɪnˈvaɪrənmənt] n. 环境 U6A
epitomize[ɪˈpɪtəmaɪz; e-] v. 摘要；概括 U4B
essential[ɪˈsenʃl] a. 必要的；重要的 U6A
esteem[ɪˈstiːm; e-] n. 尊重；尊敬 U3B
evolve[iˈvɒlv] v. 使进化；使发展 U3A
excellence[ˈeksələns] n. 优点；优秀，卓越；美德 U6A
exceptional[ɪkˈsepʃ(ə)n(ə)l; ek-] adj. 异常的；例外的 U4B
executive[ɪɡˈzekjutɪv] n. 执行者；行政官 U1B
exhausted[ɪɡˈzɔːstɪd] adj. 精疲力竭的；耗尽的 U6A
exhibition[ˌeksɪˈbɪʃn] n. 陈列；展览 U5A
exponentially[ˌekspəˈnenʃəli] adv. 成倍地；指数地 U2B
expression[ɪkˈspreʃn] n. 表达；表情 U5B

F

flexibility[ˌfleksəˈbɪləti] n. 柔韧性；灵活性 U1A
footage[ˈfʊtɪdʒ] n. 以尺计算长度；尺数；影片的镜头 U2B
foreground[ˈfɔːɡraʊnd] n. 前景；最显著的位置 U5B
foresee[fɔːˈsiː] v. 预见；预知 U2A

freak[friːk] n. 反常的事；怪物 U1B
funeral[ˈfjuːn(ə)r(ə)l] n. 葬礼 U3A
furniture[ˈfɜːnɪtʃə(r)] n. 家具 U6A

G

graphic[ˈgræfɪk] adj. 图解的；用图表示的 U6B
gravity[ˈgrævəti] n. 重力；地心引力 U2A
gross[grəʊs] v. 总共收入 U5A

H

halve[hɑːv] v. 平分；减少到一半 U2A
handicraft[ˈhandiːˌkræft] n. 手工艺 U6B
harmonious[hɑːˈməʊnɪəs] adj. 和谐的；和睦的 U4B
headquarters[ˌhedˈkwɔːtəz] n. 总部 U6B
heritage[ˈherɪtɪdʒ] n. 遗产；传统 U4A
historian[hɪsˈtɔːrɪənz] n. 历史学家 U5B
holistic[həʊˈlɪstɪk; hɒ-] adj. 整体的；全盘的 U3B
honor[ˈɒnə(r)] n. 荣誉 U1B
humanity[hjuːˈmænəti] n. 人类；人道 U6B
humble[ˈhʌmbl] adj. 谦逊的；简陋的 U1B

I

iconic[aɪˈkɒnɪk] adj. 图标的；形象的 U4A
ideal[aɪˈdɪəl; aɪˈdiːəl] adj. 理想的；完美的 U4B
identity[aɪˈdentɪtɪ] n. 身份 U3A
ideographic[ˌɪdɪəʊˈgræfɪk] adj. 表意的；表意字构成的 U3B
illustration[ˌɪləˈstreɪʃn] n. 插图；说明；例证 U6B
image[ˈɪmɪdʒ] n. 图像 U5B
immersive[ɪˈmɜːsɪv] adj. 使人身临其境的 U2B
individual[ˌɪndɪˈvɪdʒuəl] adj. 个人；个体 U5A
industrial[ɪnˈdʌstriəl] adj. 工业的；产业的 U6A
innovative[ˈɪnəveɪtɪv] adj. 创新的；革新的 U6A
inquisitive[ɪnˈkwɪzɪtɪv] adj. 好学的 U1A
insist[ɪnˈsɪst] v. 坚持 U5B
inspire[ɪnˈspaɪə] v. 启发；鼓舞 U1A
insuperable[ɪnˈsuːpərəbl] adj. 难以超越的 U3A
integrate[ˈɪntɪgreɪt] v. 使……完整 U4A
interactive[ˌɪntərˈæktɪv] adj. 互相作用的 U2B

interior[ɪnˈtɪərɪə(r)] adj. 内部的 U6A
international[ˌɪntəˈnæʃənəl] adj. 国际（上）的 U2A
intoxicate[ɪnˈtɒksɪˌkeɪt] v. 使陶醉 U1A
irreplaceable[ɪrɪˈpleɪsəb(ə)l] adj. 不能替代的 U4A

L

landscape[ˈlændskeɪp] n. 风景；风景画 U4B
linger[ˈlɪŋgə] v. 消磨；缓慢度过 U4B
literati[ˌlɪtəˈrɑːtɪ] n. 文人；文学界 U3B
literature[ˈlɪtrətʃə(r)] n. 文学 U6B

M

masterpiece[ˈmɑːstəpiːs] n. 杰作 U4A
material[məˈtɪərɪəl] n. 材料 U1A
mature[məˈtjʊə] adj. 成熟的 U1B
medium[ˈmiːdɪəm] n. 媒介；媒体 U5A
messy[ˈmesi] adj. 散乱的；麻烦的 U2A
mull[mʌl] v. 深思熟虑 U2A
mystery[ˈmɪstri] n. 秘密；谜 U5B
mystic[ˈmɪstɪk] adj. 神秘的 U5B

N

nature[ˈneɪtʃə] n. 大自然 U2A
newlyweds[nˈjuːli,wedz] n. 新婚夫妇 U2B
noble[ˈnəʊb(ə)l] adj. 高尚的；贵族的 U3A
nomadic[nəʊˈmædɪk] adj. 游牧的 U4A
nomination[ˌnɒmɪˈneɪʃn] n. 提名 U5A

O

oriented[ˈɔːrɪəntɪd] adj. 导向的；以……为方向的 U6A
original[əˈrɪdʒɪn(ə)l; ɒ-] adj. 原始的；最初的 U4A
outstanding[aʊtˈstændɪŋ] adj. 杰出的；显著的 U4A
overall[ˈəʊvərɔːl] adj. 全部的；全体的 U3B
overwhelm[ˌəʊvəˈwelm] v. 压倒；淹没 U5A

P

passion[ˈpæʃ(ə)n] n. 热情 U1A
peer[pɪə] n. 同等人；同龄人 U3A

perfect[ˈpɜːfɪkt] v. 完善 U1B
philosophy[fɪˈlɒsəfɪ] n. 哲学；哲理 U4A
physicist[ˈfɪzɪsɪst] n. 物理学家 U2A
plough[plaʊ] n. 犁；耕地 U1B
popularity[ˌpɒpjʊˈlærɪtɪ] n. 流行 U2A
preserve[prɪˈzɜːv] v. 保存 U3B
principle[ˈprɪnsəpl] n. 原则；原理 U6A
privilege[ˈprɪvəlɪdʒ] n. 特权；优惠 U2A
production[prəˈdʌkʃən] n. 产生；排演 U2A
professional[prəˈfeʃənl] adj. 专业的 U2B
profound[prəˈfaʊnd] adj. 深度的 U3A
projector[prəˈdʒektə] n. 电影放映机；幻灯机 U6A
promote[prəˈməʊt] v. 促进；提升 U6B
promotional[prəˈməʊʃənl] adj. 推广的；宣传的 U6B
publication[ˌpʌblɪˈkeɪʃn] n.（书刊等的）出版 U6B

R

range[reɪndʒ] v.（在一定范围内）变化；变动 U5B
rational[ˈræʃnəl] adj. 合理的 U2A
reconstruct[ˌriːkənˈstrʌkt] v. 重建；改造 U4A
recreational[ˌrekrɪˈeɪʃənl] adj. 娱乐的；消遣的 U4A
reflect[rɪˈflekt] v. 反映；反射 U4A
regret[rɪˈgret] n. 遗憾 U1A
release[rɪˈliːs] v. 公开 U2B
relic[ˈrelɪk] n. 遗迹；遗骸 U4B
relief[rɪˈliːf] n. 减轻 U1A
relive[riːˈlɪv] v. 再体验 U2B
remarkable[rɪˈmɑːkəbl] adj. 显著的 U2A
repel[rɪˈpel] v. 击退；抵制 U3A
representative[ˌreprɪˈzentətɪv] n. 代表 U3B
reputation[ˌrepjuˈteɪʃn] n. 名誉；声望 U2A
researcher[rɪˈsɜːtʃə(r)] n. 研究者 U5B
responsibility[rɪsˌpɒnsɪˈbɪlɪtɪ] n. 责任 U2A
rotate[rəʊˈteɪt] v.（使）旋转 U2A

S

sacred[ˈseɪkrɪd] adj. 神的；神圣的 U4B
sacrifice[ˈsækrɪfaɪs] n. 供奉 U4B

scholar[ˈskɒlə] n. 学者 U4B
sculpture[ˈskʌlptʃə] n. 雕刻 U3A
self-explanatory[ˌselfɪkˈsplænətrɪ] adj. 不解自明的；明显的 U6A
self-portrait[ˈselfˈpɔːtrɪt, -ˌtreɪt, -ˈpəʊr-] n. 自画像 U5B
significant[sɪɡˈnɪfɪkənt] adj. 重要的；有意义的 U6A
simplicity[sɪmˈplɪsətɪ] n. 简单；朴素 U6A
situate[ˈsɪtʃʊeɪt] v. 使位于；使处于 U4B
solar[ˈsəʊlə(r)] adj. 太阳的 U6B
Spanish[ˈspænɪʃ] adj. 西班牙的 U5B
specialize[ˈspeʃəlaɪz] v. 专门从事 U6B
spectacular[spekˈtækjʊlə] adj. 壮观的；惊人的 U4B
speculation[ˌspekjuˈleɪʃn] n. 思考；推断 U5B
spiritual[ˈspɪrɪtʃʊəl; -tjʊəl] adj. 精神的；心灵的 U4B
staff[stɑːf] n. 全体职工 U6B
subsequent[ˈsʌbsɪkw(ə)nt] adj. 后来的；随后的 U4A
successive[səkˈsesɪv] adj. 连续的；继承的 U4A
suitable[ˈsuːtəbəl] adj. 合适的 U2A
summit[ˈsʌmɪt] n. 顶点 U4B
superiority[suːˌpɪərɪˈɒrɪtɪ; sjuː-] n. 优越 U3A
survive[səˈvaɪv] v. 幸存；生还 U3B
sustainable[səˈsteɪnəbəl] adj. 足可支撑的；可以忍受的 U1B
swallow[ˈswɒləʊ] n. 燕子 U6B
symbolize[ˈsɪmbəlaɪz] v. 象征；用符号表现 U4B

T

technique[tekˈniːk] n. 技术 U5A
temptation[tem(p)ˈteɪʃ(ə)n] n. 引诱；诱惑物 U1B
territory[ˈterɪt(ə)rɪ] n. 领土；领域 U4A
theoretical[ˌθiːəˈretɪkəl] adj. 理论的；假设的 U2A
tingle[ˈtɪŋɡl] v. 激动 U1A
trace[treɪs] v. 追踪 U3B
transformation[ˌtrænsfəˈmeɪʃn] n. 变化；改造 U1B
transport[trænsˈpɔːt] v. 传输 U2B

U

ultimately[ˈʌltɪmɪtlɪ] adv. 最后地 U2B
unconsciously[ʌnˈkɑnʃəsli] adv. 不知不觉；无意识地 U3B
unique[juːˈniːk] adj. 独特的；稀罕的 U3A

universe[ˈjuːnɪvɜːs] n. 宇宙 U2A
upload[ʌpˈləʊd] v. 上传（或上载）数据 U2B

V

virtual[ˈvɜːtʃuəl] adj. 虚拟的 U2B
visual[ˈvɪʒuəl] adj. 视觉的；看得见的 U6B
vivid[ˈvivid] adj. 生动的；鲜明的 U1B
vocalist[ˈvəʊkəlɪst] n. 歌手；声乐家 U5B

W

well-mannered[ˈwɛlˈmænərd] adj. 行为端正的 U1A
widespread[ˈwʌɪdsprɛd] adj. 普遍的；广泛的 U4B
worship[ˈwəːʃip] v. 崇拜 U3A

附录 II 短语表

A

all stripes 所有类型 U3A
as to 至于；关于 U1B
as usual 像往常一样 U5A
ascend to 追溯；升至 U4B
at an early age 在早年 U3A
at average 平均的 U4B
attempt to 尝试；企图 U6A
attract the attention 引起注意 U5B

B

be essential to 对……是必要的 U6A
be responsible for 为……负责 U5B
be suitable for 适合 U2A
belong to 属于 U4A

C

came to a conclusion 得出结论 U5B
combine with 与……相结合 U4A
consist of 由……构成 U4A

D

depend upon 依赖；依靠 U5B
differ from 与……不同 U3B
drive off 驾车离去 U1A
due to 因为 U1B

E

earn a fame 获得名声 U4B

F

focus on 致力于 U6A

G

give rise to 使发生；引起 U3B
go for it 尝试 U1A

H

have a reputation as 有……的称呼 U2A
have concerns about 担心 U2A
have responsibility for 对……负责 U2A

I

in accordance with 依照，与……一致 U4A
in addition 除此之外 U6A
in demand 非常需要；受欢迎 U3A
in essence 本质上；其实 U3A
in memory of 纪念 U5A
in particular 尤其是 U5A
in terms of 依据；按照 U3B
in the field of 在……的领域中 U6B
integrate into 成为一体；融入 U4A
intend to 打算做 U5B

J

judge by 评判 U3A

L

lie in 在于 U3B
look down on 蔑视 U1B

M

make its debut 首次露面 U6B
mull over 仔细考虑 U2A

O

on my mind 在我心里 U1A
on the contrary 相反 U1B

P

play a role in 在……起作用 U4B
put forward 提出 U6A
put up with 忍受 U1A

R

rather than 而不是 U5A
relate to 与……相关 U6B

S

set up 建立 U2B
specialize in 专门从事于 U6B

T

take part in 参与 U6B
take sth. seriously 认真对待 U1A
the symbol of 象征 U4B
tie the knot 喜结连理 U2B
too…. to 太……而不能 U1B
trace back 追溯 U3B
track down 追寻 U2B

W

with access to 联系 U2B
without a doubt 毫无疑问 U5A
wrap up 包起来 U2B

下篇

Unit 7

Environment Protection

Warm-up Activities

I. Matching

Learn the following words and phrases about different types of weather, and match them to the pictures.

1. Tsunami(　　)　　2. Drought(　　)　　3. Thunder(　　)
4. Tornado(　　)　　5. Flood(　　)　　　　6. Earthquake(　　)

A.

B.

C.

D.
E.

F.

II. Reading

lucid　adj. 清晰的
lush　adj. 草木繁茂的
invaluable　adj. 极珍贵的

Lucid waters and lush mountains are invaluable assets. If you protect the environment, you will receive rewards from the environment.

绿水青山就是金山银山。保护生态，生态就会回馈你。

(习近平总书记在浙江省安吉县余村考查时的讲话)

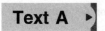

Low-carbon Life Cutting a College Student's Budget

1. The struggling college student is more than just a **stereotype**; It's a reality for many students burdened by the high payment of **tuition**, fees, and books, not to mention living **expenses**. And when mention to the form of **scholarships** and student **loans**, there are still plenty of students that have to find a job during their time in school just to make ends meet. A lack of funds may make it a lot difficult to adopt environment-friendly practices. However, there are plenty of little things you can do to live a low-carbon life* during your time on campus that won't break the bank. Many are free and some will even put money back in your pocket. Here are a few ideas you may want to consider.

2. One of the best ways to begin with is recycling. Consider it a start into low-carbon living since It's where most people begin their journey toward eco-awareness. Although your campus likely has some kinds of recycling program in place, there's nothing to stop you from setting up your own collection in order to do your part and earn a little **cash** in the process. If there is a local recycling center nearby, simply collect bags of **cans** and bottles, ask friends to save theirs so you can pick them up weekly, and make frequent trips to the recycling center to drop them off and get paid by weight. It's a great way for any **eco-minded** student to participate in keeping the planet green.

3. Of course, even students with little cash to **spare** are bound to spend here and there. For example, you have to live. And while you might think that buying things that do less **harm** to the earth is going to stress your already **strained** budget, there are several ways to get the fresh, organic produce* without **overspending**. You don't have to go to a fancy, expensive **grocery** store to find these items if there's a farmer's market in your area, where you can buy locally grown foods and get them at the **peak** of **freshness**. In addition, you might be able to argue the price a bit, especially if you wait until just before the market is closing.

4. And when it comes to spending money on consumer goods like clothing or decorations for your dormitory, second-hand is the way to go. Discount shops can provide you with clothing options at the cheaper price of new things, and with a little searching you can always find a few unique pieces at such shops. And whether you're looking for a comfortable chair or a **laptop**, used items could be what you want. You'll save some money and give otherwise **discarded** items a second life, while also decreasing the demand for new **manufacturing**. It's a win-win solution.

5. Every student can take steps to create a good future for our world. Limited funds only force you to become more creative.

Unit 7　Environment Protection

 New Words

eco-minded[ˌekəʊˈmaɪnid] adj. have mind of protect environment 有环保意识的

expense[ɪkˈspens] n. spend 费用；花费的钱；消耗；花钱的东西

stereotype[ˈsteriətaɪp] n. a very firm and simple idea about what a particular type of person or thing is like 模式化的观念（或思想）；刻板印象

tuition[tjuˈɪʃn] n. the money that you pay to be taught, especially in a college or university（尤指高校的）学费

scholarship[ˈskɒləʃɪp] n. an amount of money given to sb. by an organization to help pay for their education 奖学金

cash[kæʃ] n. money in the form of coins or bills 现金

can[kæn] n. a metal container in which food and drink is sold (盛食品或饮料的) 金属罐

spare[speə(r)] v. make sth. such as time or money available to sb. or for sth. 留出；匀出

harm[hɑːm] n. injury, damage or problems caused by sth. you do 损害；危害

strained[streɪnd] adj. (of situation) not relaxed or friendly 紧张的；不友好的

overspend[ˌəʊvəˈspend] v. spend too much money or more than you planned 超支

peak[piːk] n. the point when sb./sth. is best most successful, strongest, etc. 顶峰；高峰

freshness[freʃnəs] n. (usually of food) the state of being recently produced or picked and not frozen, dried, etc. (常指食物) 新鲜

grocery[ˈɡrəʊsəri] n. a shop that sells food and other things used in the home 食品杂货店

laptop[ˈlæptɒp] n. a small computer that you can carry with you 便携式电脑；笔记本电脑

discard[dɪsˈkɑːd] v. get rid of sth. that you no longer want or need 丢弃；抛弃

manufacture[ˌmænjuˈfæktʃə(r)] v. make goods in large quantities 大量生产；成批制造

Useful Expressions

Phrases	Examples
not to mention 更不用说	We can't afford a car, not to mention the fact that we have no garage. 我们买不起汽车，没有车库的事就更不必说了
make ends meet 勉强维持生计	Last month he couldn't make ends meet. 上个月他钱花涨了
break the bank 倾家荡产；耗尽资源	One evening at the theatre won't break the bank. 看一晚上戏不会倾家荡产的
drop…off 捎带；顺便送到	Would you drop off this material？ 请把这些材料拿去，好吗
at the peak of 顶峰	They felt very tired when they are at the peak of the mountain. 在山顶时，他们感到很疲惫

 Background Information

1. low-carbon life: 低碳生活。低碳意指较低（更低）的温室气体（二氧化碳为主）的排放。低碳生活可以理解为：减少二氧化碳的排放，低能量、低消耗、低开支的生活方式。如今，这股风潮逐渐在我国一些大城市兴起，潜移默化地改变着人们的生活。低碳生活代表着更健康、更自然、更安全，人与自然的活动更返璞归真。当今时代，随着人类社会发展，生活物质水平的提高，随之也对人类周围环境带来了影响与改变。对于普通人来说，低碳生活既是一种生活态度、生活方式，同时更是一种可持续发展的环保责任。

2. organic produce: 有机食品，也叫生态或生物食品等。有机食品是国际上对天然无污染食品比较统一的提法。有机食品通常是来自有机农业生产体系，根据国际有机农业生产要求和相应的标准生产加工的。有机食品在不同的语言中有不同的名称，国外最普遍的叫法是Organic Food，在其他语种中也有称生态食品、自然食品等。联合国粮农业和世界卫生组织（FAO/WHO）的食品法典委员会（CAC）将这类称谓各异但内涵实质基本相同的食品统称为有机食品。

Unit 7 Environment Protection

 Reading Comprehension

I. Decide whether the following statements are True (T) or False (F).

( ) 1. It's reality for many students burdened by the low cost tuition, fees and books.
( ) 2. One of the best ways to get started with is recycling.
( ) 3. Even students with much cash to spare are bound to spend here and there.
( ) 4. You have to go to fancy, expensive grocery store to find these items if there's a farmer's market in your areas.
( ) 5. When it comes to spending money on consumer goods for your dormitory, second-hand is the way to go.
( ) 6. Every students can take steps to create a better future for our planet.

II. Complete the answers to the following questions.

1. What does the author mean by saying "the struggling college student is more than just a stereotype"? (Para. 1)
   Many students need to _____ for their living in college.

2. What do many students in school have to do in order to make ends meet? (Para. 1)
   Find _____.

3. According to the author, where can you get fresh organic produce? (Para. 3)
   At a _____.

4. What can be inferred from the text? (Para. 4)
   Reducing your _____ is not as difficult as you imagine.

157

Vocabulary and Structure

Words and Phrases to Drill

budget	tuition	scholarship	cash	spare
harm	second-hand	discard	revolutionize	overspend
not to mention	make ends meet	break the bank	drop off	at the peak of

I. Choose the appropriate explanation from Column B for each of the words in Column A.

A	B
_____ 1. peak	a. injury, damage or problems caused by sth. you do
_____ 2. tuition	b. spend too much money or more than you planned
_____ 3. scholarship	c. the amount of money a person or an organization plans to spend
_____ 4. cash	d. have mind of protect environment
_____ 5. spare	e. the money you pay to be taught, especially in a college or university
_____ 6. harm	f. money in the form of coins or bills
_____ 7. expense	g. make sth. such as time or money available to sb. or for sth.
_____ 8. discard	h. the point when sb./sth. is best most successful, strongest
_____ 9. eco-minded	i. get rid of sth. that you no longer want or need
_____ 10. overspend	j. an amount of money given to sb. by an organization to help pay for their education

II. Fill in the blanks with the correct forms of the words in Column A of the above table.

1. Who is at the _____ of the mountain?
2. They are encouraged to _____ and borrow money.
3. We will _____ the old books.
4. University students should have _____ consciousness.
5. I'm sure he didn't mean any _____ .
6. Do you like to _____ all of your money?
7. He was short of _____ after the collapse of his business.
8. I want you to move into my apartment. We've a _____ room.
9. She won a _____ to study at Stanford.
10. Is this money enough for the _____ fee?

III. Compare each pair of words and choose the correct one to fill in each blank. Change the form if necessary.

1. cash   crash

   a. How can I accumulate enough _____ to get out of debt?

   b. He was killed in an air _____ .

158

2. spare   spend

   a. In her _____ time she read books on cooking.

   b. They will then have more money to _____ on other things.

3. harm   harmful

   a. Cars, trucks and buses produce exhaust nearly as _____ as the factories.

   b. I'm sure he didn't mean any _____ .

4. scholar   scholarship

   a. I made up my mind to apply for a _____ .

   b. He is a _____ .

Ⅳ. Add the suffix "ify" to the following words in brackets. Then complete the sentences with the words formed.

> **Tips:** "-ify"单词后缀意为：转为，变为。如：simple—simplify（简化）；beauty—beautify（美化）；pure—purify（净化）；ugly—uglify（丑化）等。

Sample: Her dream is to purify the water in the future for human being. (pure)

1. Try _____ to your explanation for the children. (simple)
2. The City Council has a plan to _____ the city. (beautiful)
3. The new leader hopes to _____ the country. (unit)
4. I tried to _____ her perfume. (identity)
5. We will _____ these subjects under three topics. (class)

Ⅴ. Choose the best phrase to complete each sentence.

1. We can't afford a car, _____ the fact that we have no garage.

   A. not to mention   B. not at mention   C. to mention   D. to not mention

2. Last month he couldn't _____ .

   A. make end meet   B. make ends meet   C. make ends meets   D. to make ends

3. Sustainable development will not _____ .

   A. break bank   B. break by   C. break in   D. break the bank

4. I just came by to _____ your fish tank.

   A. drop in   B. drop off   C. drop as   D. drop from

5. She want to climb to _____ the mountain.

   A. the peak of   B. peak   C. the peak   D. mountain peak

Ⅵ. Complete the following sentences by translating the Chinese given in brackets into English.

1. I had enough presence of mind _____ (没有说起我的意图).
2. Come on! One evening at the theatre _____ (不会倾家荡产的).
3. It may be difficult at times to _____ (靠你微薄的收入，做到收支相抵).
4. Sales to the British forces _____ (销售量预期会减少).

5. They want to _____ (爬到山顶).

VII. Translate the following sentences into Chinese.

1. The struggling college student is more than just a stereotype. (Para. 1)
   _____

2. One of the best ways to begin with is recycling. (Para. 2)
   _____

3. Of course, even students with little cash to spare are bound to spend here and there. (Para. 3)
   _____

4. And when it comes to spending money on consumer goods like clothing or decorations for your dormitory, second-hand is the way to go. (Para. 4)
   _____

VIII. Complete the following sentences by translating the Chinese given in brackets into English using "what."

> 关系代词 what 可以用于引导宾语从句，在句子中可表示"——的东西；——的地方；——的事情"等含义。
>
> Sample: I'll never forget <u>what she taught us</u> (她所教给我们的东西).

1. No one understood _____ (他说了什么).
2. I know _____ (他想要做什么).
3. We should do _____ (值得做的事情).
4. The picture reminded me of _____ (我曾经在湖边看到的景色).
5. The situation today is quite different from _____ (50年前的情形).

IX. Complete the following sentences by translating the Chinese given in brackets into English using "instead of… ".

> Instead of 是复合介词，意为"代替；而不是；而没有"，后面可以跟名词、代词或动名词作宾语，也可以跟介词短语。
>
> Sample: Finally, <u>instead of trying hard to be happy, as if that were the only purpose of life</u> (不再努力去追求幸福，好像它是生活的唯一目的一样), I would, if I were a boy again, try still harder to make others happy.

1. _____ (他没有回答我的问题), he began to beat about the bush.
2. Can I have chicken _____ (而不吃牛肉)?
3. In summer I often read in the open air _____ (而不是在屋子里看书).
4. I think I should go to borrow the book _____ (而不是去买这本书).
5. He will go on business to Shanghai _____ (而不是你去).

Unit 7　Environment Protection

 Dialogue Samples

Listen and read the samples carefully, and then complete the communicative tasks that follow.

Dialogue 1　The Effects of Global Warming

Paul: That's terrible! And will there be any other effects?

John: Yes, there will be many. The global weather system will change too, causing too much rain in some areas and too little in others.

Paul: Can we do something about it?

John: There's a lot we can do. First of all, we must reduce the amount of pollution coming from industries and cars and stop deforestation. Otherwise, we will suffer from our careless actions.

Dialogue 2　The Environmentally Informed

Steven: No way! Not only is smoking bad for your health, it's also the source of social problems in developing countries. Because, since profit from tobacco is very high, tobacco uses the best food-growing areas, leading to food shortages.

Austin: So for every cigarette I smoke, someone is starving?

Steven: And many tobacco planters use wood to dry tobacco leaves. You know that when you cut down a tree, you're taking another step on your way to erosion.

Austin: And erosion is also the beginning of hunger. OK, no more cigarettes and only quick showers.

Communicative Tasks

Work with your partner and take turns to start the conversations.

Task 1

Situation:

A debate between two college students about the advantages and disadvantages of building more nuclear power plants.

Tips:

Here are some things the Chinese student can say or ask:
...sound the alarm bell
meet the rising needs for...
I see what you mean, but...
There's no doubt...
With modern technologies, we can...
that doesn't mean...

Here are some things the American student can say:
from previous experiences
economic growth
one way or the other
smoke from power plants
at the expense of

Task 2

Situation:

A student discusses some resource-saving and environmental protection techniques with her host mother in Britain.

Tips:

Here are some things the waiter can say or ask:
That's incredible!
...cut down the power bill by...
Not only is it..., it's...
...to keep the air-conditioner running
Why do you...rather than...?
When do you..., you're on your way to...

Here are some things the couple can say:
Environmentally conscious
leading to...
artificial atmosphere
fresh air
not to suffer

Further Development

连读

连读的条件：相邻的两个词意思上比较紧密，同属一个意群（朗读长句子可以在一个意群结束做一个小停顿或换口气读）。

连读技巧：连读一般不重读，而是顺其自然地带过。举例如下：

1. "辅音＋元音" 的连读

It-is-an-old book. / Not-at-all. / Please pick-it-up. / Here-is-it. / Where-is my cup?

2. "辅音＋半元音" 的连读

Thank-you. / Nice to meet-you.

3. 短语或从句之间按意群停顿，意群之间即使有辅音和元音出现也不能连读。

There-is-a-book in my desk.（注意：book 和 in 不可以连读，因为二者不在同一意群）

Can you speak English or French?（注意：English 和 or 不可以连读）.

4. 失去爆破的连读

The girl in the re(d) coat was on a bla(ck) bike jus(t) now.

The ol(d) do(c)tor has a ca(t), too. We're going to work on the farm nex(t) Tuesday.

（注意：句子括号中的爆破音此时可以省略不读）

Text B

Green Economy: Farming in the Sky in Singapore

1. With a population of about five million crammed in a tiny area, Singapore has been forced to expand upwards, building **skyscrapers** to hold the country's people. Now, Singapore is applying the **vertical** model to **urban** agriculture, experimenting with **rooftop** gardens and vertical farms in order to feed its many people.

2. Currently only seven percent of Singapore's food is grown locally. The country buys most of its fresh vegetables and fruits daily from neighboring countries such as Malaysia, Thailand* and the Philippines, as well as from other places like Australia, New Zealand, Israel* and Chile.

3. A growing number of people have resulted in a rapid crowding of Singapore, as more and more towering apartment buildings shoot up. Meanwhile, **available** farmland is disappearing quickly.

4. The **solution** to the problem is to make the world's first low-carbon, water-driven **rotating** vertical farm for growing **tropical** vegetables in an urban environment. The result is a cooperative agreement between the Agri-Food and Veterinary Authority of Singapore (AVA)* and a local **firm**, Sky Greens. This aim is to spread urban farming techniques that are also environmentally friendly. With a robust economy that increases a gross **domestic** product (GDP) growing continuously, Singapore has plenty of money. "But money is **worthless** without food," according to Sky Greens Director Jack Ng.

5. "That's why I wanted to use my engineering skills to help Singapore farmers to produce more food," Ng told IPS*. It consists of lots of **aluminum** towers, some of them up to nine meters high, each containing 38-storey equipped with watering pipes for the vegetables.

6. In keeping with Sky Greens'* focus on environmental keeping, the water used to power the rotating towers is **recycled** within the system and eventually used to water the vegetables. Each tower consumes only 60 **Watts** of power daily, about the same amount as a single light bulb.

7. Ng knew that if the system was too expensive or complicated, urban farmers would not be able to survive. Therefore, he tried to design a project in which "the plant comes to you, rather than

you going to the plant". The multi-layered vegetable tower rotates very slowly, taking some eight hours to complete a full circle. As the plant travels to the top it absorbs enough sunlight and when it comes back down it is watered from a **tray** that is fed by the system that rotates the tower. This closed cycle system is easy to **maintain** and doesn't release any **exhaust**.

8. If set up on roofs of the many **multi-storey** residential blocks that house most of Singapore's population, could provide **livelihoods** for **retired** people and housewives, who would only need to spend a few hours up on the roof to attend to the system. Sky Greens towers currently produce three kinds of cabbage that are popular with the locals and these can be harvested every 28 days. They already supply NTUC* Fair Price, Singapore's largest grocery retailer that has a network of over 230 outlets and supermarkets. That is fresher because they travel a shorter distance from farm to shelf.

New Words

vertical[ˈvɜːtɪkl] adj. straight up 垂直的，竖立的；[解] 头顶的；顶点的
rotate[rəʊˈteɪt] v. turn around（使某物）旋转；使转动；使轮流，轮换
aluminum[əˈljuːmɪnəm] n. 铝
skyscraper[ˈskaɪskreɪpə(r)] n. a very tall building in a city 摩天大楼
urban[ˈɜːbən] adj. connected with a town or city 都市的；城市的；城镇的
rooftop[ˈruːftɒp] n. the outside part of the roof of a building 屋顶外部；外屋顶
available[əˈveɪləbl] adj. (of things) that you can get, buy or find（东西）可获得的；可购得的；可找到的
solution[səˈluːʃn] n. a way of solving a problem or dealing with a difficult situation 解决办法；处理手段
tropical[ˈtrɒpɪkl] adj. coming from, found in or typical of the tropics 热带的；来自热带的；产于热带的
firm[fɜːm] n. a business or company 公司；商号；商行
domestic[dəˈmestɪk] adj. of or inside a particular country, not foreign or international 本国的；国内的
worthless[ˈwɜːθləs] adj. having no practical or financial value 没用的；无价值的
recycle[ˌriːˈsaɪkl] v. treat things that have already been used so that they can be used again 回收利用；再利用
Watt[wɒt] n. a unit for measuring electrical power 瓦；瓦特（电功率单位）
tray[treɪ] n. the base for holding sth. 托盘；碟
maintain[meɪnˈteɪn] v. keep a building, a machine, etc. in good condition by checking or repairing it regularly 维修
exhaust[ɪɡˈzɔːst] n. waste gases that come out of a vehicle, an engine or a machine（车辆、发动机或机器排出的）废气
storey[ˈstɔːrɪ] n. (AmE story) a level of a building a floor 楼层
livelihood[ˈlaɪvlihʊd] n. a means of earning money in order to live 赚钱/谋生的手段；生计
retire[rɪˈtaɪə(r)] v. stop doing your job 退休

Unit 7　Environment Protection

 Useful Expressions

Phrases	Examples
in the form of 以……的形式	My garden is in the form of a square. 我的花园是方形的
equip…with 给……配备……；给……装备……	We equip our children with a good education. 我们使孩子们受到良好的教育
in keeping with 和……一致；与……协调	His actions are not in keeping with his promises. 他言行不一
with ... of… 随着	With the development of technology, mobile phone is more and more common. 随着科技的发展，手机的使用越来越普及
more and more 越来越多……	We have more and more university graduation students. 我们有越来越多的大学毕业生

 Background Information

1. Thailand: 泰国（东南亚国家）。
2. Israel: 以色列（西亚国家）。
3. Agri-Food and Veterinary Authority of Singapore(AVA)：新加坡农粮与兽医管理局。
4. Sky Greens: 天鲜公司（新加坡的一家公司）。Jack Ng: 黄顺和（为天鲜公司创始人）。
5. lPS: Inter Press Service, 国际新闻社。
6. NTUC Fair Price: 职总平价合作社，新加坡本土连锁超市。

167

Reading Comprehension

I. Decide whether the following statements are True (T) or False (F).

(   ) 1. With a population of about five million crammed in a tiny area, Singapore has been forced to expand upwards.

(   ) 2. Singapore is applying the vertical model to agriculture.

(   ) 3. Singapore imports most of its vegetables and fruits daily from neighboring countries.

(   ) 4. In Singapore, available farmland is disappearing quickly.

(   ) 5. Currently only seven percent of Singapore's food is grown locally.

II. Choose the best answer to each of the following questions.

1. What's the population of Singapore according to this passage?
   A. 5 000 000   B. 50 000 000   C. 500 000   D. 500 000 000

2. Who create the Vertical farming system called "A Go-Grow"?
   A. IS   B. jack Ng   C. A farmer   D. Obama

3. How long does the multi-layered vegetable tower to finish a full circle?
   A. 28 hours   B. 24 hours   C. 60 hours   D. About 8 hours

4. In sky Green tower, how long can we harvest the cabbage?
   A. 28 hours   B. 8 hours   C. 28 days   D. 8 days

5. How many outlets and supermarkets the NTUC Fair Price owed?
   A. over 230   B. 230   C. 220   D. 200

Grammar

Attributive Clauses

定语从句（Attributive Clauses）在句中做定语，修饰一个名词或代词，被修饰的名词、词组或代词即先行词。定语从句通常出现在先行词之后，由关系代词或关系副词引出。

1. 常见的关系代词

常见的关系代词由以下词构成：who, whom, that, whose.

限定性定语从句中的关系代词

	做主语	做宾语	做定语
指人	who/that	whom/that(可省略)	whose
指物	which/that	which/that(可省略)	whose

非限定性定语从句中的关系代词

	做主语	做宾语	做定语
指人	who	whom	whose/of whom
指物	which	which	whose/of which

which, that 用来指物（用作主语、宾语，做宾语时可以省略）。

例如：The prosperity which/that had never appeared before took on in the countryside.

农村出现了前所未有的繁荣。(which/that 在从句中做主语)

whose 表示谁（可以为人也可以为物）的（东西）。

例如：A child whose parents are dead is called an orphan.

双亲去世的孩子叫作孤儿。("whose parents"表示那个孩子的双亲)

2. 常见的关系副词

① why: 主要用于修饰表示原因的名词（主要是 the reason），同时它在定语从句中用作原因状语。

例如：We don't know the reason why he didn't show up. 我们不知道他为什么没有来。

② when: 主要用于修饰表示时间的名词，同时它在定语从句中用作时间状语。

例如：There comes a time when you have to make a choice. 你必须作出抉择的时候到了。

③ where: 主要用于修饰表示地点的名词，同时它在定语从句中用作地点状语。

例如：This is the village where he was born. 这就是他出生的村子。

British Social Life (Section A)

Social life in the UK can also be depicted in five accounts, the first of which is the two distinctions in the British society. One is the job distinction, which means the different amount of money each class earns. The other one is the class distinction, which includes the distinctive categories of the upper class, the middle class and the working class. The second is the different life styles in England, Wales, Scotland and Northern Ireland in which the diversified life is emphasized. The welfare programme is the third that prevents the British citizens from financial hardship and in turn guarantees the stability of social life in the UK. The high standard of living of the British people shows another factor in the stability of British social life. Finally, the concentration of population, especially the difference between the north and the south plays a role in the social life of citizens of the UK, although the boundary between them is hard to mark explicitly.

a. One way to classify people is by the job they do and this is used by the government in its surveys. The official classification is based upon the job a person does. The first class is professionals, e. g. accountant, doctor, dentist, solicitor. The second is managerial and technical personnel, e. g. manager, teacher, librarian, nurse, farmer. The third clerical and supervisory (non-manual) workers, e. g. shop assistant, police officer, bank clerk, and skilled manual workers, e. g. electrician, bus driver, cook. The last is the semi-skilled manual workers, e. g. postal worker, telephone operator, and unskilled manual workers, e. g. laborer, cleaner.

There is another classification to categorize the people, i. e. the upper class, the middle class and the working class, though the upper class is thought to be fairly small in number, at around two percent of the total population and the number of the working class is decreasing. Yet it is true to say that the class structure in British society is relatively obvious. The culture of a factory worker whose father is a factory worker may be quite different from that of a stockbroker whose father is a stockbroker. They tend to read different newspapers, watch different television programs, speak with a different accent, do different things in their free time and have different expectations for their children.

The class structure affects the social life in the UK and is often cited in books. There is no doubt that class awareness still exists. It is difficult to exactly convey how class is identified. Statistical information about the jobs people do and their income levels is one method. While economic criteria are one important aspect in determining class, it seems that differences in taste and behaviour are at least as significant for people in deciding whether they and others belong to a particular class.

b. The UK is one sovereign state, but as the full name of the state suggests, it is made up of England, Scotland, Wales and Northern Ireland. In each of the four lands, the differences are obvious. The nationalities of the English, the Scottish, the Welsh and the Northern Irish, rather than simply the Northern English are used to identify the British. The different clothing, accents and dialects can be seen or heard. Wherever you go, the Scottish man's tartan kilt, the-Welsh language's fathomless thicket of consonants, and the Irish dialect, are some of the easy distinctions. In addition the recent groups of immigrants have brought with them their cultures, such as Muslims. The Muslim ways of life are quite different from those of the British Christian life. Therefore, a Muslim woman in London does not have the same experience of life as the English man in Scotland. And the everyday life of an Ulsterman in Belfast varies considerably from that of a Welsh farmer.

Unit 8

Modern Life

Warm-up Activities

I. Matching

Learn the following words about different types of convention, and match them to the pictures.

1. Gun power(   )   2. Printing(   )
3. Compass(   )   4. Paper(   )

1.    B.

C.    D.

II. Reading

Science and technology is the first development force. It's high time to develop high technology and realize industrialization.

科技是第一生产力。发展高科技、实现产业化。
（邓小平）

development force 生产力
realize   v. 实现
industrialization   n. 产业化

Text A

Taking the Sweat Out of Online Shopping

1. It's fair to say that the Internet has **revolutionized** our shopping habits. In the past we had no choice but to **traipse** up and down the high street looking for the best deal, now we can do it from the comfort of our **armchairs**. But there are **disadvantages** too. The high street is not a big **scale**. You can see the shops you want to go to and simply head in their direction. But the Internet is too vast to **contemplate** and you go to the shops that you want to visit. If you don't know where to go, then you could end up with a worse deal than you would have got using up your shoe **leather**. There are now websites around which try to guide people through the online **maze**. One of these, Haggle4me*, aims to get you the best possible deal.

Bargain hunt

2. The idea is very simple. You put in the best price you've found. For example, It's a new television for $600. Other visitors to the website then search the web using their contacts and try to get you a better deal. It means that they find the same TV for $500. That means you've saved $100. As long as you've saved at least $20, then you pay a fifth of the saving to the **haggler** who found the deal (in this case, $20). The haggler then pays a quarter of the fee to the website (in this example, $5).

3. There seems to be little to lose as long as you try to find the best price you can in the first place. If you put in a manufacturer's **recommended** retail price (RRP), for example, the savings might be huge but then the haggler's fee would be much larger too. You can often beat the RRP very easily by simply using one of the many price **comparison** websites out there (Kelkoo* or PriceRunner*, for example).

4. That brings us to the big **drawback** of Haggle4me: time. Most of us are **impatient** and once we've decided we want something, we want it there and then. But to give the hagglers a chance to get you a better deal, you need to give them time—the more the better. And that's obviously going to

delay your **purchase**.

Easy way to Taobao*

5. As well as buying things online, you can also sell your unwanted items. The online **auction** site, Taobao(or Xianyu), is one of the net's major success stories. But listing your items can take a long time, especially if you haven't done it before. And you'll need to monitor the auction, answer any questions from potential buyers, and **arrange** delivery or collection. Also, people without a computer can't take advantage of it at all.

6. To solve these potential problems, a new type of business is springing up—and this time It's happening on the high street. Chains of shops will take your **unwanted** items and then list them on Taobao for you. They do all the hard work, including the description, photographing your item and posting it afterward.

7. But again, there's a catch. Generally they take a third of the sale price as their commission, with the minimum commission of $15. So with lower value items, you could end up getting little or even nothing. The new ideas for buying and selling online work well for those who don't have time—or inclination—to do the work themselves.

New Words

recommend[ˌrekəˈmend] v. persuade sb. 推荐；劝告；使显得吸引人；托付

haggler[ˈhælə] n. sb. who argues to agree on the price of sth. 议价者

revolutionize[ˌrevəˈluːʃənaɪz] v. (BrE revolutionise) completely change the way that sth. is done 革命，变革

traipse[treɪps] v. walk slowly when you are tired and unwilling 疲惫地走；磨蹭

armchair[ˈɑːmtʃeə(r)] n. a comfortable chair with sides on which you can rest your arms 扶手椅

disadvantage[ˌdɪsədˈvɑːntɪdʒ] n. sth. that makes sb./sth. less effective, successful or attractive 不利因素

scale[skeɪl] n. the size or extent of sth. 规模；程度

contemplate[ˈkɒntəmpleɪt] v. think about whether you should do sth. or how you should do sth. 考虑；思量

leather[ˈleðə(r)] n. material made by removing the hair or fur from animal skins and preserving the skins using special processes 皮；皮革

maze[meɪz] n. a complex system of paths in which it is easy to get lost 迷宫

bargain[ˈbɑːɡən] n. a thing bought for less than the usual price 便宜货；廉价货

comparison[kəmˈpærɪsn] n. an occasion when two or more people or things are compared 对比，比较

drawback[ˈdrɔːbæk] n. a disadvantage or a bad feature of sth. 不利因素；缺点；毛病

impatient[ɪmˈpeɪʃnt] adj. annoyed because of delays, mistakes, etc. 不耐烦的

purchase[ˈpɜːtʃəs] n. the act or process of buying sth. 采购；购买

unwanted[ˌʌnˈwɒntɪd] adj. if sth. is unwanted, you do not want it 不需要的；多余的

auction[ˈɔːkʃn] n. a public occasion when things are sold to the people who offer the most money for them 拍卖

arrange[əˈreɪndʒ] v. make plans for sth. to happen 准备；安排

Useful Expressions

Phrases	Examples
use up 用完；耗尽	Does burning candle use up some air inside the glass? 燃烧的蜡烛会用尽杯里的空气吗
but then 然而；另一方面	At first she demurred, but then finally agreed. 她开始表示反对，但最终还是同意了
there and then 在当时；当场；当即	There and then he made his decision. 他当时就做出了决定
spring up 迅速出现；突然兴起	Doubts have begun to spring up in my mind. 我突然起了疑心
take advantage of 利用	Students should take advantage of our libraries. 学生们要充分利用图书馆

 Background Information

1. Haggle4me: 一个比价服务网站。
2. Kelkoo: 法国的一个比价服务网站。
3. PriceRunner: 瑞典的一个比价服务网站。
4. Taobao: 淘宝网是亚太地区较大的网络零售、商圈，由阿里巴巴集团在 2003 年 5 月创立。淘宝网是中国深受欢迎的网购零售平台，拥有近 5 亿的注册用户数，每天有超过 6 000 万的固定访客，每天的在线商品数已经超过了 8 亿件，平均每分钟售出 4.8 万件商品。随着淘宝网规模的扩大和用户数量的增加，淘宝也从单一的 C2C 网络集市变成了包括 C2C、团购、分销、拍卖等多种电子商务模式在内的综合性零售商圈，目前已经成为世界范围的电子商务交易平台之一。

Reading Comprehension

I. **Decide whether the following statements are True (T) or False (F).**

(   ) 1. If you want to shop online, you should hunt for the shops that you want to visit.
(   ) 2. Haggle4me is a website helping people to get through the online maze.
(   ) 3. The haggler pays a quarter of the total price of goods to the website.
(   ) 4. You should give the haggler more money in order to get a better deal.
(   ) 5. It will take a long time to list the unwanted items before selling them on Taobao.
(   ) 6. People without a computer can't make use of the online auction site, Taobao.
(   ) 7. Chains of shops often take a small percentage of the sale price as their commission.
(   ) 8. People who can buy and sell online by themselves will probably get the best deal.

II. **Complete the answers to the following questions.**

1. Is it fair to say that the Internet has revolutionized our shopping habits. (Para. 1)
   _____, _____.

2. What disadvantages in the high street? (Para. 1)
   The high street is on a _____ small _____.

3. What can you sell online? (Para. 5)
   You can also sell your _____ items.

4. Which people are suitable for shopping on the Internet? (Para. 7)
   For those who don't have _____ or _____, to do the work themselves.

Unit 8 Modern Life

 Vocabulary and Structure

Words and Phrases to Drill

maze	scale	bargain	comparison	impatient
purchase	drawback	auction	unwanted	arrange
use up	but then	there and then	spring up	take advantage of

I. Choose the appropriate explanation from Column B for each of the words in Column A.

A	B
_____ 1. maze	a. a disadvantage or a bad feature of sth.
_____ 2. scale	b. if sth. is unwanted, you do not want it
_____ 3. bargain	c. a complex system of paths in which it is easy to get lost
_____ 4. comparison	d. the size or extent of sth.
_____ 5. impatient	e. an occasion when two or more people or things are compared
_____ 6. purchase	f. a thing bought for less than the usual price
_____ 7. drawback	g. a thing bought for less than the usual price
_____ 8. unwanted	h. wanting sth. to happen as soon as possible
_____ 9. auction	i. a public occasion when things are sold to the people who offer the most money for them
_____ 10. arrange	j. make plans for sth. to happen

II. Fill in the blanks with the correct forms of the words in Column A of the above table.

1. That hat was a good _____ .
2. We'll _____ them for charity.
3. I will _____ for someone to take you round.
4. Everything has its _____ .
5. She felt _____ .
6. He is _____ as the first hour passes and then another.
7. How emissions of heat-trapping gases can be reduced on a global _____ .
8. We got lost in the _____ .
9. Clothes are the best _____ , with many items marked down.
10. This dress is really cheaper by _____ .

III. Compare each pair of words and choose the correct one to fill in each blank. Change the form if necessary.

1. arrange   arrangement
   a. It is not for me to _____ such matters.
   b. He has made every _____ to meet any emergency.

179

2. compare   comparison

   a. _____ the following passages.

   b. By _____ with London, Paris is small.

3. auction   action

   a. It was a rare pleasure to see him in _____ .

   b. They've put the contents of their house up for _____ .

4. patient   impatient

   a. A _____ will usually listen to the doctor's advice.

   b. I'd been waiting for twenty minutes and I was getting _____ .

Ⅳ. Add the prefix "-en" to the following words in brackets. Then complete the sentences with the words formed.

> **Tips:** Tips: 后缀 "-en" 接在某些名词后构成动词，有 "使" "使……变成" 等含义。如：frighten(恐吓), hasten(加快), heighten(提高), lengthen(延长), strengthen(加强) 等。

Sample: You can lengthen your holidays. (lengthen)

1. He heard her breathing _____ . (deep)
2. Why does the sun lighten our hair, but _____ our skin? (dark)
3. We _____ in experiences by traveling. (broad)
4. Newspaper as good reading materials can _____ our knowledge. (rich)
5. I actually felt my heart _____ . (quick)

Ⅴ. Choose the best phrase to complete each sentence.

1. Does burning candle _____ some air inside the glass?

   A. use up   B. use out   C. using up   D. to use up

2. The new company did well at first, _____ ran into trouble.

   A. then but   B. but then   C. but   D. to then but

3. _____ he asked her to marry him.

   A. Here   B. Here and there   C. There and then   D. There

4. Some weeds _____ in only one night.

   A. to spring up   B. in spring   C. spring out   D. spring up

5. We should _____ our public transport.

   A. take advantage of   B. advantages

   C. takes advantage of   D. take advantage

Ⅵ. Complete the following sentences by translating the Chinese given in brackets into English.

1. Doubts have begun to _____ (突然起了) in my mind.

2. Many felt that he should have _____ (当场辞职).

3. At first she demurred(反对), _____ (但最终还是同意了).

4. It isn't them who _____(把全球的资源耗费殆尽的).
5. You should _____(充分利用) our club to communicate with other students.

VII. Translate the following sentences into Chinese.

1. It's fair to say that the Internet has revolutionized our shopping habits. (Para. 1)
   _____

2. There seems to be little to lose as long as you try to find the best price you can in the first place. (Para. 3)
   _____

3. Most of us are impatient and once we've decided we want something, we want it there and then. (Para. 4)
   _____

4. As well as buying things online, you can also sell your unwanted items. (Para. 5)
   _____

VIII. Complete the following sentences by translating the Chinese given in brackets into English using the structure "so that".

> so that 引导目的状语从句，意为"以便；为了；目的是"，其从句中常用 may, might, should, can, could, will, would 等。
>
> Sample: Hopes and dreams and aspirations must be revisited often <u>so that we won't lose sight of things that are really important to us</u>(这样，我们就不会忘记那些对我们而言真正重要的东西).

1. A teacher must speak clearly _____(以便学生能充分理解).
2. Please get prepared _____(这样，我们就可以随时出发).
3. I stayed on _____(使他不至于觉得孤单).
4. I put your keys in the drawer _____(这样就不会丢了).
5. They got up very early _____(以便能赶上火车).

IX. Complete the following sentences by translating the Chinese given in brackets into English using "who".

> who 引导定语从句时，其先行词往往是指人的名词。who 在从句中作主语，不可以省略。
>
> Sample: Men were hunters <u>who made specific plans about how to catch and kill animals for food</u>(他们要详细计划如何捕杀猎物).

1. Yesterday I help _____(一个迷路的老人).
2. The man behind you is Tom's father _____(他是一个医生).
3. He is _____(那个看上去长得有点像你的人).
4. I once met this man _____(他给我讲过一个奇怪的故事).
5. _____ (在农场劳作的那个农民) has a lot of money.

Dialogue Samples

Listen and read the samples carefully, and then complete the communicative tasks that follow.

Dialogue 1 Making reservation

Jim: Maple Travel Agency. May I help you?

Bowie: I would like to reserve a ticket, please.

Jim: Is it one way or round trip?

Bowie: One way, please.

Jim: What date are you flying?

Bowie: July 1st.

Jim: Would you like to fly early in the morning or late in the afternoon?

Bowie: An early flight would be fine.

Jim: OK, no problem.

Dialogue2 At the Airport Terminal

(At the Counter)

Tom: Excuse me, where is the American Airlines' counter?

Bob: Go down that way. It's to your left.

David: (at the airlines' counter) May I help you?

Tom: I have an e-ticket, I don't know how it works.

David: Well, if you have an e-ticket and have no luggage to check in, you don't need to wait in line. Just go to an e-machine over there and input your ID number, the machine will print out a boarding pass for you.

Tom: But I have baggage to check in.

David: well, Then I'll need your ID and ticket, please.

Tom: Here you are.

Communicative Tasks

Work with your partner and take turns to start the conversations.

Task 1

Task 2

Situation:

Situation:

A costumer wants to book a ticket to the New York. And he is at the counter.

A man was late for his plane, and he wants to change to another plane.

Tips:

Tips:

Here are some thing she can say or ask:
Excuse me.
Can you help me, please?
I want to book a ticket to …
How much is the ticket?
Is there any cheaper one?

Here are some things the staff can say or ask:
I feel sorry for that.
It is OK. Don't worry.
I will deal with this.
You can transfer to another plane.
I will book a new ticket for you.

Here are some things the staff in the airport can say:
How can I help you?
Sorry, we haven't any left.
Yes, we do have some left.
It is about …dollars.

Here are some things the man can say:
Oh, that is terrible.
I am late for the plane.
What should I do?
Can I change another plane.

Further Development

同化

音的同化也是一种连读的现象,两个词之间非常平滑地过渡,导致一个音受临音影响而变化。音的同化主要是以下3种方式。

(1) 辅音 [d] 与 [j] 相邻时,被同化为 [dʒ]:Would you…?.
(2) 辅者 [t] 与 [j] 相邻时,被同化为 [tʃ]:Can't you…?.
(3) 辅音 [s] 与 [j] 相邻时,被同化为 [ʃ]:Miss you.

Text B

The Dangers of Cell Phone Use

1. Cell phones are a danger on the road in more ways than one. Two new studies show that talking on the phone while traveling, whether you're driving or on foot, is increasing both pedestrian deaths and those of drivers and passengers, and recommend not use cell phone use by both pedestrians and drivers.

2. New studies from Rutgers University*, Newark*, connected the impact of cell phones on accident **fatalities** with the number of cell phones in use, showing that the current increase in deaths **attributed** to cell phone use follows a period when cell phones actually helped to reduce pedestrian and traffic fatalities. However, this **reduction** in fatalities disappeared once the number of phones in use reached a "critical mass" of 100 million, the studies found.

3. The studies looked at cell phone use and car accidents from 1975 to 2002, and factored in a number of variables, including vehicle speed, alcohol consumption, seat belt use, and miles driven. The studies found the cell phone-fatality **correlation** to be true even when taking into consideration speed, alcohol consumption and seat **belt** use.

4. The studies determined that, at the current time, cell phone use has a "significant **adverse** effect on pedestrian safety" and that "cell phones and their usage above a critical **threshold** adds to **fatal** accidents." In the late 1980s and part of the 1990s, before the number of phones **exploded**, cell phone use actually had a "life-saving effect" in pedestrian and traffic accidents. "Cell phone users were able to quickly call for medical **assistance** when involved in an accident. This quick medical **response** actually reduced the number of traffic deaths for a time," the studies **hypothesized**.

5. However, this was not the case when cell phones were first used in the mid-1980s, when they caused a "life-taking effect" among pedestrians, drivers and passengers in vehicles. In those early days, when there were fewer than a million phones, fatalities increased, because drivers and pedestrians probably were still adjusting to the **novelty** of using them, and there weren't enough cell phones in use to make a difference in **summoning** help following an accident.

6. The "life-saving effect" occurred as the volume of phones grew into the early 1990s, and increasing cell phones were used to call for assistance following accidents, leading to a drop in fatalities. But this "life-saving effect" was canceled out once the number of phones reached a "critical mass" of about 100 million and the "life-taking effect"-increased accidents and fatalities-**outweighed** the benefits of quick access to 911 services, according to the studies.

7. The studies looked at pedestrian fatalities related to cell phone use and examined all cell **phone-related** traffic fatalities. The researchers of those studies use **econometric** models to analyze data from a number of government and private studies, including those by the National Highway Traffic Safety Administration*, the Department of Transportation* and the US Census Bureau*, among others.

8. The researchers recommend that governments consider more **aggressive** policies to reduce cell phone use by both drivers and pedestrians, to reduce the number of fatalities.

Unit 8　Modern Life

 New Words

attribute[əˈtrɪbjuːt] v. sth. belongs to sb. 认为某事［物］属于某人［物］
belt[belt] n. the long stuff for purpose use 腰带；腰带
phone-related[fəʊn rɪˈleɪtɪd] adj. sth. about phone 与手机相关的
fatality[fəˈtæləti] n. a death caused by an accident, a war, violence or disease（事故、战争、暴力或疾病导致的）死亡
reduction[rɪˈdʌkʃn] n. the process or result of making sth. smaller or less in amount, size, importance, etc. 降低；减少；缩小
correlation[ˌkɒrəˈleɪʃn] n. a connection between two things in which one thing changes as the other does 相互关系；相关性
adverse[ˈædvɜːs] adj. negative and unpleasant, not likely to produce a good result 不利的
threshold[ˈθreʃhəʊld] n. the level at which sth. starts to happen or have an effect 起始点
fatal[ˈfeɪtl] adj. causing or ending in death 致命的
explode[ɪkˈspləʊd] v. increase suddenly and very quickly in number 激增
assistance[əˈsɪstəns] n. help or support 帮助；援助；支持
response[rɪˈspɒns] n. a reaction to sth. that has happened or been said 反应；响应
hypothesize[haɪˈpɒθəsaɪz] v. suggest a possible explanation for sth. when you are not definitely know about it 假设；假定
novelty[ˈnɒvlti] n. the excitement or interest that sth. new or unusual creates 新鲜感；新奇感
summon[ˈsʌmən] v. call for or try to obtain sth. 呼吁；请求
outweigh[ˌaʊtˈweɪ] v. be greater or more important than sth. 重于；大于；超过
econometric[ɪkɒnəˈmetrɪk] adj. of or relating to econometric, which is the application of mathematics and statistics to the study of economic and financial data 计量经济学的
aggressive[əˈgresɪv] adj. acting with force and determination in order to succeed 积极的；志在必得的

187

Useful Expressions

Phrases	Examples
attribute to 归因于；归功于	He has the attribute to confront with misfortunes with great optimism. 他很乐观地积极地面对不幸
factor in 计入	Obesity is a major risk factor in many diseases. 肥胖是引发多种疾病的重要因素
take…into consideration 考虑到，顾及	Time factor is what we must first take into consideration. 时间因素是我们必须首先考虑的
cancel out 抵消	Did the two groups actually cancel out? I hope not. 这两组人的力量果真相互抵消了吗？我希望并不如此
according to 根据	According to the weather report, we'll have rain tomorrow. 根据天气预报，明天有雨

 Background Information

1. Rutgers University: 罗格斯大学（美国大学），简称 RU 或 Rutgers，全名为新泽西州立罗格斯大学（Rutgers, The State University of New Jersey）。罗格斯大学的前身是成立于 1766 年的皇后学院（Queen's College），是一所在世界上享有盛名的顶尖公立研究型大学，也是新泽西州规模最大的高等学府，其学术声誉在州内仅次于普林斯顿大学（Princeton University）。

2. Newark: 纽瓦克（美国城市）。

3. National Highway Traffic Safety Administration: （美国）国家公路交通安全管理局。

4. Department of Transportation: （美国）运输部。

5. US Census Bureau: 美国人口普查局。美国人口普查局是专门提供人口和经济方面数据的机构。这些数据是需要其他部门的协助、帮忙提供的，它对于人口和经济的掌管是有好处的。这些数据包括人口数目、经济指标、美国商业统计、工业报告等。作为美国商务部下属的一个机关，它的任务由美国宪法注明：必须至少每十年进行一次人口普查，相应的美国众议院的成员数由这个调查结果决定；除此之外，它还提供美国国家、人民和经济的统计数据。

Unit 8 Modern Life

 Reading Comprehension

I. Decide whether the following statements are True (T) or False (F).

( ) 1. The studies looked at cell phone use and car accident from 2002 to 2008.

( ) 2. There was the case when cell phones were first used in the mid-1980s.

( ) 3. Governments consider policies to reduce cell phone use by both drivers and pedestrians.

( ) 4. The researchers recommend that governments consider less aggressive policies to reduce cell phone use by both drivers and pedestrians.

II. Choose the best answer to each of the following questions.

1. The expression "factor in" in the third paragraph most probably means _____.
   A. conclude　　　B. result in　　　C. include　　　D. obtain

2. According to the studies from Rutgers University, cell phones actually helped reduce pedestrian and traffic fatalities before _____.
   A. cars explode
   B. government considered
   C. people afford to buy phones
   D. phones in use reached a "critical mass" of 100 millions

3. Why did cell phones fail to cause a "life-saving effect" in the mid-1980s?
   A. because cell phones were not widely used and people were not used to using them
   B. Because medical service was not available at that time
   C. Because cell phone use was reduced by governments' aggressive policies
   D. Because people couldn't be put through after accidents

4. Which of the following statements is NOT true according to the text?
   A. Cell phone use once had a "life-saving effect" in both pedestrian and traffic accidents
   B. Factors like vehicle speed, alcohol consumption, seat belt use and miles driven were proved to be more related to traffic fatalities than cell phone use
   C. Cell phones' "life-saving effect" was replaced by their "life-taking effect"
   D. In spite of the benefits of quick access to medical service, cell phone use had a "life-taking effect" after the number of phones exploded

5. What can be inferred from the text?
   A. Medical assistance may give priority to cell phone-related accidents
   B. The number of phones may drop sharply in the future
   C. Cell phones' "life-saving effect" may outweigh their "life-taking effect" in the future
   D. Drivers who use cell phones while driving may get more severe punishment in the future

Grammar

Emphatic Pattern

英语有许多方式表示强调,可利用重读或加强语气,增加一些特殊词汇,倒装、前置以及强调句型来达到强调的目的。这里重点讨论强调句型。

1. 强调句型"It is(was) + 被强调部分 + that(who) + 句子的其余部分"

It 在句中无意义,只起引出被强调部分的作用。被强调部分是物时,只能用 that;被强调的部分指人时,除可用 that 外,还可换用 who(强调宾语指人时也可用 whom).

例如:

Tom was reviewing his lessons in the reading-room for the whole afternoon in order to pass the English exam. 为了通过英语考试汤姆在阅览室复习了一下午的功课。

It was Tom who/that was reviewing his lessons in the reading-room for the whole afternoon in order to pass the English exam. 汤姆为了通过英语考试,在阅览室复习了一下午的功课。

It was in the reading-room that Tom was reviewing his lessons for the whole afternoon in order to pass the exam. 为了通过英语考试,汤姆一下午都是在阅览室复习功课。

It was for the whole afternoon that Tom was reviewing his lessons in the reading-room in order to pass the exam. 为了通过英语考试,汤姆在阅览室复习功课,他整整复习了一个下午。

It was in order to pass the exam that Tom was reviewing his lessons in the reading-room for the whole morning. 汤姆整整一个下午都在阅览室复习功课,为的是通过英语考试。

2. 使用强调句型的注意事项

① 去掉强调结构 It is(was)…that(who)…后,剩下的词仍能组成一个完整的句子。这是判断是不是强调句型的关键。试比较:

It is strange that he didn't come yesterday. (很奇怪,他昨天没来。)

It is you and Tom that didn't come yesterday. (是你和汤姆昨天没来。)

第一个句子去掉 It is…that…后,句子结构不完整,是主语从句;第二个句子去掉 It is…that…后,句子变为"you and Tom didn't come yesterday",仍是一个表意完整的句子,是强调句。

② 强调时间或地点状语时,不用 when 或 where 来代替 that. 只有指人时可用 who 代替 that.

③ it 后面的 be 动词只能用一般现在时 is 或一般过去式 was.

④ that 或 who 后面必须主谓一致。如:

It is I who/that am an English teacher. (当英语老师的人是我。)

It is that boy who/that speaks English best in the class. (班上英语讲得最好的是那个男孩。)

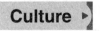

British Social Life (Section B)

c. The third is the fact that the UK is a welfare state which was established after the Labour Party came to power in 1945. Post-war welfare has been a combination of public and private provision. There are three main areas of welfare provision: health, housing and social security. The National Health Service provides free medical treatment for all the people in the country. It is one of the largest employers in the world with more than a million employees and is based on need rather than the ability to pay, which is financed mainly out of general taxation and the remainder out of national insurance contributions. Because of the increasing cost of the provision, the use of the private sector in health care and private non-medical services is encouraged. If a person is ill, the hospital not only gives him or her medical care but also provides him or her with food.

Housing in the UK is either privately owned or provided by funds from the British government which acts as a controller of the proportion of private and public housing provision. Different types of housing tend to be found in different parts of a city ranging from the detached house with a large garden in the suburbs to the small terraced house in the inner city. Government policies ensure the provision of adequate housing and the minimal standards of housing for British citizens. Today about 30% of British households rent a flat or a house from the local authority and over 65% of households own their houses. The local authority administers the housing benefit for those who are on low incomes or those who are unexpectedly or temporarily out of work through illness. The Department of Social Security processes the unemployment benefit and income support. Those who become unemployed can claim both housing benefit and unemployment benefit. The sum differ between a single man or a couple with children, which is payable weekly and for up to a year in any one period of unemployment. Begging is illegal in the UK, which is thought degrading to the beggar and embarrassing to everyone else. Income support is given to those who are working on a low wage with a family to support. Other benefits available include sickness benefit, widow's pension and disablement allowance. In all these ways and others, almost every British citizen is prevented from financial hardship. The welfare state in the UK affects the social life and the life style of the British people.

d. The living standards affect the life of a country. The standard of living in the UK is rather high. According to a United Nation report in 1992 the UK ranked tenth out of 160 countries. The high percentage of ownership of houses is one of the factors. Every family either has a house of its own or a rented one. The availability of certain durable modern goods is growing, for example, 98% of the people have television, 88% have telephones, 83% own a freezer or fridge freezer, 67% own a car or van, 68% have a video, 21% own a computer. These statistics demonstrate the high living standard in the UK. What is regarded as a necessity in one country will not be regarded as such in another. Someone who is poor in a developed country may well be considered rich in a developing country. Marked improvements in the standard of living in the UK took place during the 20th century. These improvements have changed the way of life in the UK considerably.

e. Finally the concentration of population in the UK. The economic difference between north and south is another distinction which marks British society, a distinction which can be seen in many societies but is perhaps particularly obvious in the UK, i. e. the difference between the capital and the rest of the country. London is in the south of the country, and is dominant in the United Kingdom in all sorts of ways. It is by far the largest city in the country, with about one seventh of the nation's population; it is the seat of government; it is the cultural centre, home to all the major newspapers, TV stations, and no doubt the widest selection of galleries, theatres and museums. Also it is the business centre, headquarters of the vast majority of Britain's big companies; it is the financial centre of the nation, and one of the three major international financial centres in the world. As such it combines the functions of New York, Washington and Los Angeles, in one city. To some extent the rest of the country lives in its shade.

Unit 9

Chinese Festivals

Warm-up Activities

Ⅰ. **Matching**

Learn the following phrases about different festivals, and match them to the pictures.

1. Spring Festival (　　)　　　　2. Lantern Festival (　　)
3. Tomb-sweeping Festival (　　)　4. Dragon Boat Festival (　　)
5. Double Ninth Festival (　　)　　6. Mid-Autumn Festival (　　)

A.

B.

C.

D.

E.

F.

Ⅱ. **Reading**

seize　v. 抓住
greet　v. 迎接；欢迎
arrival　n. 到达；抵达

Let's seize the day and live it to the full, and greet the arrival of the year 2020 together. I wish you all a happy new year!

让我们只争朝夕，不负韶华，共同迎接2020年的到来。祝大家新年快乐！

（习近平总书记2020年新年贺词）

Text A

Chinese Qixi Festival

1. Chinese Qixi Festival, the most romantic of all the traditional holidays in China, falls on the 7th day of the seventh lunar month. So it is also called Double Seventh Festival. Each year, some big companies organize a variety of activities, and people send gifts to their lovers. As a result, the festival is also considered to be Chinese "Valentine's Day". The Qixi Festival is derived from a beautiful legendary love story about Niulang (Cowherd) and Zhinü (Weaving Maid), which has been passed down from generation to generation.

2. Long, long ago, there was an upright and kind man called Niulang (Cowherd) who did not live a happy life. His only companion was his old ox. One day, a fairy named Zhinü (Weaving Maid) fell in love with him, so she descended down to earth secretly to get married. The Cowherd farmed in the field and the Weaving Maid wove at home. They led a happy life and gave birth to a boy and a girl.

3. Unluckily, the Jade Emperor and the Empress of Heaven* discovered their union and ordered the troops from Heaven to take the Weaving Maid back. With the help of his ox, the Cowherd flew to Heaven with his children. Meanwhile when he was about to find his wife, the Empress of Heaven took off her gold hairpin and used it to draw a line, which suddenly turned into a celestial river in the sky.

4. The couple was **separated** by the river (The Milky Way) forever and could only **shed** their tears. Then tens of thousands of magpies were touched by their **faithful** love, so they came to establish a bridge across the Milky Way to help them meet each other. The Empress of Heaven was finally moved and allowed them to meet each other on the seventh day of the seventh lunar month.

5. The festival is in mid-summer when the weather is very hot. On this particular night every year when the sky is dotted with stars, people can see the Milky Way **spanning** from the north to the south. On the opposite sides of it there are two bright stars which watch each other from afar.

6. During the Qixi festival, people usually look up into the sky, praying for good luck and health. Young women, in particular, would beg Weaving Maid for **wisdom**, so that they can have a lively mind, a quick hand and a happy marriage. That's why the festival has another name "Qiqiao

Festival". On this day, girls and women like to show their **embroidery** and use **ingredients** such as oil, flours, sugar and honey to make various kinds of delicious foods to celebrate the festival. This custom dates back to China's Han Dynasty. But with the changing of times, these traditional customs have been weakened in cities and these activities are disappearing.

  7. On May 20, 2006, the Qixi Festival was included by the State Council into the first **batch** of the country's **intangible** cultural heritage* list. The legend of Cowherd and Weaving Maid, a symbol of faithful love, is still **circulated** among the folk and still remains in the hearts of people.

New Words

lunar[ˈluːnə(r)] adj. Lunar means relating to the moon 月球的；月亮的
variety[vəˈraɪəti] n. several different sorts of the same thing（同一事物的）不同种类
legendary[ˈledʒəndri] adj. mentioned in stories from ancient times 传奇的；传说的
upright[ˈʌpraɪt] adj. (of a person) behaving in a moral and honest way（人）正直的；诚实的
companion[kəmˈpæniən] n. a person or an animal that travels with you or spends a lot of time with you 旅伴；伴侣；陪伴
fairy[ˈfeəri] n. (in stories) a creature like a small person, who has magic powers 小仙人；仙子
weave[wiːv] v. to make cloth, a carpet, a basket, etc. by crossing threads or strips across, over and under each other by hand or on a machine called a loom（用手或机器）编；织
troops[truːp] n. [pl.] soldiers, especially in large groups 军队；部队；士兵
hairpin[ˈheəpɪn] n. a small thin piece of wire that is folded in the middle, used by women for holding their hair in place 发夹
celestial[səˈlestiəl] adj. [usually before noun] (formal or literary) of the sky or of heaven 天空的
separate[ˈseprət] v. to move apart; to make people or things move apart（使）分离；分散
shed[ʃed] v. (formal or literary) if you shed tears, you cry 流；洒
faithful[ˈfeɪθfl] adj. staying with or supporting a particular person, organization or belief 忠实的；忠诚的
span[spæn] v. to stretch right across sth., from one side to the other 横跨；跨越
wisdom[ˈwɪzdəm] n. the ability to make sensible decisions and give good advice because of the experience and knowledge that you have 智慧；才智；精明
embroidery[ɪmˈbrɔɪdəri] n. the skill or activity of decorating cloth in this way 刺绣技法
ingredient[ɪnˈɡriːdiənt] n. one of the things from which sth. is made, especially one of the foods that are used together to make a particular dish 成分；（尤指烹饪）原料
batch[bætʃ] n. a number of people or things that are dealt with as a group 一批
intangible[ɪnˈtændʒəbl] adj. that does not exist as a physical thing but is still valuable to a company 无形的（指没有实体存在的资本性资产）
circulate[ˈsɜːkjəleɪt] v. if a story, an idea, information, etc. circulates or if you circulate it, it spreads or it is passed from one person to another 传播；流传；散布

Useful Expressions

Phrases	Examples
derive from 由……起源	Some ancient Greek philosophy seems to derive from the Oriental theory. 古希腊人的一些哲学理论似乎源自东方
pass down 使流传	This title will only pass down through the male line. 这个头衔将只能传给男性后裔
descend to 降临；下降	Don't descend to his level. 别降低到他那水准
date back to 追溯到……；从……开始	My family has a vase, which is said to date back to Ming Dynasty. 我家有个花瓶，据说是从明代传下来的
beg...for 乞讨；恳求	Now you're making me beg you for this. 现在你要我求你是吧

Background Information

1. Jade Emperor and Empress of Heaven: 玉皇大帝，即"昊天金阙无上至尊自然妙有弥罗至真玉皇上帝"，是道教神话传说中天地的主宰，又称"太上开天执符御历含真体道昊天玉皇上帝""玉皇大天尊""高天上圣大慈仁者玉皇大天尊玄穹高上帝""玄穹高上帝""天公""老天爷"。王母娘娘，另称"九灵太妙龟山金母""太灵九光龟台金母""瑶池金母""西王母""金母""王母""西姥"等，是古代中国神话传说中掌管不死药，罚恶、预警灾厉的长生女神。

2. intangible cultural heritage: 非物质文化遗产。根据联合国教科文组织的《保护非物质文化遗产公约》定义：非物质文化遗产指被各群体、团体，有时为个人所视为其文化遗产的各种实践、表演、表现形式、知识体系和技能及其有关的工具、实物、工艺品和文化场所。各个群体和团体随着其所处环境、与自然界的相互关系和历史条件的变化不断使这种代代相传的非物质文化遗产得到创新，同时使他们自己具有一种认同感和历史感，从而促进了文化多样性和激发人类的创造力。公约所定义的"非物质文化遗产"包括以下方面：口头传统和表现形式，包括作为非物质文化遗产媒介的语言；表演艺术；社会实践、仪式、节庆活动；有关自然界和宇宙的知识和实践；传统手工艺。

Unit 9　Chinese Festivals

 Reading Comprehension

Ⅰ. **Decide whether the following statements are True (T) or False (F).**
(　) 1. Chinese Qixi Festival falls on the 7th day of the sixth lunar month.
(　) 2. The Qixi Festival is based on a beautiful legendary love story about Cowherd and Weaving Maid.
(　) 3. The Cowherd fought in the war and the Weaving Maid wove at home.
(　) 4. The Jade Emperor discovered their union and ordered a soldier from Heaven to take the Weaving Maid back.
(　) 5. Every day, people can see the Milky Way spanning from the east to the west.
(　) 6. On May 20, 2006, the Qixi Festival was included by the State Council into the first batch of the country's intangible cultural heritage list.

Ⅱ. **Complete the answers to the following questions.**
1. Which festival is the most romantic of all the traditional holidays in China? (Para. 1)
　　_____ is the most romantic of all the traditional holidays in China.
2. Why did the Weaving Maid descend down to earth secretly? (Para. 2)
　　Because she _____.
3. What did the Cowherd do with the help of his ox? (Para. 3)
　　With the help of his ox, the Cowherd _____ with his children.
4. What do girls and women like to show during the Qixi Festival? (Para. 6)
　　Girls and women like to show _____.

Vocabulary and Structure

Words and Phrases to Drill

lunar	variety	upright	weave	separate
faithful	wisdom	ingredient	intangible	circulate
derive from	pass down	descend to	date back to	beg...for...

Ⅰ. Choose the appropriate explanation from Column B for each of the words in Column A.

A	B
_____ 1. lunar	a. spreads or it is passed from one person to another
_____ 2. variety	b. several different sorts of the same thing
_____ 3. weave	c. to move apart; to make people or things move apart
_____ 4. separate	d. relating to the moon
_____ 5. upright	e. (of a person) behaving in a moral and honest way
_____ 6. circulate	f. that does not exist as a physical thing but is still valuable to a company
_____ 7. intangible	g. the ability to make sensible decisions because of the experience and knowledge that you have
_____ 8. wisdom	h. one of the things from which sth. is made
_____ 9. faithful	i. staying with or supporting a particular person, organization or belief
_____ 10. ingredient	j. to make cloth, a carpet, a basket, etc. by crossing threads or strips across, over and under each other by hand or on a machine called a loom

Ⅱ. Fill in the blanks with the correct forms of the words in Column A of the above table.

1. The Spring Festival is the _____ New Year.
2. People change their mind for a _____ of reasons.
3. Sit in a relaxed _____ posture.
4. She is skilled at _____ .
5. Rural communities are widely _____ .
6. We must be honest and _____ to the people.
7. Experience is the mother of _____ .
8. Our skin cream contains only natural _____ .
9. There are _____ benefits.
10. The document was _____ to all members.

Ⅲ. Compare each pair of words and choose the correct one to fill in each blank. Change the form if necessary.

1. variety　various
   a. The music itself has so much _____ .
   b. The methods are many and _____ .

2. faithful   faith
   a. Dogs are _____ animals.
   b. I don't think his _____ should be ridiculed.
3. intangible   tangible
   a. Stocks and bonds are _____ property.
   b. The tension between them was almost _____ .
4. circulate   circulation
   a. Draughts help to _____ air.
   b. The newspaper has proved unable to maintain its _____ figures.

IV. Add the suffix "-ful" to the following words in brackets. Then complete the sentences with the words formed.

> **Tips:** "-ful"一般作为后缀加在名词后，构成形容词，表示充满……的、有……倾向的、有……性质的、充满……的。如 colorful, 多彩的；beautiful, 美丽的；useful, 有用的等。

Sample: Don't just sit watching television—make yourself useful! (use)
1. Thanks to her _____ handling of the affair, the problem was avoided. (skill)
2. She gave me a _____ look. (mean)
3. He took a _____ of the stew and ate it. (spoon)
4. They were _____ in winning the contract. (success)
5. He felt bright and _____ and full of energy. (cheer)

V. Choose the best phrase to complete each sentence.
1. Many English words are _____ Latin and Greek words.
   A. derived from   B. derive of   C. derive into   D. derive to
2. I hope that we can _____ the excellence of traditional Chinese culture better.
   A. pass on   B. pass down   C. pass onto   D. pass over
3. We're not going to _____ this level.
   A. descend   B. descend from   C. descend to   D. descend over
4. Most of the buildings _____ the 16th century.
   A. date of   B. date from   C. date to   D. date back to
5. He falls at her feet to _____ her _____ her forgiveness.
   A. pray…of…   B. pray… with…   C. beg…against…   D. beg…for…

VI. Complete the following sentences by translating the Chinese given in brackets into English.
1. These stories _____ (根据他在长征中的经历写成的).
2. They often use folk songs to _____ (来传递历史).
3. In Chinese legend, the immortals _____ (是不能随便下凡的).
4. Chinese acrobatic has a long history which can _____ (可追溯到两千多年前).
5. May I _____ (请求你捐助吗)?

VII. **Translate the following sentences into Chinese.**

1. Chinese Qixi Festival, the most romantic of all the traditional holidays in China, falls on the 7th day of the seventh lunar month. (para. 1)

2. The Qixi Festival is derived from a beautiful legendary love story about Niulang and Zhinü. (para. 1)

3. On May 20, 2006, the Qixi Festival was included by the State Council into the first batch of the country's intangible cultural heritage list. (para. 7)

4. The legend of Cowherd and Weaving Maid is still circulated among the folk. (para. 7)

VIII. **Rewrite the following sentences into emphatic sentences by adding "do/does/did."**

> 英语中表示强调的方法之一是在动词前加助动词 do/ does/ did，其中助动词的时态要根据句子的时态来确定。
> Sample: I care about you, Mike, and hope we can still be friends.
> I do care about you, Mike, and hope we can still be friends.

1. Our country develops much faster than before.

2. He felt hurt, even betrayed.

3. Some people believe that nuclear power poses a threat to world peace.

4. She sings the song well.

5. I was impolite and I beg your pardon.

IX. **Complete the following sentences by translating the Chinese given in brackets into English using "no matter how / where/ when, etc".**

> 词组 no matter 与疑问词 who, what, where, when, how 等连用，意味"无论，不管"。
> Sample: But one thing I would encourage parents to do is to remind their kids that no matter which athletes they look up to(无论他们崇拜哪些运动员), there are no perfect human beings.

1. Don't open the door, _____(不管谁来).
2. Don't trust him, _____(无论他说什么).
3. _____ (无论你在哪里工作), you can always find time to study.
4. _____ (无论你有多么忙), your kids deserve more quality time with you.
5. _____ (无论你多大), you can learn to draw.

Dialogue Samples

Listen and read the samples carefully, and then complete the communicative tasks that follow.

Dialogue 1　Talking about shopping

Tom: So, Francis, do you enjoy shopping?

Francis: Yes, when I'm in the mood for it. Definitely.

Tom: Do you usually follow fashion?

Francis: No, because I prefer comfortable clothing.

Tom: So, are you a bargain shopper?

Francis: I try to be but if there is something that I really want to have, I will save up and buy it.

Tom: What sort of thing would you save up to buy?

Francis: I saved up to buy a nice yellow hat and I've had that now for three years, so it was definitely a good purchase. It was about a hundred dollars.

Tom: Wow, that is a lot.

Francis: Mm.

Dialogue 2　Talking about shopping online

Tom: Have you ever bought anything online?

Francis: No, I haven't, but one of my best friends has bought dresses, shoes and hats, yeah, she really loves shopping online because it is convenient.

Tom: Has she encountered problems while shopping online?

Francis: She hasn't had any problems at all.

Tom: So how come you don't shop online?

Francis: I like to have contact with sales people and try clothes on. What if the clothes don't fit?

Tom: Right. Right.

Communicative Tasks

Work with your partner and take turns to start the conversations.

Task 1

Situation:

Lin wants to buy a tie, so he goes to the department store.

Tips:

| Here are some things Lin can say or ask:

I'm just looking. / I'm just browsing.

I don't care for it too much.

Do you have this tie in red?

Could you show me that one? |

| Here are some things the saleswoman can say or ask:

Welcome to Macy's, How can I help you?

Is there anything I can do for you?

These ties are on sale now.

The regular price used to be $15, and now we're selling them at $10 dollars for one and $15 dollars for the pair. |

Task 2

Situation:

Zhang is selecting a new pair of pants in the department store.

Tips:

| Here are some things Zhang can say or ask:

I'd like to have a look if you don't mind.

I'm interested in this new type of pants.

I'd like this one. May I try it on?

Do you carry hundred percent cotton pants? |

| Here are some things the salesman can say or ask:

Do you find anything you like?

This color is very popular.

I think we're out of your size.

Check back next Sunday. |

Further Development

失音

失音，就是某一个或者几个音脱落，把单词、短语和句子快速连缀成串。单词间的失音有四种类型。

类型一：前一词以"持续音+/t/ /d/"结尾，后一词以辅音开头，则其中/t/ /d/失音，例如：

    refused both   last class   bend back   settled there

类型二：前一词以"破音/擦音+/t/ /d/"结束，后一词以辅音开头，则其中/t/ /d/失音，例如：

    kept quiet   rubbed gently

    fetched me   parched throat

注：后一词如始于 h 则/t/ /d/很少脱落，例如：kept her waiting.

类型三：动词否定结尾的缩写形式 n't 中的/t/失音（无论后一词以元音还是辅音开头），例如：

    Doesn't she know?

    He wouldn't overeat.

类型四：前一词以/t/ 结束，后一词以/t/ 或 /d/开头，则前面的/t/往往失音，例如：

    I've got to go.

    What do you want?

Text B

The Spring Festival

1. For several thousands years, Chinese people have developed many traditional festivals including the Spring Festival, the Lantern Festival, the Qingming Festival, the Dragon Boat Festival, the Qixi Festival, the Mid-Autumn Festival and the Double Ninth Festival. Those traditional festivals are colorful and rich in **content**. Among them, the Spring Festival is the most significant one for Chinese people. It is the time for family members to gather just as westerners do on Christmas. Also, it is time for bidding farewell to the old and ushering in the new. Now the Chinese government **stipulates** that people have seven days off for the Chinese New Year.

2. There are many legends about the origin of nian*. According to the most famous legend, in ancient China there lived a **fierce monster** nian living deep at the **bottom** of the sea. On the day of every New Year's Eve, nian would **devour** people. So on this day, people from all villages would run away to **avoid** the **calamity**.

3. One New Year's Eve, villagers of the Peach Blossom Village planned to leave the village quickly as usual when there came an old man with **graceful** white beard. A grandmother living at the east end of the village gave the old man some food and advised him to go and hide in the mountains with the villagers. But he just wanted to stay at her house for the night and promised to **scare** away the monster.

4. Around midnight the monster **invaded** the village and found it was quite different. The house of the grandmother was **brilliantly illuminated**, with red paper **stuck** on the doors. As the monster **approached** the door of the grandmother's house, there came the exploding sounds, which scared him away.

5. The next day when villagers came back and found everything safe, they were quite surprised. They swarmed into the grandmother's house, only to find that the doors were struck with red paper, the **embers** of a pile of bamboo were still giving out the exploding sounds of bang-bong, and a few

candles were still glowing in the room. It turned out that the red colour, exploding and flame were what nian feared the most. In order to celebrate the arrival of the auspiciousness, the villagers put on their new clothes and visited their relatives and friends. These customs and activities were soon spread to the other villages.

6. From then on, red is considered as an **auspicious** color. People let off **firecrackers** and fireworks for bidding farewell to the old year and welcoming the new year. In addition, people keep their houses brilliantly illuminated and stay up late into the night watching together the Spring Festival Gala* on CCTV and waiting for the New Year's bell at midnight.

7. The Spring Festival has 4 000-years of history in China. As a **witness** of the historical transformations China has experienced, it embodies the **continuity** of the Chinese civilization. Wherever there are Chinese people, the Spring Festival is celebrated.

New Words

content[ˈkɒntent] n. the subject matter of a book, speech etc（书、讲话等的）主题；主要内容

stipulate[ˈstɪpjuleɪt] v. to state clearly and firmly that sth must be done 规定；明确要求

fierce[fɪəs] adj. angry and aggressive in a way that is frightening 凶猛的；凶狠的；凶残的

monster[ˈmɒnstə(r)] n. (in stories) an imaginary creature that is very large, ugly and frightening （传说中的）怪物；怪兽

bottom[ˈbɒtəm] n. lowest part 底部

devour[dɪˈvaʊə(r)] v. to eat all of sth. quickly, because you are very hungry 狼吞虎咽地吃光

avoid[əˈvɔɪd] v. to prevent sth. bad from happening 避免；防止

calamity[kəˈlæməti] n. an event that causes great damage to people's lives, property, etc. 灾难

graceful[ˈgreɪsfl] adj. moving in a controlled, attractive way 优美的；优雅的；雅致的

scare[skeə(r)] v. to frighten sb. 惊吓；使害怕；使恐惧

invade[ɪnˈveɪd] v. to enter a country, town, etc. using military force in order to take control of it 武装入侵；侵略；侵犯

brilliant[ˈbrɪliənt] adj. very bright (of light or colours)（光线或色彩）明亮的；鲜艳的

illuminate[ɪˈluːmɪneɪt] v. to shine light on sth. 照明；照亮；照射

stick[stɪk] v. to fix sth to sth. else, usually with a sticky substance; to become fixed to sth. in this way 粘贴；粘住

approach[əˈprəʊtʃ] v. to come near to sb./sth. in distance or time 靠近；接近

ember[ˈembə(r)] n. a piece of wood or coal that is not burning but is still red and hot after a fire has died 余火未尽的木块（或煤块）

auspicious[ɔːˈspɪʃəs] adj. showing signs that sth. is likely to be successful in the future 吉祥的

firecracker[ˈfaɪəkrækə(r)] n. a small firework that explodes with a loud noise 鞭炮；爆竹

witness[ˈwɪtnəs] n. a person who sees sth. happen 目击者；见证人

continuity[ˌkɒntɪˈnjuːəti] n. the fact of not stopping or not changing 连续性；持续性

Useful Expressions

Phrases	Examples
bid farewell 告别	Shanghai is bidding farewell to the World Expo-a six-month event showcasing China's rise in the world. 上海已宣告世博会的结束，本次为期六个月的展览向世界展示了中国的崛起
usher in 迎来	America must play its role in ushering in a new era of peace. 美国必须为迎来一个和平的新纪元施展自己的作用
have…off 休假	Any time you have off now will have to be made up another day. 现在你休息的时间都得在以后补回来
swarm into 蜂拥而至	The children swarmed into the zoo. 孩子们成群地进入了动物园
turn out 证明是	His forecast turned out to be quite wrong. 他的预测最后证明是大错特错

 Background Information

1. nian: 年兽，是民间神话传说中的恶魔。从先秦至清，历代神话、志怪、传奇、逸事笔记，如《山海经》《搜神记》《聊斋志异》均无记载。有三种可能：年兽只是近现代人结合春节爆竹驱邪等风俗杜撰传说，以讹传讹；年兽为某地乡土传说，现代人妙笔生花，经网络传播而广为流传；确有典籍记载，只是目前还未找到。相传古时候每到年末的午夜，年兽就会进攻村子，凡被年兽占领的村子都遭受残酷的大屠杀，年兽头上的犄角就是屠杀武器。屠杀结束后，年兽会吃掉所有人的头颅。为了防止有人诈死或侥幸逃脱，年兽假装离开村子后折回来屠杀幸存者，甚至让村子发生剧烈的晃动，就连婴儿、孩童都难以幸免。人们利用年兽的两大弱点，放爆竹（会吓走年兽）、贴春联，以驱赶年兽的进攻。

2. the Spring Festival Gala: 中央电视台春节联欢晚会，简称为央视春晚或春晚，是中央电视台在每年除夕之夜为了庆祝新年而开办的综合性文艺晚会。起源于1979年，正式开办于1983年，2014年被定位为国家项目。央视春晚涵盖小品、歌曲、歌舞、杂技、魔术、戏曲、相声剧等多种艺术形式，把现场观众和电视机前的观众带入狂欢之中，以打造"普天同庆，盛世欢歌"的节日景象。央视春晚于每年除夕晚20:00在中央电视台综合频道、综艺频道、中文国际频道、军事频道、农业频道、少儿频道等现场直播。

Reading Comprehension

I. **Decide whether the following statements are True (T) or False (F).**

( ) 1. For several thousands years, Chinese people have developed 7 traditional festivals.

( ) 2. It is time for bidding farewell to the old and ushering in the new.

( ) 3. Now the Chinese government stipulates that people have seven days off for the Lantern Festival.

( ) 4. In China, green is the considered as an auspicious color.

( ) 5. On New Year's Eve, people stay up late into the night listening to the classical music.

II. **Choose the best answer to each of the following questions.**

1. What would nian climb up to the shore to do on the day of every New Year's Eve?
   A. find his companion
   B. help people
   C. scare people away
   D. devour people

2. The old beggar with graceful white beard promised to _____ .
   A. stay in the grandmother's house
   B. hide in his own house to keep away from the monster
   C. flee to the remote mountains to avoid the calamity
   D. scare away the monster

3. According to Paragraph 4 and 5, what did nian fear the most ?
   A. red colour
   B. exploding
   C. flame
   D. above all

4. Why did people let off firecrackers and fireworks in ancient China?
   A. for bidding farewell to the old year and welcoming the new year.
   B. to drive away wild animals and evil spirits.
   C. to visit their relatives and friends.
   D. for the sake of health and wealth.

5. The Spring Festival _____ .
   A. has 5 000-years of history in China
   B. embodies the amazing continuity of the Chinese civilization
   C. helps maintain the political identity of the Chinese nation
   D. is celebrated everywhere

Grammar

Subject-Verb Agreement

主谓一致就是主语和谓语动词在人称、数和意义等方面保持一致。

1. 主谓一致原则

(1) 语法一致原则。

语法一致，指谓语动词和主语在单数或复数形式上是一致的。

例如：Experience has taught me that life can be very unfair.

(2) 意义一致。

意义一致，是指谓语动词的单数或复数取决于主语表达的概念，而不是形式。主语形式虽是单数，但意义是复数，谓语动词也采取复数形式。而有些主语形式虽是复数，但意义上看作单数，谓语动词也采取单数形式。

例如：Economics is not difficult for him to learn.

(3) 就近原则。

就近原则，是指主语有两个以上时，谓语动词要与其最接近的名词或代词的数保持一致。

例如：There is an apple, two peaches on the table.

There are two peaches, an apple on the table.

2. 主谓一致的用法

(1) 名词做主语时的主谓一致。

可数名词做主语，动词可用单数或复数形式；不可数名词做主语，动词只能用单数形式。

例如：Time is precious.

Two thousand miles is a long distance.

集体名词一般都看作复数。

例如：Most people have taken part in the activity.

有些集体名词表示物体的总称，通常做不可数名词，谓语动词用单数，如 equipment, furniture, merchandise 等。

例如：The furniture was easy to transport.

有些集体名词，如 audience, family, group 等，侧重整体时，谓语用单数，侧重个体中的各个成员时，谓语用复数。

例如：His family are all fond of football.

The family is tiniest cell of the society.

(2) 代词做主语时的主谓一致。

由 anyone, anything, anybody, no one, nothing, everyone, everybody, everything, someone, somebody, each, either, neither 等不定代词做主语，谓语动词使用单数形式。

例如：Someone is standing at the door.

none 做主语，谓语动词单复数形式由 of 后名词的单复数而定。none 后接可数名词复数时，动词可用单数或复数，接不可数名词时，动词用单数。

例如：None of the food was delicious.

　　　None of the teachers is/are absent today.

both 做主语，谓语动词用复数。

例如：Both of you are beautiful.

all, most, half 等做主语时，采用意义一致原则来确定动词的单复数形式。

例如：All is well that ends well.

　　　All are eager to reach an agreement.

(3) 并列结构做主语时的主谓一致。

由 and 或 both...and 连接两个单数形式的名词词组做主语时，一般谓语动词用复数形式。例如：A young man and a girl want to go there.

在 each...and each..., no...and no... 等结构之后，谓语动词用单数形式。

例如：No man and no animal is to be found on the moon.

"名词 + and + 名词"做主语，表示同一人、同一概念或事物时，谓语动词用单数形式。

例如：A writer and educator is giving a lecture now.

由 not only...but also, either...or, neither...nor 或 or 连接的并列主语，通常根据就近一致原则，动词的单复数形式由最接近它的名词词组的单复数形式决定。

例如：Either the players or the coach is responsible for the defeat.

由 as well as, together with, besides, like, along with, with but, except, accompanied by, rather than, including 连接两个名词做主语，谓语单复数形式应由连接词前的名词而定。

例如：Tom, along with his friends, goes skating every Saturday.

Unit 9 Chinese Festivals

Talking About the Weather

The British people tend to have conversations relating to weather. Talking about weather is a common topic in the UK. Weather is the first thing they usually talk about. When you come across a friend and do not know how to start your conversation, you could say, "It is a nice day, isn't it ?" or "It looks like rain", or you might say, "I hope the rain lets up soon", or something like that. So weather is often talked about in the UK. James and George are talking about today's weather, so now let's see how they start their conversation.

James: Oh, what a terrible day today! It's so hot, I can hardly bear it.

George: Yes. There is hardly a breath of air.

James: Do you know today's temperature? The weatherman predicted that it would be 31 ℃.

George: But it seems much higher than that. What's the weather forecast for tomorrow?

James: They say that the temperature will climb to 32 ℃.

George: Oh, what a terrible day!

Why do the British people prefer to talk about weather? Two reasons are as follows. One is the uncertainty of the weather. The four seasons in China are clear and distinct: warm spring, hot summer, cool autumn and cold winter. The weather does not change much in a week or in a day. But in the UK the weather is frequently changing. Some people even say, "One can experience four seasons in the course of a single day!" So you may laugh when you see in London that the people are wearing raincoats or taking umbrellas on a bright sunny day. Another reason is that talking about weather seems a friendly and safe way of communicating, because the conversation, unlike discussing politics, may not be heated.

Unit 10

Chinese Kung Fu

Warm-up Activities

I. Matching

Learn the following phrases about boxing and warrior, and match them to the pictures.

1. crane boxing (　　)　　2. tiger boxing (　　)　　3. snake boxing (　　)
4. mantis boxing(　　)　　5. monkey boxing (　　)　　6. Dragon Warrior (　　)

A.

B.

C.

D.

E.

F.

II. Reading

Kung fu novels must depict justice and righteousness. The good fight the wicked. Traditional values are shown through the characters and their stories, not by lecturing readers.

武侠小说一定要描绘出正义与正气。邪不压正。传统价值观要通过角色及其故事体现出来,而不是对读者说教。

（金庸）

justice　n. 公平；公正
righteousness　n. 正义
wicked　adj. 邪恶的；恶毒的

Text A

The Schools of Chinese Kung Fu

1. Chinese Kung Fu has a long history and is one of the important forms of traditional Chinese culture. It can be divided into many schools due to historical development and **geographical distribution**. Some schools are named after the mountains and rivers, such as Wudang and Emei; some after their grandmaster, such as Yung Chun; still some after animal actions such as monkey fist. The five most famous schools are Shaolin, Wudang, Emei, Kongtong and Kunlun.

Shaolin School

2. Popular sayings include "all kung fu comes out of Shaolin" and "Shaolin kung fu excels in the world", **indicating** the influence of Shaolin kung fu among martial arts*. As the **mainstream** of Chinese kung fu, Shaolin kung fu has the longest history and the most various fist fighting techniques. The Shaolin Temple on Songshan Mountain in Dengfeng of Henan Province is the **cradle** of Shaolin kung fu.

3. The Shaolin Temple was set up during the Northern Wei Dynasty. An Indian monk came to China and then another monk, Bodhidharma*, traveled to the Shaolin Temple teaching Chan Buddhism*. Through continuous development, Shaolin School, which has absorbed the **essence** of different schools, has 708 forms of kung fu at the present time.

Wudang School

4. There is a saying which goes like this, "Wudang is respected in the south and Shaolin in the north," showing the two schools' **status** and impact in the world of Chinese kung fu. Wudang **applies** such **philosophical theories** as tai chi, yin and yang, the Eight **Trigrams*** and the Five Elements* into the principles of practice and fighting skills. Wudang kung fu is characterized by natural relaxation and being soft on the outside and tough on the inside.

5. When people talking about the history of Wudang School, Zhang Sanfeng would be the first name that comes to your mind. He created Neijiaquan* of the Wudang School, which is proper for **self-defense** and health.

Emei School

6. The Emei School is named after Emei Mountain in Sichuan Province. The **religious** cultures of Daoism* and Buddhism*, together with the folk customs of Sichuan, have exerted a profound influence on this school. It **advocates** the **combination** of both **dynamic** and **static** movements.

7. According to the novel written by the famous Chinese writer Jin Yong, the school was said to

be founded by Guo Xiang, the daughter of Guo Jing and Huang Rong. She was traveling the world but her sudden **enlightenment** changed her into a nun and then she set up Emei School. The Emei School made progress during the Wei and Jin dynasties and saw an **unprecedented** development during the Ming and Qing dynasties.

8. Apart from Shaolin, Wudang and Emei, there are some other important schools including Kongtong School and Kunlun School. Kongtong School combines Daoism with martial arts, and fighting techniques with body-building exercises. And fist fighting techniques of Kunlun School are **vigorous** and strong with fast and fierce movements. There is also a good saying, "Martial arts originate in China, but it belongs to the world", so they are great national and international cultural legacy.

New Words

geographical [ˌdʒiːəˈɡræfɪkl] adj. concerned with or relating to geography 地理（学）的

distribution [ˌdɪstrɪˈbjuːʃn] n. the way that sth. is shared or exists over a particular area or among a particular group of people 分配；分布

indicate [ˈɪndɪkeɪt] v. to show that sth. is true or exists 表明；显示

mainstream [ˈmeɪnstriːm] n. the ideas and opinions that are thought to be normal because they are shared by most people 主流思想；主流群体

cradle [ˈkreɪdl] n. A cradle is a baby's bed with high sides. Cradles often have curved bases so that they rock from side to side 摇篮

essence [ˈesns] n. The essence of something is its basic and most important characteristic which gives it its individual identity 实质；本质；精髓

status [ˈsteɪtəs] n. Your status is your social or professional position 社会地位；专业资格

apply [əˈplaɪ] v. If you apply something such as a rule, you use it in a situation or activity. 应用

philosophical [ˌfɪləˈsɒfɪkl] adj. concerned with or relating to philosophy 哲学的

theory [ˈθɪəri] n. A theory is a formal idea that is intended to explain something 理论；学说

trigram [ˈtraɪɡræm] n. each of the eight figures formed of three parallel lines, each either whole or broken, combined to form the sixty-four hexagrams of the I Ching (《易经》中的) 卦

self-defense [ˌselfdɪˈfens] n. the act of defending yourself 自卫；正当防卫

religious [rɪˈlɪdʒəs] adj. You use religious to describe things that are connected with religion or with one particular religion 宗教的；信教的

advocate [ˈædvəkeɪt] v. to support sth. publicly (formal) 拥护；支持；提倡

combination [ˌkɒmbɪˈneɪʃn] n. the act of mixing together two or more things 结合；联合；混合

dynamic [daɪˈnæmɪk] adj. always changing and making progress 动态的；发展变化的

static [ˈstætɪk] adj. not moving, changing or developing 静止的；静态的；停滞的

posture [ˈpɒstʃə(r)] n. the position in which you hold your body when standing or sitting 姿势

enlightenment [ɪnˈlaɪtnmənt] n. the process of understanding sth. 启迪；启发；开导；开明

unprecedented [ʌnˈpresɪdentɪd] adj. that has never happened, been done or been known before 前所未有的；空前的；没有先例的

vigorous [ˈvɪɡərəs] adj. very active, determined or full of energy 充满活力的；果断的

Useful Expressions

Phrases	Examples
divide into 分成；分为	The physical benefits of exercise can be divided into three factors. 运动对身体的好处可以分为 3 个方面
name after 以……的名字起名	The machine is named after its inventor. 这部机器是以其发明者的名字命名的
be characterized by 以……为特征	The education system is characterized by an emphasis on success in exams. 这种教育制度以强调考试成绩为特征
together with 与；和……一同	He works well together with them. 他同他们一起工作得不错
exert a profound influence on 对……产生深远影响	The concise aesthetics exert a profound influence on the modern interior design. 简约之美对现代室内设计具有深刻的影响

 Background Information

1. martial arts: 武术是古代军事战争一种传承的技术。习武可强身健体，亦可防御敌人进攻。

2. Bodhidharma: 菩提达摩，南北朝禅僧，略称达摩或达磨。据记述，南印度人，属刹帝利种姓，通彻大乘佛法，为修习禅定者所推崇。北魏时，曾在洛阳、嵩山等地传授禅教。

3. Chan Buddhism: 禅宗又名佛心宗。禅宗不是汉传佛教，又不离汉传佛教，是中国化后的佛教——禅宗。《六祖坛经》等是禅宗的佛经。《百丈清规》是禅宗的律。

4. the Eight Trigrams: 八卦是中国道家文化的深奥概念，是一套用四组阴阳组成的形而上的哲学符号，其深邃的哲理解释自然、社会现象。

5. the Five Elements: 五行是中国古代道教哲学的一种系统观，广泛用于中医、堪舆、命理、相术和占卜等方面。

6. Neijiaquan: 内家拳相对于外家拳而言，是阴阳学说的又一实践。

7. Daoism: 道教是中国本土宗教，以"道"为最高信仰。道教在中国古代鬼神崇拜观念上，以黄、老道家思想为理论根据，承袭战国以来的神仙方术衍化形成。

8. Buddhism: 佛教距今已有两千五百多年，是由古印度迦毗罗卫国（今尼泊尔境内）王子乔达摩·悉达多所创（参考佛诞）。西方国家普遍认为佛教起源于印度。

Reading Comprehension

Ⅰ. **Decide whether the following statements are True (T) or False (F).**

(　　) 1. Chinese kung fu can be divided into many schools due to political development.

(　　) 2. The five most famous schools are Shaolin, Wudang, Emei, Kongtong and Kunlun.

(　　) 3. An Indian monk, Batuo, traveled to the Shaolin Temple teaching Chan Buddhism.

(　　) 4. Emei applies such philosophical theories as tai chi, yin and yang, the Eight Trigrams and the Five Elements into the principles of practice and fighting skills.

(　　) 5. The Emei School made progress during the Wei and Jin dynasties and saw an unprecedented development during the Ming and Qing dynasties.

(　　) 6. And fist fighting techniques of Kunlun School are vigorous and strong with fast and fierce movements.

Ⅱ. **Complete the answers to the following questions.**

1. Which schools enjoy a worldwide fame? (Para. 1)

   _____ enjoy a worldwide fame.

2. Where is the Shaolin Temple, the cradle of Shaolin kung fu, located? (Para. 2)

   It is located _____.

3. What does Wudang apply into the principles of practice and fighting skills? (Para. 4)

   Such philosophical theories as _____.

4. What is Emei School named after? (Para. 6)

   It is named after _____.

Unit 10 Chinese Kung Fu

 Vocabulary and Structure

Words and Phrases to Drill

religious	geographical	advocate	combination	unprecedented
apply	indicate	cradle	theory	vigorous
divide into	name after	be characterized by	together with	exert a profound influence on

I. Choose the appropriate explanation from Column B for each of the words in Column A.

A	B
_____ 1. religious	a. to use something in a situation or activity
_____ 2. apply	b. to describe things that are connected with religion
_____ 3. geographical	c. to show that sth. is true or exists
_____ 4. indicate	d. concerned with or relating to geography
_____ 5. advocate	e. a baby's bed with high sides
_____ 6. cradle	f. to support sth. publicly
_____ 7. combination	g. a formal idea or set of ideas that is intended to explain something
_____ 8. theory	h. the act of joining or mixing together two or more things to form a single unit
_____ 9. unprecedented	i. very active, determined or full of energy
_____ 10. vigorous	j. that has never happened, been done or been known before

II. Fill in the blanks with the correct forms of the words in Column A of the above table.

1. It is _____ more diverse than any other continent.
2. A survey of retired people has _____ that most are independent and enjoying life.
3. The Yellow River was the _____ of Chinese civilization.
4. These ideas are often difficult to _____ in practice.
5. He taught us music _____ .
6. She held her _____ belief.
7. We _____ a peaceful settlement of international disputes.
8. An alloy is a _____ of two or more different metals.
9. China's industry is developing at an _____ rate.
10. His calligraphy is _____ and forceful.

III. Compare each pair of words and choose the correct one to fill in each blank. Change the form if necessary.

1. geographical   geography
   a. _____ was my weak subject.
   b. The _____ location is important for me.
2. apply   application
   a. Students learned the practical _____ of the theory.
   b. In this way they can better _____ theory to practice.

221

3. combination   combine
   a. We shall _____ the three departments.
   b. These paints can be used individually or in _____ .
4. vigorous   vigor
   a. Since then, the Chinese society has shown _____ and creativity.
   b. She had a _____ opponent.

IV. **Add the suffix "-able" to the following words in brackets. Then complete the sentences with the words formed.**

> **Tips:** "-able"是一个形容词后缀，意为"that can be-ed, 可以被……的"，一般用在及物动词的后面。"-able"还有一个变体"-ible"。

Sample: We spent a most agreeable day together! (agree)
1. She was efficient and _____ . (rely)
2. It became _____ to eat certain kinds of fish. (fashion)
3. He had suffered _____ injuries. (terror)
4. He made us a _____ offer for the painting. (reason)
5. The area is _____ for its scenery. (remark)

V. **Choose the best phrase to complete each sentence.**
1. Administratively, the country is _____ 50 states.
   A. divided into   B. divide into   C. divided from   D. divide from
2. The college is _____ George Washington.
   A. named under   B. name after   C. named after   D. name under
3. These changes will _____ the economic development in Guangdong province.
   A. make difference   B. make sense
   C. exert impact of   D. exert a profound influence on
4. I, _____ Tom, went to the party last night.
   A. together   B. altogether   C. together with   D. as well
5. Traditional Chinese realistic painting _____ fine brushwork and close attention to detail.
   A. is characterized from   B. characterizes
   C. is characterized of   D. is characterized by

VI. **Complete the following sentences by translating the Chinese given in brackets into English.**
1. We will _____ (把学生分成六组).
2. The building is _____ (以邵逸夫的名字命名).
3. The paintings _____ (特征是内容丰富，情节生动).
4. I am _____ (同你在一起).
5. For college students to do a part-time job will _____ (对今后生活具有深远的影响).

Ⅶ. **Translate the following sentences into Chinese.**

1. Chinese kung fu has a long history and is one of the important forms of traditional Chinese culture. (para. 1)
   _____

2. Wudang applies such philosophical theories as tai chi, yin and yang, the Eight Trigrams and the Five Elements into the principles of practice and fighting skills. (para. 4)
   _____

3. The religious cultures of Daoism and Buddhism, together with the folk customs of Sichuan, have exerted a profound influence on Emei school. (para. 6)
   _____

4. Fist fighting techniques of Kunlun School are vigorous and strong. (para. 8)
   _____

Ⅷ. **Complete the following sentences by translating the Chinese given in brackets into English using "be likely to".**

> be likely to 表示"可能……"。
> Sample: If you feel good about your outward appearance <u>then you are more likely to feel the same inwardly</u>(那你在内心也很可能自我感觉良好).

1. Tom says that _____(他有可能在年底以前做出最后的决定).
2. It is said that _____(她很有可能出国深造).
3. We are glad to know that _____(他非常有可能成为下一任校长).
4. You have to get up early, because _____(校车可能早上七点钟就出发了).
5. _____ (他不太可能完成这个任务) within such a short time.

Ⅸ. **Complete the following sentences by translating the Chinese in brackets into English using the expression "as if".**

> 在 as if 引导的状语从句中,可用虚拟语气来表达所述事情与实际不符。
> Sample: He had gone to France determined to live there exactly <u>as if he were in England</u>(就好像他在英国似的) and had judged it entirely from his own English viewpoints.

1. I've loved you _____(就像你是我家的一员).
2. They talked _____(就像多年的老朋友一样).
3. He behaved _____(就像他是这个房子的主人).
4. He spoke to me _____(就像我是聋子似的).
5. He acts _____(就像他是一个专家似的).

Dialogue Samples

Listen and read the samples carefully, and then complete the communicative tasks that follow.

Dialogue 1 Inquiring at the bank

Bank clerk: Good afternoon, may I help you?

Tom: Good afternoon. I want to open an account, please.

Bank clerk: I can help you with that. Would you like to open a savings account or a checking account?

Tom: Is there any difference?

Bank clerk: Of course. You can use a checking account to pay for your bills, and a savings account can earn interest.

Tom: I think I need both.

Bank clerk: There's a service charge for the checking account but no charge for the savings.

Tom: Is there any minimum requirement for the first deposit?

Bank clerk: 5 hundred dollars is the minimum.

Dialogue 2 Opening an account

Brian: I would like to open an account. What should I do?

Bank clerk: First, I need your personal information. Please fill in this form showing your name and address. Your signature is needed here, and here.

Brian: …OK.

Bank clerk: OK. Now It's all set. A checkbook will be delivered to you for free, and you'll receive it in 7 working days.

Brian: You mean it will be delivered to my address?

Bank clerk: Yes, the address you put on the application form.

Brian: Great! Thanks.

Communicative Tasks

Work with your partner and take turns to start the conversations.

Task 1

Situation:

Lily wants to withdraw some money, so she goes to the bank.

Tips:

Here are some things Lily can say or ask:
I want to withdraw some money from my peony card.
I'd like to withdraw some money from my passbook.
Okay. Here they are.

Here are some things the bank clerk can say or ask:
Please fill out a withdrawal slip. How much do you want?
Please show me your ID card and enter your secret code.
Please wait for a while.

Task 2

Situation:

Wang wants to remit 5 000 yuan in cash to his friend in Beijing.

Tips:

Here are some things Wang can say or ask:
How long does it take?
Can you send it there in a quicker way?
How much does it cost?

Here are some things the bank clerk can say or ask:
Our bank provides "remittance express" for individuals.
The remittance will arrive within 24 hours.
The service commission is 1%.
Please fill in the remittance slip in triplicate.

Further Development

浊化

（1）清辅音浊化只是一种发音现象，不是规则。

（2）浊化发音的时候，按照字典里的标注读，但其变化要按照英语的习惯。

（3）清辅音浊化不仅仅包括 s 后面的清辅音被浊化，很多时候不加 s 也可能被浊化。如 water, happy, meeting, walking 等，地道英语一般将这些单词中间那个清辅音发成对应的浊辅音了。

（4）s 后面的清辅音浊化可归纳为：如果清辅音后面是一个元音，前面有一个 s，那么无论是在单词的最前面还是中间，只要是在重读音节或次重读音节里，一般都读成对应浊辅音，如 strike，要变成"dr"所发的那个音（如 dream 中的"dr"所发的音）。再比如 speak, stand, sky。

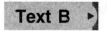

Chinese Kung Fu

1. The term kung fu refers to the martial arts of China, also called Wushu and Quanfa. **Originally**, it can refer to any skill **achieved** through practice, not necessarily martial arts. There are hundreds of styles of kung fu, and are practiced all over the world, with each having its own techniques. The origin of kung fu dates back to over 1 600 years ago in the Shaolin Temple, where monks practiced kung fu for health and self-defense during their **quest** for enlightenment.

2. The first Shaolin temple was established in 377 AD in Henan province. In 527 AD, one famous monk coming from India, Bodhidharma, visited the temple for religious teaching, but he found the monks in the temple had trained their minds, but not their bodies so they were weak and in poor health. To find a way to give the monks strength and **vitality**, Bodhidharma locked himself in a room for nine years of **meditation**. His resulting work, *Yi Jin Jing**, a series of exercises which developed strength, vitality, and **internal** energy, is considered the original Shaolin martial art.

3. Nowadays, kung fu has been recognized around the world. When mentioning it, people all over the world may think of the well-known movie *kung fu Panda*. In fact, kung fu was first **popularized** by the outstanding person Bruce Lee in the western world. His 1973 film "Enter the Dragon"* was an international box office hit. After the Bruce Lee film, there came lots of martial arts films popularized in the west by Hollywood.

4. In 1976, another great movie "Shaolin Temple" came out by the Chinese director Chang Cheh*. This is a **classic** movie that focused on **discipline** and **trial** in contrast to the skills that were in focus in the Bruce Lee film. In the story, the temple **disciples** with years of **repetitive** labor like cooking and carrying water **gradually acquire** kung fu skills without their knowing it. Now kung fu has been further popularized by the kung fu movies by the actors and martial artists like Jackie Chan and Jet Li. Can you just list some other popular kung fu movies?

5. In fact, kung fu has found place in popular culture. It had influenced the ancient Chinese **Opera**, a form of **drama**, even in the Tang Dynasty. Martial arts in literature date back to the 2nd and 3rd century BC and were later popularized in the Tang and Ming Dynasties. The **genre** of literature describing martial arts is known as "wuxia", which means "martial arts heroes". Jin Yong* is widely regarded as the finest Chinese wuxia writer. He wrote 15 tales, of which one was a short story and the other 14 were novels of various lengths. His works include *The Smiling, Proud Wanderer*; *The Legend of the **Condor** Heroes*; *The Condor and The Lovers*; ***Eightfold** Path of the Heavenly Dragon*; *Duke of Mount Deer*; *Flying Fox of Snowy Mountain*.

6. The popular opinions about kung fu are influenced by these works. Since the 1970s, kung fu has been **globalized** via books, TV shows and movies.

New Words

originally[əˈrɪdʒənəli] adv. used to describe the situation that existed at the beginning of a particular period or activity, especially before sth. was changed 起初；原来

achieve[əˈtʃiːv] v. If you achieve a particular aim or effect, you succeed in doing it or causing it to happen, usually after a lot of effort. （经努力）完成；达到；获得

quest[kwest] v. A quest is a long and difficult search for something. （长期艰难的）追求；探索

vitality[vaɪˈtæləti] n. If you say that someone or something has vitality, you mean that they have great energy and liveliness. 活力；生命力；热情

meditation[ˌmedɪˈteɪʃn] n. the practice of thinking deeply in silence 冥想；沉思；深思

internal[ɪnˈtɜːnl] adj. Internal is used to describe things that exist or happen inside a country or organization. 国内的；内政的；（组织）内部的

popularize[ˈpɒpjələraɪz] v. to make a lot of people interested in it 使受喜爱；使受欢迎

classic[ˈklæsɪk] adj. A classic film, piece of writing, or piece of music is of very high quality （电影、著作、音乐）经典的；典范的；最优秀的

discipline[ˈdɪsəplɪn] n. the practice of training people to obey rules and orders and punishing them if they do not 训练；训导；纪律；风纪

trial[ˈtraɪəl] n. the process of testing the ability, quality or performance of sb./sth. 试验；试用

disciple[dɪˈsaɪpl] n. a person who believes in and follows the teachings of a religious or political leader 信徒；门徒；追随者

repetitive[rɪˈpetətɪv] adj. repeated many times 多次重复的

gradually[ˈɡrædʒuəli] adv. slowly, over a long period of time 逐渐地；逐步地；渐进地

acquire[əˈkwaɪə(r)] v. to gain sth. by your own efforts, ability or behaviour （通过努力）获得

opera[ˈɒprə] n. a dramatic work in which all or most of the words are sung to music 歌剧（剧本）

drama[ˈdrɑːmə] n. plays considered as a form of literature 戏剧文学；戏剧艺术；戏剧

genre[ˈʒɒ̃rə] n. (formal) a particular type or style of literature, art, film or music that you can recognize because of its special features 体裁

condor[ˈkɒndɔː(r)] n. a large bird of the vulture family 大秃鹰（主要栖居在南美洲）

eightfold[ˈeɪtfəʊld] adj. having eight units or components 八倍的；八层的

globalize[ˈɡləʊbəlaɪz] v. operate all around the world （使）全球化；全世界化

Useful Expressions

Phrases	Examples
refer to 指的是	That remark does not refer to her. 那句话不是指她说的
not necessarily 未必；不一定	Speed and safety are not necessarily incompatible. 速度和安全未必不相容
a series of 一系列；一连串	A series of technical foul-ups delayed the launch of the new product. 一系列技术问题延误了新产品的上市
come out 出现；出版	The book comes out this week. 这本书本周出版
in contrast to 相比之下	In contrast to the previous year the situation is much better now. 与1年前相比，现在情况已经好多了

 Background Information

1. Yi Jin Jing：《易筋经》。据清代学者凌廷堪的《校礼堂文集》、周中孚的《郑堂读书记》、康戈武的《中国武术实用大全》、周明和周稔丰的《易筋洗髓经（修订本）》以及《中国大百科全书·体育卷》等书考证，均认为《易筋经》系明朝天启四年（1624）天台紫凝道人托名达摩所作。《易筋经》表达了道教练气求长生的一种境界，里面含有大量道教词汇和修炼内容。

2. Enter the Dragon：《龙争虎斗》。《龙争虎斗》是1973年嘉禾影业和华纳影业联合制作的一部动作电影，由高洛斯（罗伯特·克洛斯）执导，李小龙、石坚、约翰·萨克松等主演。

3. Chang Cheh：张彻是20世纪60年代、70年代香港影坛最有影响力的人物之一，被称为"香港电影一代枭雄"。他对电影所做的贡献，恐怕连今天的徐克、王家卫也都望尘莫及。

4. Jin Yong：金庸，原名查良镛，1924年3月10日生于浙江省海宁市，1948年移居香港。当代知名武侠小说作家、新闻学家、企业家、政治评论家、社会活动家，"香港四大才子"之一。他的作品包括：《笑傲江湖》《射雕英雄传》《神雕侠侣》《天龙八部》《鹿鼎记》《雪山飞狐》等。

Unit 10　Chinese Kung Fu

 Reading Comprehension

Ⅰ. **Decide whether the following statements are True (T) or False (F).**
(　) 1. The term kung fu refers to any skill achieved through practice, not necessarily martial arts.
(　) 2. The first Shaolin temple was established in 377 AD in Hebei province.
(　) 3. Kung fu was first popularized by the outstanding person Jackie Chan in the western world.
(　) 4. Martial arts in literature date back to the 2nd and 3rd century BC and were later popularized in the Tang and Ming Dynasties.
(　) 5. Jin Yong is widely regarded as the finest Chinese wuxia writer.

Ⅱ. **Choose the best answer to each of the following questions.**
1. Why did monks in the Shaolin Temple practice kung fu ?
　A. for health and self-defense　　B. for health and confidence
　C. for fighting and self-defense　　D. for fighting and confidence
2. Why did Bodhidharma lock himself in a room for nine years of meditation?
　A. To find a way to give the monks strength and vitality
　B. To find a way to avoid the realistic society
　C. To find a way to make himself as strong as possible
　D. To find a way to get rid of trouble
3. When did lots of martial arts films become popularized in the west by Hollywood?
　A. After the Jin Yong film　　B. After the Bruce Lee film
　C. After the Jackie Chan film　　D. After the Jet Li film
4. Which of the following novels was not written by Jin Yong?
　A. The Smiling, Proud Wanderer　　B. The Condor and The Lovers
　C. Duke of Mount Deer　　D. Shaolin Temple
5. How has kung fu been globalized since the 1970s?
　A. via books, newspapers and journals　　B. via books, songs and dances
　C. via drama, music and movies　　D. via books, TV shows and movies

Grammar

Adjective and Adverb

1. 形容词

形容词是用来修饰名词或代词的词，一般放在其所修饰的名词之前，在句中用作定语、表语、补语、状语等，多数形容词具有比较等级。

形容词做表语，表明主语的性质和特征，放在连系动词之后。

例如：Computer is very important in our everyday life.

形容词做定语，修饰名词或不定代词，通常放在名词之前，不定代词之后。

例如：What a terrible news!

形容词做宾语补足语，放在宾语之后，与其构成复合宾语。

例如：We must keep our house clean and tidy.

2. 副词

副词修饰动词、形容词或其他副词，表示动作、状态的特征或某种性质的程度。

根据其用途与含义，副词可分为下列六大类。

（1）时间副词。常用的有 before, then, soon, already, yet 等。

（2）地点副词。常用的有 there, up, above, below, outside 等。

（3）疑问副词。常用的有 what, how, why 等。

（4）方式副词。常用的有 quickly, conveniently 等。

（5）程度副词。常用的有 so, quite, enough 等。

（6）频度副词。常用的有 always, usually, hardly, never 等。

Culture ▶

Three Royal Traditions

There are three important traditions in the British royal family. The first one is playing the flute, which is inherited from Queen Victoria. Every morning, the Queen listens to the playing of a flute by the royal flutist who does so outside the dining-hall for a quarter of an hour.

The second of the royal traditions is the changing of the Queen's guard. The ceremonies take place in two places, including Buckingham Palace and Whitehall. Both take place at eleven a. m. weekdays and at ten on Sunday. The Queen's guards, dressed in red coats and black trousers, a white belt, white gloves, with a glittering sword on the waist and a tall black fur hat on the head, hold this colourful military ceremony in front of Buckingham Place. The daily ceremony takes place in front of the Horse Guard building. Many people come here and see the ceremony from all over the world every year.

The third royal ceremony involves the queen. In fact, the British Queen makes a parliamentary speech, which is rather solemn. She starts out from Buckingham Palace sitting in a brilliant carriage and eventually arrives at the Place of Westminster. Sitting on the throne in the House of Lords, she sends a messenger with a black walking stick in her hand to the House of Commons on the other end of the Palace to inform them of the Queens's speech. But what you should know is that the gate of the Commons is closed. When the messenger gets there, he knocks at the door three times with his stick. When the Speaker permits, the guard opens the gate and lets him in, and he conveys the Queen's words. Then all the members of the House of Commons will be led to the House of Loads and attend the speech.

Unit 11

Designers and Musicians

Warm-up Activities

I. Matching

Learn the following words about different types of instruments, and match them to the pictures.

1. grand piano (   )   2. cello (   )   3. guitar (   )
4. saxophone(   )   5. flute (   )   6. drum set (   )

A.    B.    C.

D.   E.    F.

II. Reading

March of the Volunteers
《义勇军进行曲》
National Anthem 国歌

Arise! All who refuse to be slaves! Let our flesh and blood become our new Great Wall!

起来！不愿做奴隶的人们，把我们的血肉铸成我们新的长城！

Text A ▶

The Golden Age of Design

1. The golden age of design has been announced many times over the past couple of decades—four, by my count. Now, this **previous momentum** paired with technology, **community** and big business has fueled something new: an unheard-of belief in the power of design to not only **elevate** an idea, but be the idea.

2. First, at the turn of the 21st century, it became a **democratic** affair. Daily supplies were made more beautiful and more readily **accessible**, and suddenly it was no longer acceptable for things to be ordinary. The second arrived by way of products such as the iPod, which **represented** the possibility of form as actual function. "Design," Steve Jobs* said in 2003, is "not just what it looks like and feels like. Design is how it works". And the business world became aware of what design could do for profits.

3. These days, engineering-centric Silicon Valley* sees design as something that no longer just adds value, but actually creates it. The idea that design can **generate** profit is now being **embraced** by venture **capitalists**, too. "People who make things generally have not been in the seat of power because they're busy making things."—that's starting to change.

4. This design moment is also about a different marketplace—that of ideas. One of design's most important functions is to help people deal with change. We're living in a time of "acknowledged **urgency**". As a result, design has become **incredibly multifaceted** in recent years, covering subfields such as interaction design, critical design, environmental design, social design, biodesign and service design, to name just a few. It's become a medium for expressing ideas, raising questions and addressing social and individual anxieties.

5. So is design a business builder or idea spreader? Both, often at the same time. In earlier moments, the **democratization** of design was about what we could buy. Now it's about what we can

make and how we can sell. Today's design student may be less interested in building a **portfolio** than in simply crowdfunding an idea. How design has moved "from the aesthetic, to the **strategic**, to the **participatory**"? The "open source" ideology we normally associate with certain corners of tech culture has made its way into design. Engineering and design are **melding**; code-enterprises are making objects; and object makers are hardwiring all kinds of things with code. Style, **functionality** and engineering are now one and the same, and even **mundane** objects are **virtuously** designed.

6. What is certain is that all these combined elements—style, function, social impact, creativity and profit motive—have yielded an original vision of what design is and why it matters. Design has fundamentally changed the way we experience the world, from the way we **interact** with objects to our expectations about how organizations are structured. It's a new and exciting moment for design—that is, until the next one comes along.

Unit 11 Designers and Musicians

 New Words

previous[ˈpriːvɪəs] adj. having happened or existed before the event, time, or thing that you are talking about now 以前的；早先的

momentum[məˈmentəm] n. the ability to keep increasing or developing 势头；动力

community[kəˈmjuːnətɪ] n. all the people who live in a particular area, country, etc. when talked about as a group 社区

elevate[ˈelɪveɪt] v. to give a promotion to or assign to a higher position 提升；举起

democratic[deməˈkrætɪk] adj. controlled by representatives who are elected by the people of a country 民主的；民主政治的；大众的

accessible[əkˈsesɪb(ə)l] adj. capable of being reached 易接近的；可进入的；可理解的

represent[reprɪˈzent] v. to take the place of or be parallel or equivalent to 代表；表现

generate[ˈdʒenəreɪt] v. to bring into existence 使形成；发生；生殖；产生物理反应

embrace[ɪmˈbreɪs; em-] v. include in scope; include as part of something broader 拥抱；包含

capitalist[ˈkæpɪt(ə)lɪst] n. a person who owns or controls a lot of wealth and uses it to produce more wealth 资本家

urgency[ˈɜːdʒ(ə)nsɪ] n. pressing importance requiring speedy action 紧急；紧急的事

incredibly[ɪnˈkredəblɪ] adv. not easy to believe 难以置信地；非常地

multifaceted[mʌltɪˈfæsɪtɪd] adj. having many aspects 多层面的

portfolio[pɔːtˈfəʊlɪəʊ] n. a large, flat, thin case for carrying loose papers drawings or maps 公文包；文件夹

strategic[strəˈtiːdʒɪk] adj. relating to or concerned with strategy 战略上的；战略的

participatory[pɑːtɪsɪˈpeɪtərɪ] adj. affording the opportunity for individual participation 供人分享的；吸引参与的

meld[meld] v. lose its distinct outline or shape; blend gradually 合并；混合

functionality[fʌŋkʃəˈnælətɪ] n. capable of serving a purpose well 功能

mundane[ˈmʌndeɪn] adj. belonging to this earth or world 世俗的；平凡的

virtuously[ˈvɜːtjuəslɪ] adv. in a moral manner 合乎道德地；品性正直地；善良地

interact[ɪntərˈækt] v. act together or towards others or with others 互相影响；互相作用

Useful Expressions

Phrases	Examples
become aware of 知道；发觉	When I keep my positive attitude I sooner or later become aware of how to solve the problems. 当我保持积极的态度我迟早会知道如何去解决问题
deal with 处理；对付	How do we deal with these new challenges? 我们该如何处理这些新挑战呢
to name just a few 仅举几例；等等	Compared with books, the Internet enjoys many obvious advantages such as high speed, great efficiency, to name just a few. 与书本相比，互联网具有许多明显的好处，比如说高速、高效，等等
associate with 与……联系在一起	Who you associate with influences your thoughts, actions and behavior. 你和谁来往会影响你的思想、活动和行为
interact with 与……相互作用； 与……相互影响	We interact with our environment. 我们与环境相互影响

 Background Information

1. Steve Jobs: 史蒂夫·乔布斯（1955年2月24日—2011年10月5日），出生于美国加利福尼亚州旧金山，美国发明家、企业家，美国苹果公司联合创办人。乔布斯被认为是计算机业界与娱乐业界的标志性人物，先后领导和推出了麦金塔计算机（Macintosh）、iMac、iPod、iPhone、iPad等风靡全球的电子产品，深刻地改变了现代通信、娱乐、生活方式。乔布斯同时也是前Pixar动画公司的董事长及行政总裁。2011年10月5日，史蒂夫·乔布斯因患胰腺癌病逝，享年56岁。

2. Silicon Valley: 硅谷位于美国加利福尼亚州的旧金山经圣克拉拉至圣何塞近50千米的一条狭长地带，是美国重要的电子工业基地，也是世界最为知名的电子工业集中地。它是随着20世纪60年代中期以来，微电子技术高速发展而逐步形成的，其特点是以附近一些具有雄厚科研力量的美国一流大学斯坦福、伯克利和加州理工等世界知名大学为依托，以高技术的中小公司群为基础，并拥有思科、英特尔、惠普、朗讯、苹果等大公司，融科学、技术、生产为一体。目前它已有大大小小电子工业公司达10 000家以上。

Unit 11 Designers and Musicians

 Reading Comprehension

I. Decide whether the following statements are True (T) or False (F).
(   ) 1. The golden age of design has been announced only once over the past decades.
(   ) 2. The first golden age of design became a democratic affair in the middle of 21st century.
(   ) 3. The business world became aware of what design could do for profits.
(   ) 4. These days, engineering-centric Silicon Valley sees design as something that adds value.
(   ) 5. Design's become a medium for expressing ideas, raising questions and addressing social and individual anxieties.
(   ) 6. In earlier moments, the democratization of design was about what we could sell.
(   ) 7. Style, functionality and engineering are now one and the same.

II. Complete the answers to the following questions.
1. What has the previous momentum paired with fueled something new? (Para. 1)
   The previous momentum paired with _____, _____ and _____ has fueled something new.
2. What is being embraced by venture capitalists? (Para. 3)
   The idea that design can generate _____.
3. What is design's most important function? (Para. 4)
   One of design's most important functions is to _____.
4. What have yielded an original vision of what design is and how it matters? (Para. 6)
   All these combined elements—_____, _____, _____, _____ and _____.

Vocabulary and Structure

Words and Phrases to Drill

previous	interact	democratic	represent	generate
embrace	inspiration	incredibly	combine	strategic
become aware of	deal with	associate with	interact with	to name just a few

I. Choose the appropriate explanation from Column B for each of the words in Column A.

A	B
_____ 1. strategic	a. put or add together
_____ 2. previous	b. to give a promotion to or assign to a higher position
_____ 3. combine	c. to bring into existence
_____ 4. elevate	d. not easy to believe
_____ 5. inspiration	e. act together or towards others or with others
_____ 6. generate	f. having happened or existed before the event, time, or thing that you are talking about now
_____ 7. incredibly	g. allowing a choice
_____ 8. interact	h. relating to or concerned with strategy
_____ 9. alternative	i. to take the place of or be parallel or equivalent to
_____ 10. represent	j. a good idea about what you should do, write, say, etc. especially one which you get suddenly

II. Fill in the blanks with the correct forms of the words in Column A of the above table.

1. Why not _____ traditions of the past with the innovations of the future?
2. He changed his _____ decision.
3. Many poets and artists have drawn their _____ from nature.
4. The computer bug _____ chaos in the office.
5. You must be around other people and _____ with them.
6. The general laid down a few _____ targets on the map.
7. When a(n) _____ explanation arises, there is no longer any need for God.
8. We _____ 47 nations from every region of the world.
9. Soon they will _____ you to a high rank in their society.
10. The fact is _____ exaggerated.

III. Compare each pair of words and choose the correct one to fill in each blank. Change the form if necessary.

1. inspire   inspiration
    a. Wildlife has been a source of fascination and _____ for artists for thousands of years.
    b. We need someone who can _____ the team.

2. credit   incredible
    a. I left my _____ card at home.
    b. I hope you will take the challenge and find _____ joy in the process.
3. interact   interaction
    a. There could be more than one _____ between the consumer and provider.
    b. Staff members train the visitors on how to safely _____ with the animals.
4. generate   generation
    a. Tourism _____ income for local communities.
    b. Like most of my _____, I had never known the war.

IV. **Add the suffix "-ous" to the following words in brackets. Then complete the sentences with the words formed.**

> **Tips:** -ous 或-ious 加在名词、动词之后，意为"充满……的"、"具有……特征的"，构成的新词为形容词。如：danger + ous = dangerous(危险的)；generate + ous = generous(慷慨的)。

Sample: I hope people will be <u>courageous</u> enough to speak out against this injustice. (courage)
1. The _____ actress is now appearing at the Capital Theatre. (fame)
2. This film has some mildly _____ moments. (humor)
3. _____ attempts have been made to hide the truth. (number)
4. Her mother was hard-working and _____ for her 4 children. (ambition)
5. There are _____ ways to answer your questions. (vary)

V. **Choose the best phrase to complete each sentence.**
1. They suddenly _____ people looking at them.
    A. become aware of   B. became aware that
    C. become awareness of D. became aware of
2. Let me _____ the customer's complaint.
    A. deal with   B. deal to   C. handle with   D. manage to
3. After the meeting, the youths started to _____ the older members.
    A. interact with   B. interact to   C. interact by   D. interact on
4. Don't _____ dishonest boys.
    A. associate to   B. combine with   C. associate with   D. relate by
5. Now every year, we perform to the public such classic shows as Peter Pan, Nutcracker, Cinderella, and Alice in Wonderland, _____ .
    A. to name after   B. to name just a few
    C. to name just a couple   D. to name a little

VI. Complete the following sentences by translating the Chinese given in brackets into English.

1. _____ （商业界意识到了）what design could do for profits.

2. One of design's most important functions is _____ （帮助人们应对变化）.

3. Design has become incredibly multifaceted in recent years, covering subfields such as interaction design, critical design, environmental design, _____ （社会设计、生物设计和服务设计等）.

4. The "open source" ideology _____ （我们通常认为与科技文化角落相联系的）has made its way into design.

5. Design has fundamentally changed the way we experience the world, _____ _____ （从我们与产品对象的交互方式到我们对组织构成的期许）.

VII. Translate the following sentences into Chinese.

1. An unheard-of belief in the power of design to not only elevate an idea, but be the idea. (Para. 1)
   _____

2. Daily supplies were made more beautiful and more readily accessible, and suddenly it was no longer acceptable for things to be ordinary. (Para. 2)
   _____

3. These days, engineering-centric Silicon Valley sees design as something that no longer just adds value, but actually creates it. (Para. 3)
   _____

4. It's become a medium for expressing ideas, raising questions and addressing social and individual anxieties. (Para. 4)
   _____

VIII. Combine the following sentences using "unless".

> 连词 unless 意为"除非……""如果不……"，多引导否定意义的真实条件句，或非真实条件句。
>
> Sample: You don't hurry up. You will miss the bus.
>   You will miss the bus unless you hurry up.

1. You don't work harder. You'll fail in chemistry again.
   _____

2. You don't oil the motor regularly. It won't run smoothly.
   _____

3. You will never get anywhere. You don't set your goal.
   _____

4. I wouldn't be saying this. I am not sure of the facts.
   _____

5. They couldn't have arrived at the site instantly. The police hadn't had a helicopter.

IX. Combine the following sentences using Non-finite Attributive Clauses.

> 非限定性定语从句用来修饰先行词或整个主句，起补充或说明主句的作用，用逗号与主句隔开。应注意的是这类从句不能使用关系代词 that 和关系副词 why 来引导。
>
> Sample: Our guide was an excellent cook.   He was a French Canadian.
>   Our guide, who was a French Canadian, was an excellent cook.

1. He lent me a thousand dollars. A thousand dollars was exactly the amount I needed.

2. Tony has two sisters. They are working in the city.

3. Alice failed in the experiment. The fact surprised all of us.

4. The book was borrowed from Jane. Jane telephoned me just now.

5. We are going to visit the Louvre. It is one of the world-famous museums.

Dialogue Samples

Listen and read the samples carefully, then complete the communicative tasks that follow.

Dialogue 1   A Job Interview

Peter: Tell me something about yourself, please.

David: My name is David and I live in Beijing. My major is electrical engineering.

Peter: What kind of personality do you think you have?

David: Well, I approach things very enthusiastically, and I don't like to leave things half-done. I'm very organized and extremely capable.

Peter: What are your weaknesses and strengths?

David: Well, I'm afraid I'm a poor speaker, however I'm fully aware of this, so I've been studying how to speak in public. I suppose my strengths are that I'm persistent and a fast-learner.

Peter: Do you have any licenses or certificates?

David: I have a driver's license, and I am a CPA (Certified Public Accountant).

Peter: How do you relate to others?

David: I'm very co-operative and have good spirit for teamwork.

Dialogue 2   A Job Interview

Jack: I see from your resume that you have been working for a while.

Frank: Yes, I worked for two years with an American Company.

Jack: Tell me what you know about our company please.

Frank: Well, the company was founded in New York in 1950 by Mark Ward, who was the first president. It has 1 billion dollars in capital; it employs 5 000 people, and it is the largest company in its field in the States.

Jack: What do you know about our major products and our share of the market?

Frank: The products are mostly marketed in Europe and the United States but have sold very well here in China. So, I think in the future you'll find China to be a profitable market as well.

Jack: What made you decide to change your job?

Frank: I would like to get a job in which I can further develop my career.

Jack: May I ask you why you left the former company?

Frank: Because I want to change my working environment and seek new challenges.

Communicative Tasks

Work with your partner and take turns to start the conversations.

Task 1

Situation:

The Director of HR is interviewing a college graduate in HCG Company.

Tips:

> **Here are some things the Director of HR can say or ask:**
>
> I'm in charge of the interview. My name is …
>
> I've read your letter of application. You don't seem to have any working experience.
>
> Why did you apply for the internship in this company?

> **Here are some things the college graduate can say:**
>
> But the ridge training at my college should make up for my lack of working experience.
>
> I am interested in your company for several reasons…
>
> With my strong academic background, I'm capable and competent.

Task 2

Situation:

An applicant with some experience is talking with the interviewer.

Tips:

> **Here are some things the interviewer can say or ask:**
>
> What is your working experience?
>
> How will your experiences benefit this company?
>
> Are you aware of the aspects of this position and do you feel you are qualified?

> **Here are some things the applicant can say:**
>
> I've worked for IBM for 3 years.
>
> I know the marketing from top to bottom. That will increase your profit margin and keep the shareholders satisfied.
>
> I understand my qualification and your needs by researching your company.

Further Development

英美发音的主要差别（一）

1. 开口由小变大即英 [ɑː]—美 [æ]

字母 a 在 [s][θ][n] 前，英式英语读 [ɑː]，而美式英语则读 [æ]，例如

单词	英式英语	美式英语	单词	英式英语	美式英语
ask	[ɑːsk]	[æsk]	last	[lɑːst]	[læst]
pass	[pɑːs]	[pæs]	past	[pɑːst]	[pæst]
class	[klɑːs]	[klæs]	grass	[grɑːs]	[græs]
path	[pɑːθ]	[pæθ]	bath	[bɑːθ]	[bæθ]
dance	[dɑːns]	[dæns]	chance	[tʃɑːns]	[tʃæns]

因此，My father read my palm calmly in Chicago plaza.

英式英语读音为 [maɪ ˈfɑːðə riːd maɪ pɑːlm ˈkɑːmlɪ ɪn ʃɪˈkɑːgəʊ ˈplɑːzə]

美式英语读音为 [maɪ ˈfæðə riːd maɪ pælm ˈkæmlɪ ɪn ʃɪˈkægəʊ ˈplæzə]

2. 字母 r 的发音

在英式英语中，字母 r 只有在元音之前才发音，在元音之后不发音。而在美式英语中，字母 r 无论在何处都要发 [r] 音。如：car 英式英语音标为 [kɑː]，美式英语音标为 [kɑːr]. farm 英式英语音标为 [fɑːm]，美式英语音标为 [fɑːrm].

3. 辅音由清变浊，即英清→美浊

[t] 作为词词尾音时，英式英语发成清音，而美式英语则将清音浊化。例如：

letter 英 [ˈletə]→美 [ˈledə]；writer 英 [ˈraɪtə]→美 [ˈraɪdə]

Betty bought a bit of butter. 英 [ˈbetɪ ˈbɔːtə bɪtəv ˈbʌtə] - 美 [ˈbedɪ ˈbɔːdə bɪdəv ˈbʌdə]

再如 [p] 与 [k] 音

shopping　　　　英 [ˈʃɒpɪŋ] - 美 [ˈʃɒbɪŋ]

Micky　　　　　英 [ˈmɪkɪ] - 美 [ˈmɪgɪ]

Text B

Different Types of Composers

1. I can see three different types of composers in musical history, each of whom creates music in a somewhat different fashion.

2. The type that has fired public imagination most is that of the **spontaneously** inspired composer—the Franz Schubert* type, in other words. All composers are inspired, of course, but this type is more spontaneously inspired. Music simply wells out of him. He can't get it down on paper fast enough. You can almost tell this type of composer by his fruitful **output**.

3. In a sense, men of this kind begin not so much with a musical theme as with a completed composition. They **invariably** work best in the shorter forms. It is much easier to **improvise** a song than it is to improvise a **symphony**. It isn't easy to be inspired in that spontaneous way for long periods at a stretch. Even Schubert was more successful in handling the shorter forms of music.

4. Beethoven* belongs to the second type—the **constructive** type, one might call it. This type serves as an example of the **creative** process in music better than any other, because in this case the composer really does begin with a musical theme. In Beethoven's case there is no doubt about it, for we have the notebooks in which he put the themes down. We can see from his notebooks how he worked over his themes. He was the type that begins with a theme; makes it a **preliminary** idea; and upon that composes a musical work, day after day, in painstaking fashion. Most composers since Beethoven's day belong to this second type.

5. The third type of composer I can only call, for lack of a better name, the **traditionalist** type. Men like Palestrina* and Bach belong in this category. They both are **characteristic** of the kind of composer who is born in a particular period of musical history, when a certain musical style is about to reach its fullest development. The creative act with Palestrina is not the **thematic** conception so much as the personal **treatment** of a well-established pattern. And even Bach*, who composed forty-eight of the most various and inspired themes in his Well Tempered Clavichord, knew in advance the general formal mold that they were to fill.

6. One might add, for the sake of completeness, a fourth type of composer—the pioneer type: men like Gesualdo in the seventeenth century, Moussorgsky and Berlioz in the nineteenth, Debussy and Edgar Varese in the twentieth. It is difficult to **summarize** the composing methods of so **diversified** a group. One can safely say that their approach to composition is the opposite of the traditionalist type. They clearly oppose **conventional** solutions of musical problems. In many ways, their attitude is experimental—they seek to add new **harmonies**, new **sonorities**, new formal principles. The pioneer type was the characteristic one at the turn of the seventeenth century and also at the beginning of the twentieth century, but it is much less **evident** today.

Unit 11 Designers and Musicians

 New Words

composer[kəm'pozɚ] n. someone who composes music as a profession 作曲家；音乐家

spontaneously[spɒn'teɪnɪəslɪ] adv. without advance preparation 自发地；自然地；不由自主地

output['aʊtpʊt] n. the amount of sth. that a person, a machine or an organization produces 输出，输出量；产量；出产

invariably[ɪn'veərɪəblɪ] adv. without variation or change, in every case 总是；不变地；一定地

improvise['ɪmprəvaɪz] v. to invent music, the words in a play, a statement, etc. while you are playing or speaking, instead of planning it in advance 即兴创作；即兴表演

symphony['sɪmf(ə)nɪ] n. a long complicated piece of music for a large orchestra, in three or four main parts 交响乐；谐声，和声

constructive[kən'strʌktɪv] adj. having a useful and helpful effect rather than being negative or with no purpose 建设性的；推定的；构造上的；有助益的

creative[kriː'eɪtɪv] adj. having the skill and ability to produce sth. new, especially a work of art; showing this ability 创造性的

preliminary[prɪ'lɪmɪn(ə)rɪ] adj. happening before a more important action or event 初步的；开始的；预备的

traditionalist[trə'dɪʃənəlɪst] n. a person who prefers tradition to modern ideas or ways of doing things 传统主义者；因循守旧者

characteristic[kærəktə'rɪstɪk] adj. typical or distinctive 典型的；特有的

thematic[θɪ'mætɪk] adj. connected with the theme or themes of sth. 主题的，主旋律的；题目的

treatment['triːtm(ə)nt] n. care provided to improve a situation 治疗；处理；对待

summarize['sʌməraɪz] v. to give a summary of sth. 总结；概述

diversify[daɪ'vɜːsɪˌfaɪ] v. to change or to make sth. change so that there is greater variety 多样化

conventional[kən'venʃ(ə)n(ə)l] adj. following what is traditional or the way sth. has been done for a long time 符合习俗的，传统的；常见的；惯例的

harmony['hɑːmənɪ] n. the way in which different notes that are played or sung together combine to make a pleasing sound 和声；协调；和睦；融洽

sonority[sə'nɒrɪtɪ] n. having the character of a loud deep sound 响亮；响亮程度，宏亮度

evident[ˌevɪd(ə)nt] adj. clear; easily seen 明显的；明白的

Useful Expressions

Phrases	Examples
well out 喷涌而出	Tears welled out of her face. 她的眼泪喷涌而出
at a stretch 一口气	Today I really swam to my heart's content. I did 3 000 metres at a stretch. 今天我一口气游了三千米，真过瘾
put down 记下；放下	We've put down on our staff development plan for this year that we would like some technology courses. 我们已经在今年的员工发展计划中写到我们希望有一些技术培训课程
in advance 提前；预先	Everything has been fixed in advance. 一切都是事先确定好了的
for the sake of 为了	We can't risk big things for the sake of small ones. 我们不能因小失大

Background Information

1. Franz Schubert: 弗朗茨·舒伯特（1797年1月31日生于维也纳，1828年11月19日逝于维也纳，享年31岁），奥地利籍 Germanen（日耳曼人），作曲家。他是早期浪漫主义音乐的代表人物，也被认为是古典主义音乐的最后一位巨匠。

2. Beethoven: 路德维希·凡·贝多芬（1770年12月16日—1827年3月26日），出生于德国波恩，维也纳古典乐派代表人物之一，欧洲古典主义时期作曲家，世界音乐史上最伟大的作曲家之一。贝多芬一生创作题材广泛，重要作品包括9部交响曲、1部歌剧、32首钢琴奏鸣曲、5首钢琴协奏曲、多首管弦乐序曲及小提琴、大提琴奏鸣曲等。

3. Palestrina: 帕莱斯特里那（1525年—1594年2月2日），意大利文艺复兴时期作曲家，被广泛认为是文艺复兴时期最杰出的作曲家之一。

4. Bach: 约翰·塞巴斯蒂安·巴赫（1685年3月21日—1750年7月28日），巴洛克时期的德国作曲家，杰出的管风琴、小提琴、大键琴演奏家，被普遍认为是音乐史上最重要的作曲家之一，并被尊称为"西方近代音乐之父"，也是西方文化史上最重要的人物之一。

Unit 11 Designers and Musicians

 Reading Comprehension

I. Decide whether the following statements are True (T) or False (F).

(   ) 1. According to the author, there are three different types of composers in musical history.

(   ) 2. The type that has fired public imagination most is that of the spontaneously inspired composer—the Franz Schubert type.

(   ) 3. The spontaneously inspired composer begins not so much with a musical theme as with a completed composition.

(   ) 4. The creative act with Palestrina is the thematic conception but not the personal treatment of a well-established pattern.

(   ) 5. The pioneer type of composer is the opposite of the traditionalist type.

II. Choose the best answer to each of the following questions.

1. What type of composer has fired public imagination most?
   A. The spontaneously inspired type
   B. The constructive type.
   C. The traditionalist type
   D. The pioneer type.

2. What kind of music was Schubert good at handling?
   A. Symphony
   B. The theme music
   C. The shorter forms of music
   D. Songs

3. What can we infer from Para. 5?
   A. The composers like Palestrina and Bach were living in the period of fullest development of musical history
   B. The creative act with Palestrina is the thematic conception
   C. We are living in a traditional musical period
   D. Bach didn't knew the general formal mold when he composed his Well Tempered Clavichord

4. What did Beethoven begin with when he composed a musical work?
   A. A poem   B. A song   C. A Symphony   D. A theme

5. When did the pioneer type become characteristic?
   A. In the late 17th century
   B. At the beginning of 20th century
   C. In the late 20th century
   D. Both A and B

Practical Writing

Letter of Complaining

投诉信

投诉信用于对对方公司的服务、产品等不满意时，它一般包括三部分，即投诉内容、投诉原因以及期望得到的结果。

常用句型：

① I am writing to complain about…
我写信的目的是投诉……

② I am writing to inform you that I am dissatisfied with the service of your hotel.
我写信是向你投诉你们酒店的服务。

③ I request the immediate replacement of the damaged goods.
我要求立即调换受损物品。

④ I understand you will give immediate attention to this matter.
我想你们会立即对此问题给予关注。

⑤ I would like a refund, or…
我想退款，或是……

⑥ I would like to have this matter settled be the end of…
我希望该问题能在……之前得到解决。

Sample

Sep. 21st

The Manager
Spring Department Store
Stacy St. N. Y

Dear Sir or Madam,

I am writing to complain about the quality of the sweater(code: NE36574) I bought yesterday from you.

In my opinion, the sweater is not worth the $30 I paid for it. I haven't even worn it and it already has some stains on it, something like spots of ink. The stains couldn't have been made by me, since the labels are still on the sweater.

I have kept all the receipts. It's a brown sweater for men, made by JSW Company.

I would like a refund, or have my new sweater cleaned. And I would like to have this matter settled be the end of this week.

I look forward to hearing from you at your earliest convenience.

Yours faithfully,
John Smith

Letter of Apology
道歉信

道歉信通常包括三部分内容：表示歉意，道歉的缘由；出现差错的原因，提出弥补措施；请求原谅。道歉信语言要真挚，解释的理由要真实。好的道歉信不仅会获得对方的谅解，还会增进彼此的感情。

常用句型：

① I must apologize for any inconvenience it may have caused you.

为此事可能给您带来的不便，深表歉意。

② We hope that this has not caused you any inconvenience.

我们希望这没有给你们带来不便。

③ We are sorry to hear that some of the books we sent you were incorrectly bound.

我们很遗憾获悉我方所寄的部分书籍装订有误。

④ Unfortunately, some mistakes were made and the goods have been improperly delivered.

很遗憾，发生了某些误会，以致错发了货物。

⑤ We are very sorry that we are not in a position to place orders with you for these books.

很抱歉我们不能向你们订购这些书本。

⑥ I regret to inform you that I can not attend the meeting on Friday.

很遗憾地告知你我不能参加周五的会议了。

⑦ We frankly admit that we were at fault and we are anxious to correct the consequences. Please accept our regrets.

我们承认过失在于我方，我们愿意弥补损失。请接受我们的道歉。

⑧ With apologies once again. / With many apologies.

再次表示抱歉。/十分抱歉。

Sample

Jan. 31st

Dear Susan,

I'm awfully sorry I forgot to meet you at the railway station yesterday. We had an end-of-term party in our dormitory the night before. I was so proud of the final exam results that I drank like a fish all night. I felt dizzy all day yesterday and had little sense of what I should do. It was in the evening that I realized I forgot to meet you at the railway station. Since then, I've tried to call you several times, but I feel you are still angry with me and wouldn't answer my phone call.

I promise this will not happen and wish you would forgive me.

Yours,
Linda

Culture

Three Don'ts
Taboos

The British people have the queue habit. If you have watched a TV news program about the UK or have seen an English film, you probably know of the people lining up one after another, getting on the bus, getting on the train or buying something, such as a newspaper. There is seldom any jumping of the queue. If somebody jumps the queue, the British people look down upon him or her. They think that he or she is ill—bred, and take a remarkably dim view of such behavior.

In the UK and the USA, you should never ask a woman her age. Women do not like others to know their ages. They think it is very impolite of you to ask their ages.

Don't try to bargain in the UK when you do the shopping. The British do not expect or welcome bargaining. Sometimes they consider it losing face. If it is a question of some expensive artwork or a large quantity of antique furniture or silver, you might try to work out a sensible overall price with your salesman. The British people seldom bargain. They just buy what they want at what they think a reasonable price and take such a practise for granted.

Some other DON'TS and superstitions:

(1) To get out of bed on the wrong side means you will have a bad day.

(2) It is unlucky to have a black cat cross the road in front of you.

(3) The bride should not see the husband on the morning before the wedding.

(4) Cattle lying down indicate rain.

(5) A cricket in the house is good luck.

(6) To pass under a ladder brings bad luck.

(7) Lighting three cigarettes from one match brings bad luck to the third person.

(8) To break a mirror brings seven years' bad luck.

(9) Carrying a rabbit's foot brings good luck.

(10) Opening an umbrella in the house is bad luck.

Unit 12

Dreams and Career

Unit 12 Dreams and Career

Warm-up Activities

I. Matching

Learn the following words and phrases about the majors of Arts, and match them to the pictures.

1. Furniture Functional Design (　　)
2. Public Space Design (　　)
3. Arts and Crafts (　　)
4. Landscape Architecture (　　)
5. Animation (　　)
6. Film and Television Performance (　　)

A.

B.

C.

D.

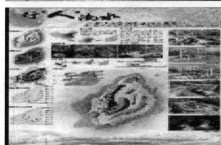
E.

F.

II. Reading

China's Spirit—the patriotism-imbued national spirit; reform and innovation as the core spirit of the times.

"中国精神"，是以爱国主义为核心的民族精神和以改革创新为核心的时代精神。

spirit　n. 精神
patriotism　n. 爱国主义
reform and innovation 改革创新
　　core　adj. 核心的

Text A

From a Tattoo* Artist to a Fashion Designer

1. At 15, Saira Hunjan took her mother along to meet the person with whom she would do work in the school holidays. "You know there's going to be a lot of **swearing**," he warned the mother and daughter. So began Ms Hunjan's career as a tattoo artist.

2. As a teenager Ms Hunjan was **fascinated** by the traditions of body **adornment**, particularly Indian **decorative** art, **fabric** patterns and temples. She was "forever drawing", first on paper then on herself before moving on to the arms and legs of willing friends. After buying a tattoo magazine she knew what she wanted to do. While studying for a fine arts degree at Camberwell College of Art she was also **apprenticed** to a studio in Surrey. This involved "cleaning, making tea, earning my keep and proving that I really wanted to do this. Then alongside I learnt to tattoo". First, she practiced on bananas and grape, before moving on to friends and colleagues at the tattoo **parlour**.

3. The work can be **emotionally** intense for both tattooist and **client**. Tattoos can mark the start of a new life after a break-up or a memorial to a dead friend or relative. Today she has a two-year waiting list and can **command** "at least" £100 an hour. But, having moved to Wales from London "to get out of all the craziness and connect with nature", she has branched into other areas. **Collaborating** with leather goods maker Ettinger, she has produced wallets and purses as well as working on **swimwear**, tents and prints. In doing so she has joined a small but growing number of tattoo artists who are **extending** their creative skills beyond body adornment to **luxury** goods.

4. Tattoo artists should look beyond body art if they want a long-term future. There has been a **massive explosion** in tattooing in the last ten years. People's attitudes have changed—the **generation** have grown up with it on TV, websites and blogs. From a small niche area it has grown

massively to become part of a youth movement. The elite will always be in demand. At the top end, the market is now international. "It's not about walking into your nearest studio," says Ms Hunjan, "It's about 'selecting an artist' and getting on a train or flying to a different country because this is who you want to work on you."

5. Moving into other areas is not just about increasing one's career **longevity**, it is about **sustaining** job satisfaction. You can't be creative and inspired all the time. When you do any job you experience—like in relationships—love and passions. It's a **rollercoaster**. There's times when you are inspired and others when you can't find the motivation. It's easy to fall into **apathy** but it's up to you to keep yourself going.

New Words

tattoo[tæˈtuː] n. a picture or design that is marked permanently on a person's skin by making small holes in the skin with a needle and filling them with colored ink 文身；刺青

swear[sweə] v. to use rude or offensive language, usually because you are angry 咒骂

fascinate[ˈfæsɪneɪt] v. to attract or interest sb. very much 着迷；迷住；神魂颠倒

adornment[əˈdɔːnmənt] n. the action of decorating with something colorful and interesting 装饰；装饰品

decorative[ˈdekərətɪv] adj. decorated in a way that makes it attractive; intended to look attractive or pretty 装饰性的；装潢用的

fabric[ˈfæbrɪk] n. material made by weaving wool, cotton, silk, etc., used for making clothes, curtains, etc. and for covering furniture 织物；布

apprentice[əˈprentɪs] v. be or work as an apprentice 当学徒

parlour[ˌpɑːlə] n. a room in a private house where people can sit and talk and relax 客厅；工作室

emotionally[ɪˈməʊʃənəli] adv. with regard to emotions 感情上；情绪上；令人激动地

client[ˈklaɪənt] n. someone who pays for goods or services 客户

command[kəˈmɑːnd] v. to tell sb. to do sth. 命令，指挥；控制

collaborate[kəˈlæbəreit] v. to work together with sb. in order to produce or achieve sth. 合作

swimwear[ˈswɪmweə] n. clothing that you wear for swimming 游泳衣

extend[ɪkˈstend; ek-] v. to make sth. longer or larger 延伸；扩大；推广

luxury[ˈlʌkʃ(ə) rɪ] n. something that is an indulgence rather than a necessity 奢侈品

massive[ˈmæsɪv] adj. extremely large or serious 大量的；巨大的，厚重的；魁伟的

explosion[ɪkˈspləʊʒ(ə) n] n. a large, sudden or rapid increase in the amount or number of sth. 猛增

generation[dʒenəˈreɪʃ(ə) n] n. all the people living at the same time or of the same age 一代人

longevity[lɒnˈdʒevɪtɪ] n. the fact of lasting a long time 持久；长寿

sustain[səˈsteɪn] v. to provide enough of what sb./sth. needs in order to live or exist 维持；支撑

rollercoaster[ˈrəʊləˈkəʊstə] n. a track at a fairground that goes up and down very steep slopes and that people ride on in a small train for fun and excitement 过山车

apathy[ˈæpəθɪ] n. the trait of lacking enthusiasm for or interest in things generally 冷漠，无兴趣，漠不关心；无感情

Useful Expressions

Phrases	Examples
be fascinated by 被迷住	In the city center of Xi'an, I'm sure you will be fascinated by the building behind us. 来到西安，您肯定会被我们身后的这座建筑所吸引
get out of 摆脱；逃避	It's amazing what people will do to get out of paying taxes. 人们为逃税而做出的种种事情令人吃惊
connect with 与……连接	This sentence does not seem to connect with the context. 这个句子似乎与上下文脱节
branch into 进入	Ultimately, we hope to branch into the Asian market. 最终，我们希望进入亚洲市场
collaborate with 合作	Try to collaborate with and get to know other co-workers, so that they don't feel excluded. 试着和同事合作了解，这样他们就不会觉得排挤

Background Information

Tattoo: 文身俗称刺青，作为人类历史文化的一部分，延续至今已有两千多年。第一种是毛利人流传下来的，用鲨鱼牙齿及动物骨刺捆上木棒蘸上墨水，用小锤敲击入肤。第二种是用数根针绑在一起捆在木棒上，手工点刺入肤。第三种是用电机带动针刺入皮肤，此种方法是当今文身师常用的方法。

Reading Comprehension

Ⅰ. Decide whether the following statements are True (T) or False (F).
( ) 1. Ms Hunjan began her career as a tattoo artist when she was a college student.
( ) 2. As a teenager Ms Hunjan was fascinated by the body adornment.
( ) 3. Hunjan drew her picture on the arms and legs of willing friends at the beginning.
( ) 4. Both tattooist and client can be emotionally intense for the work.
( ) 5. Hunjan moved to Wales from London to branch into other areas.
( ) 6. Tattoo artists should stay focus if they want a long-term future.
( ) 7. Moving into other areas is only about increasing one's career longevity.

Ⅱ. Complete the answers to the following questions.
1. What was fascinated Hunjan when she was a teenager? (Para. 2)
   She was fascinated by the traditions of body adornment, particularly _____,
   _____ and _____.
2. What can tattoos mark? (Para. 3)
   Tattoos can mark the start of _____ after a break-up or a
   _____ to a dead friend or relative.
3. How is the top market of tattoo? (Para. 4)
   At the top end, the market is now _____.
4. What are the purpose of moving into other areas? (Para. 5)
   Moving into other areas is not just about increasing one's _____, it is
   about sustaining _____.

Vocabulary and Structure

Words and Phrases to Drill

swear	decorative	apprentice	emotionally	command
extend	massive	explosion	longevity	sustain
be fascinated by	get out of	connect with	branch into	collaborate with

I. Choose the appropriate explanation from Column B for each of the words in Column A.

A	B
_____ 1. swear	a. to tell sb. to do sth.
_____ 2. decorative	b. be or work as an apprentice
_____ 3. apprentice	c. extremely large or serious
_____ 4. emotionally	d. a large, sudden or rapid increase in the amount or number of sth.
_____ 5. command	e. to use rude or offensive language, usually because you are angry
_____ 6. extend	f. the fact of lasting a long time
_____ 7. massive	g. to provide enough of what sb./sth. needs in order to live or exist
_____ 8. explosion	h. with regard to emotions
_____ 9. longevity	i. decorated in a way that makes it attractive; intended to look attractive or pretty
_____ 10. sustain	j. to make sth. longer or larger

II. Fill in the blanks with the correct forms of the words in Column A of the above table.

1. I started off as a(n) _____ and worked my way up.
2. The school is _____ the range of subjects taught.
3. He died six weeks later of a _____ heart attack.
4. She fell over and _____ loudly.
5. The company _____ losses of millions of dollars.
6. We wish you both health and _____ .
7. He _____ his men to retreat.
8. The curtains are for purely _____ purposes and do not open or close.
9. 300 people were injured in the _____ .
10. They are _____ mature and should behave responsibly.

III. Compare each pair of words and choose the correct one to fill in each blank. Change the form if necessary.

1. decorate   decorative
   a. The curtains are for purely _____ purposes and do not open or close.
   b. They _____ the room with flowers and balloons.

2. emotion   emotional
   a. He lost control of his _____ .
   b. He is a very _____ man.
3. explode   explosion
   a. Bombs were _____ all around the city.
   b. The study also forecast an _____ in the diet soft-drink market.
4. sustain   sustainable
   a. _____ development of society and environment is closely related to human culture.
   b. If you _____ something, you continue it or maintain it for a period of time.

IV. **Add the suffix "-ly" to the following words in brackets. Then complete the sentences with the words formed.**

> **Tips:** "-ly"作为副词后缀，几乎可以加在一切形容词后面，表示状态（如cheerfully）、方式（如financially）、程度（如greatly）、方向（如northwardly）、次序（如thirdly）、时间（如recently）等。另外，"-ly"也可加在名词后面充当形容词后缀。

Sample: Each morning he <u>leisurely</u> has his breakfast and reads the morning paper. (leisure)
1. The survey showed tourists most often complain of _____ taxi drivers. (sure)
2. We believe in giving _____ and effectively to leave a lasting impact on the society. (sustainable)
3. It was the most unexpected piece of news one could _____ imagine. (possible)
4. The book explains grammar _____ and clearly. (simple)
5. I'm always _____ busy on Thursdays. (terrible)

V. **Choose the best phrase to complete each sentence.**
1. He seems to be fixed and _____ the portrait.
   A. fascinated on   B. interested by   C. fascinated by   D. interested on
2. It's amazing what people will do to _____ paying taxes.
   A. get out of   B. get up of   C. go out by   D. go up to
3. Your online social networks enable you to _____ people who have interests similar to yours.
   A. interact with   B. connect to   C. interact by   D. connect with
4. When you wish to start a conversation with an English speaker, the weather offers opportunities to _____ other areas of discussion.
   A. break into   B. branch out   C. branch into   D. break up
5. I can permit them to _____ the main office and share information in real time.
   A. collaborate on   B. collaborate with   C. collaborate in   D. collaborate to

VI. **Complete the following sentences by translating the Chinese given in brackets into English.**
1. As a teenager Ms Hunjan _____ (非常迷恋传统的身体纹绘艺术).

2. Having moved to Wales from London "_____"(为了摆脱喧嚣、亲近大自然), she has branched into other areas.

3. _____(通过与皮具制造商艾丁格合作), she has produced wallets and purses as well as working on swimwear, tents and prints.

4. There has been _____(文身行业突飞猛进的发展) in the last ten years.

5. Moving into other areas is not just about increasing one's career longevity, _____ _____(还是为了维持对工作的满意度).

VII. Translate the following sentences into Chinese.

1. The work can be emotionally intense for both tattooist and client. (Para. 3)

2. In doing so she has joined a small but growing number of tattoo artists who are extending their creative skills beyond body adornment to luxury goods. (Para. 3)

3. Tattoo artists should look beyond body art if they want a long-term future. (Para. 4)

4. From a small niche area it has grown massively to become part of a youth movement. The elite will always be in demand. (Para. 4)

5. It's easy to fall into apathy but it's up to you to keep yourself going. (Para. 5)

VIII. Combine the sentence beginnings in Column A with the endings in Column B to form complete sentences.

Column A	Column B
It is good for you…	…winning a marathon is another.
Being able to run fast is one thing, …	… don't quit.
Talking to him…	…to do some exercise.
When faced with failure…	…is like talking to a wall.

IX. Combine the sentence beginnings in Column A with the endings in Column B to form complete sentences.

Column A	Column B
It would be hard…	… do we hear such fine singing from school choirs(合唱团).
They are the ones…	… when it is better to be a listener.
There are times…	… to say which is better.
Seldom…	… who are in charge of the picture show.

Dialogue Samples

Listen and read the samples carefully, then complete the communicative tasks that follow.

Dialogue 1　Future Job

Smith: Hi, Jack. How are you getting along?

Jack: I'm OK. Graduation season is coming.

Smith: Yes, how time flies. We will graduate soon. Well, have you thought about your future job?

Jack: Of course. I have thought about it, I want to be a civil servant.

Smith: Wow, really? That's a good idea. But it is said that being a civil servant is not easy.

Jack: Well, it is difficult to pass the examinations. But there are many benefits of being a civil servant, such as the salary, the holiday, the welfare, etc. Do you have any plans for your future?

Smith: Yes, I want to be a psychiatrist, and it is why I choose my major.

Jack: You are outstanding and enthusiastic, and it suits you.

Smith: Oh, It's time to attend the lecture. Let's talk about it next time.

Jack: OK, see you.

Smith: Bye.

Dialogue 2　Your Dream Career

Jesse: I would like to be an international correspondent in the future, how about you?

James: I have wanted to be a teacher from childhood. Well, your dream sounds great.

Jesse: Yeah, it is a glamorous job being an international correspondent, I can travel around the world and get updated information to the people all over the world.

James: Maybe English is necessary for you. It is the basic language of communication all over the world.

Jesse: I see, you want to be an English teacher, don't you?

James: Yes, I hope I can go back to my hometown and teach the children there. It is difficult for them to learn English. So I hope I can help by teaching English.

Jesse: Wow, that is really a great dream. Let's study hard from now on to make our dreams come true.

James: Yeah, keep studying and working hard to make our dreams come true.

Communicative Tasks

Work with your partner and take turns to start the conversations.

Task 1

Situation:

Father and daughter are discussing the son's future career.

Tips:

Here are some things the father can say:
It is time we talked about…
…is definitely for…
…to get into…
be good at math and chemistry.
That sounds boring.

Here are some things the daughter can say:
to make good use of…
promising career.
after graduating from college…
to love colors and shapes…
prizes in drawing competitions…

Task 2

Situation:

Two students are talking about success in their study.

Tips:

Here are some things student A can say:
I just can't get over …
He was known for …
…must be kind of …
That's a good question.
…can do a lot to fill in the gap.

Here are some things student B can say:
Many famous person, such as …
The man who is "above average"
99% perspiration, 1% inspiration
turn out to be…
to persist in

269

Further Development

英美发音的主要差别（二）

其他发音差异情况有以下几点。

1. 元音字母 e

在非重读音节中，英式英语读作［ɪ］，而美式英语则读成［e］。如 experience 的英式英语音标为［ɪkˈspɪəriəns］，而美式英语音标则为［eksˈpɪəriəns］。

2. 元音字母 i

在单词 direct, director, direction, directly 中的字母 i，英式英语中读作［ɪ］，美式英语中则读作［aɪ］。如 direct 的英式英语音标为［dɪˈrekt］，美式英语音标则为［daɪˈrekt］。

3. 元音字母 o

在非重读音节中，英式英语多不发音，而美式英语则都发音。例如：

history[ˈhɪstri]（英音）　　　　　[ˈhɪstəri]（美音）
factory[ˈfæktri]（英音）　　　　　[ˈfæktəri]（美音）
dictionary[ˈdɪkʃənri]（英音）　　　[ˈdɪkʃəneri]（美音）

4. 元音字母 u

在单词 difficult 中，英式英语读作［ˈdɪfɪkəlt］，而美式英语则读作［ˈdɪfɪkʌlt］。

5. 辅音连缀 wh 的发音

英式英语读［w］，美式英语读［hw］，但在字母 a, e, i, o 前都读［h］，例如：
what, where, which, somewhere, meanwhile, overwhelm, whole.

6. either 和 neither 的发音

either 和 neither 的英式英语音标为［ˈaɪðə］和［ˈnaɪðə］，美式英语音标为［ˈiːðɚ］和［ˈniːðɚ］。

7. 重音位置的差异

美国人常将单词的重音放在开头，而英国人则不然。例如：
magazine[ˌmæɡəˈziːn]（英音），[ˈmæɡəziːn]（美音）。

Text B

Derivative Occupation

1. As soon as the sky clears one rainy summer day in Guangzhou, plus-size modeling hopeful Wang Jialin hurries out for a test photo shoot. Passersby **stare** as she poses on the busy street.

2. "I'm used to it," the 20-year-old **mumbles**. At 165 centimeters tall and weighting 94 kilograms, she stands out in Chinese crowds. The long black floral dress she wears is size 5XL, while most stores only carry small, medium, and large.

3. Wang had never considered becoming a model until her mother, who works in the clothing **export** industry, came across a plus-size modeling agent and suggested that her daughter give it a try.

4. "Chinese people think of beauty as slenderness," Wang tells Sixth Tone*. She doesn't remember anyone ever telling her she was pretty until she met modeling **agent** Huang Fei.

5. Huang is one of the plus-size modeling industry's **pioneering** agent. She sees plus-size modeling not only as a business **opportunity** with real growth **potential**, but also as a way to change popular **perceptions** around fatness, beauty, and health.

6. In China, plus-size modeling is a **relatively** new business that only **surfaced** around 2010. Now, the city of Guangzhou has become the center of the plus-size modeling industry due to the southern coastal region's **flourishing garment** export sector and its status as a **hub** for online women's fashion **retailers**. Plus-size models can make over 10 000 yuan ($1 470) per month, twice the **average** monthly salary in the city, according to state news **agency** Xinhua.

7. However, strict beauty standards apply, even in the plus-size modeling world. Huang looks for pretty girls who are at least 1.65 meters tall; are under 25 years old; and have a relatively **slender**

waist, a long neck, and—most importantly—a small, **photogenic** face. "These requirements rule out most big girls who want to be models," she says.

8. In China, plus-size models are a new occupation group. This is not only the introduction of western fashion, but also the rise of online shopping and the demand of foreign trade.

9. Taking a broad view at the world, aesthetics of fashion has been changing quietly. Thus the plus size has gained more and more recognition and popularity. For example, Britain is the birthplace and main market of Victoria's Secret*. As a brand of Limited Brands*, Victoria's Secret has more than 1 000 stores in the United States and Canada. In March 2015, Victoria's Secret cooperated with an Italian company to expand its European market. But there is a same problem in the United States, Britain and Europe—the **obesity** rate is very high. It is essential to adapt to the local environment if you want to **exploit** the markets in these countries. That is an obvious transformation for Victoria's Secret, which has been walking along the "small size" route. There is no doubt that the "plus-size" route carried out by Victoria's Secret is to please the market. Whether it works or wins the favor of British people remains to be a "secret" for a period of time.

Unit 12　Dreams and Career

New Words

derivative[dɪˈrɪvətɪv] adj. copied from sth. else; not having new or original ideas 派生的

occupation[ˌɒkjʊˈpeɪʃ(ə)n] n. a job or profession 职业

stare[steə] v. to look at sb./sth. for a long time 凝视；盯着看

mumble[ˈmʌmb(ə)l] v. to speak or say sth. in a quiet voice in a way that is not clear 含糊地说话

export[ˈekspɔːt; ɪkˈ-] n. to sell and send goods to another country 输出；出口

pioneer[paɪəˈnɪər] v. open up and explore a new area, take the lead or initiative in 首创；先驱

agent[ˈeɪdʒ(ə)nt] n. a person whose job is to act for, or manage the affairs of other people in business, politics, etc. 代理人；代理商

opportunity[ˌɒpəˈtjuːnətɪ] n. a time when a particular situation makes it possible to do or achieve sth. 时机；机会

potential[pəˈtenʃl] n. the possibility of sth. happening or being developed or used 潜能；可能性

perception[pəˈsepʃ(ə)n] n. the way you notice things, especially with the senses 知觉

relatively[ˈrelətɪvlɪ] adv. to a fairly large degree, especially in comparison to sth. else 相当地；相对地，比较地

surface[ˈsɜːfɪs] v. appear or become visible 浮出水面

flourish[ˈflʌrɪʃ] v. to develop quickly and be successful or common 繁荣，兴旺；茂盛；活跃

garment[ˈɡɑːm(ə)nt] n. a piece of clothing 衣服；服装

hub[hʌb] n. the central and most important part of a particular place or activity 中心

retailer[ˈriːteɪlə] n. a person or business that sells goods to the public 零售商

average[ˈæv(ə)rɪdʒ] adj. calculated by adding several amounts together, finding a total, and dividing the total by the number of amounts 平均的；普通的

agency[ˈeɪdʒ(ə)nsɪ] n. a business or an organization that provides a particular service especially on behalf of other businesses or organizations 代理，中介；代理处，经销处

slender[ˈslendə] adj. thin in an attractive or elegant way 细长的；苗条的；微薄的

photogenic[ˌfəʊtə(ʊ)ˈdʒenɪk] adj. looking attractive in photographs 上相的；适于摄影的

obesity[ə(ʊ)ˈbiːsɪtɪ] n. more than average fatness 肥大；肥胖

exploit[ˈeksplɔɪt; ɪkˈsplɔɪt] v. to develop or use sth. for business or industry 开发，开拓；开采

Useful Expressions

Phrases	Examples
stand out 突出；超群	Every tree, wall and fence stood out against dazzling white fields. 每棵树、每堵墙和每道栅栏都在白得耀眼的田野映衬下十分夺目
come across 偶遇；偶然发生	I came across a group of children playing. 我碰到一群正在玩耍的小孩
rule out 排除……的可能性	The Prime Minister is believed to have ruled out cuts in child benefit or pensions. 据信首相已经排除了削减儿童救济金或养老金的可能
take a view at 看一看	We took a view at the development process of foreign policy, trying to learn from those experiences. 我们看了下国外政策的发展进程，试图从中获取经验
adapt to 适应	We have tried to adapt to local customs. 我们努力去适应当地的风俗习惯

 Background Information

1. Sixth Tone: 第六声，澎湃新闻国际版。澎湃新闻是上海报业集团改革后公布的第一个成果。澎湃新闻主打时政新闻与思想分析，生产并聚合中文互联网世界中优质的时政思想类内容。澎湃新闻结合互联网技术创新与新闻价值传承，致力于新闻追问功能与新闻跟踪功能的实践。澎湃新闻有网页、Wap、App 客户端等一系列新媒体平台。比较有影响力的栏目包括中国政库、中南海、打虎记、人事风向、一号专案、舆论场、知识分子等。2017 年 10 月 28 日，澎湃新闻荣获"2017 中国应用新闻传播十大创新案例"。

2. Victoria's Secret: 维多利亚的秘密是美国的一家连锁女性成衣零售店，主要经营内衣和文胸等。产品种类包括了女士内衣、文胸、内裤、泳装、休闲女装、女鞋、化妆品及各种配套服装、豪华短裤、香水以及相关书籍等，是全球最著名的性感内衣品牌之一。

3. Limited Brands: 公司创办人 Leslie Wexner 于 1963 年创办了第一家服装专卖店。Wexner 凭借极具超群的品位和敏锐的商业嗅觉，将经营的品牌定位于青少年尤其是年轻女性。准确的产品开发和天才的经营使 Limited 一炮而红。公司旗下包括 Victoria's Secret、Bath & Body Works 和 the Express 等连锁店。

Unit 12 Dreams and Career

 Reading Comprehension

Ⅰ. **Decide whether the following statements are True (T) or False (F).**

(   ) 1. Huang is the plus-size modeling industry's pioneering agent.

(   ) 2. In China, plus-size modeling is a relatively new business that only surfaced around 2010.

(   ) 3. Plus-size models are a new occupation group only because of the introduction of western fashion.

(   ) 4. France is the birthplace and main market of Victoria's Secret.

Ⅱ. **Choose the best answer to each of the following questions.**

1. According to Wang Jialin, what do Chinese people think of beauty?
   A. Fatness   B. Slenderness   C. Height   D. Appearance

2. Which is not the reason that Guangzhou has become the center of the plus-size modeling industry?
   A. The southern coastal region's flourishing garment export sector
   B. Its status as a hub for online shopping
   C. It is the women's fashion retailers
   D. The weather in Guangzhou is warm

3. What is the most important factor of being a plus-size model?
   A. A small, photogenic face   B. At least 1.65 meters tall
   C. Under 25 years old   D. Having a relatively slender waist, a long neck

4. Why has plus size gained more and more recognition and popularity?
   A. Because people of southern cities are tall and strong
   B. Because plus-size models are popular in Guangzhou
   C. Because aesthetics of fashion has been changing quietly
   D. Because the opportunities of employment are fewer and fewer

5. Why did Victoria's Secret choose the route of "plus-size"?
   A. Because they want to please the market in Europe
   B. Because they aren't required in America
   C. Because they want to open the market in Asia
   D. None of above

Practical Writing

Resume

个人简历

简历（resume，英文也常简化为 C.V.），指简单的个人经历。招聘单位往往要求谋职者提供简历。简历通常包括以下几项：姓名、地址、电话、出生日期、学历、工作经历等。此外，还可以加上婚姻状况、国籍、现任职务、职称、科研课题或方向，参加何学术团体，掌握何种外语，留学、进修、工作国别、兴趣爱好及证明人姓名等。

（1）姓名。

中国人姓名的写法与大多数西方人不同，不是名在前、姓在后，而是姓在前、名在后。为了避免误会，可以在姓后加一逗号：如 Wang, Ming；或大写姓的每一个字母，即 WANG Ming。

（2）地址。

可以既写单位地址或临时住址，又写家庭住址；写临时住址时，应注明至何时为止。如：Temporary address: 17 University Ave. Providence, RI 02906 (until Dec. 31, 1999).

（3）电话。

办公室电话号码后应加（O）或（W），住宅电话号码后加（H）。

（4）婚姻状况（Marital Status）.

未婚用 Single，已婚用 Married，离异用 Divorced. No/Two Children 表明无子女或有子女两人。

（5）学历（Education）.

一般按时间顺序由近及远填写，从最后就读的学校及学习时期写起。需要记住的是在填写工作经历、获奖情况以及发表著作各项时，应采用同样的写法，按时间顺序由近及远地填。如：

2019　　M. A. in Computer Science, Tsinghua University

2015　　B. A. in Mathematics. Lanzhou University

（6）工作经历。

除时间段以外，还应写单位名称以及担任的职务或职称。如：

2021—　　　　Associate Professor of Economics, Wuhan University

2009—2020　　Lecturer, Henan University

（7）受何奖励（Award/ Honors and Scholarships）.

包括获得的奖学金、科研基金或资助荣誉称号或会员资格、发明奖、优秀科研成果奖等。如：

2019　　　　　Excellent Student, ×× × University

2017—2018　　Fulbright Award, United States State Department

　　　　　　　Exchange Program, Washington, USA

(8) 掌握何种外语（Languages）.
如：Chinese and English (fluent in both speaking and writing), French (reading only)
(9) 证明人（References/ Referees）.
证明人指能提供有关你的情况或为你写推荐信的人，通常要求两三名。切记事先应征得证明人的同意方可填写他们的姓名。除姓名外，还应填写证明人的职务、地址以及电话号码。如：

Prof. Tan Yonggang (Chairman)
Department of Foreign language and Literature
Hubei University
Baoyiyan, Wuchang
Hubei 430062
P. R. C
Telephone: 611903 Ext. 565

(10) 简历常用词汇如下。

简历：Resume	姓：family name/ surname	名：first name	地址：address
电话：telephone number		工作经历：work experience	
教育背景：educational background/education			
个人简况：personal information/data			
求职意向：job objective		籍贯：native place	
国籍：nationality		民族：nation	
外语技能：foreign language skills		邮政编码：postal code	
性别：gender		婚姻状况：marital status	
必修课程 required courses		专业课程 specialized courses	
选修课程 selected courses		主修 major	
优秀学生干部 excellent student leader		班长 Monitor	
奖学金 scholarship		解决问题能手 problem solver	
充满创意 creative thinker		组织力高 organized	

Sample

Personal Information

Name: Xue Wu   Health: Excellent
Gender (Sex) : Male   Age: 21
Place of Birth: Nanjing, Jiangsu, China   Marital Status: Single
Address: No. 45 Zhongshan Road Nangjing   Zip Code: 475003
Tel: (025) 365-8096   Mobile Phone: 1373-785-1234
E-mail Address: Xue2012@ 163. com
Job Objective: interior designer

Education

09, 2018—07, 2021　　Shenyang Institute of Technology

Major

interior design

Part-time Work Experience

08, 2020—08, 2021　　Risheng Decoration Engineering Co. Ltd.　　Assistant designer

Language Proficiency

English: Accurate & Fluent　　　CET4:　Excellent　　　CET6: Excellent

Computer Proficiency

Pass the National Computer Rank Test (second grade of database technology)

Familiar with CVB, ASP, SQL, SERVER 2000, Special interest in the development of JAVA.

Other Specialties

Knowledge of commerce and foreign trade, and with special interest.

Self-judgment

Honest, energetic, fashion minded, having strong ambition and determination to succeed; pleasant personality; prepared to work hard, ability to learn; creative while possessing a great team spirit.

Advertisement

广告

广告是商品、器物、服务的宣传方式，旨在使消费者对某种商品、器物或服务产生兴趣，从而促使他们进行消费。因此，广告必须具有吸引力，要能引起广大消费者的兴趣，促使他们在接触广告之后就能产生强烈的购买欲望。这就决定了广告英语必须达到迅速影响和劝告的作用。

广告语言的最大特点是具有鼓动性和吸引力。人称以第三人称为主，时态以一般现在时为主。

广告一般分标题、正文和随文三个部分。标题词数要少，要能引起读者的兴趣。正文要对标题进行阐释和证实，内容要有吸引力。随文又叫附文，是传达企业名称、地址、购买商品的方法等附加广告信息的文字，一般出现在广告的结尾。

Sample

假设你是李华，你现在为新开业的瘦身餐馆以"Once tasted, always loved"为题写一则英文广告。餐馆提供平衡的饮食，以饺子为特色，饭菜健康美味。该餐馆设在湖边，风景优美。电话：5558888。

要求：1. 介绍餐馆的特色和优势。
　　　2. 可适当增加细节，使行文连贯。

Once tasted, always loved

Have you ever dreamed of becoming slim while enjoying delicious food? Then come to our slimming restaurant, which is the home of balanced food.

Our restaurant specializes in dumplings and noodles, which are our local favorite dishes. Mouthwatering salads containing fibers and vitamins are also included in our menu. Moreover, the prices of our dishes are reasonable, and for the first week we are offering a discount of 20%. Once you have tried our food, you will never want to go anywhere else!

Located by the lake, our restaurant is a perfect place for you to have an excellent meal while enjoying great views. Why not pay us a visit? Telephone number: 5558888.

Culture

Love of Privacy

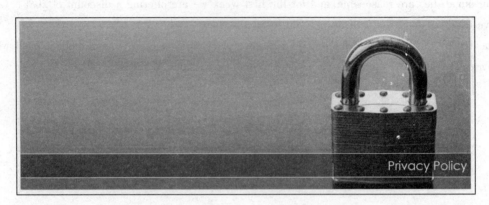

The right to privacy and personal freedom is unquestioned by the British and the Americans. Perhaps it is the lack of space that has fostered and maintained their fierce individualism in the UK. There is a common saying among the British people, "My home is my castle. The wind can come in, but the Kings and Queens and human beings can never come in without my permission."

When an English man moves into a new house, the first thing he does is to build a fence around the house to separate himself from his neighbors. So deeply does the British man immerse himself in his private interests that he sometimes can quite ignore the fact that the world is rocking precariously, everything is unimportant just as long as nothing disturbs his favorite "nesting castle".

The same goes with the American people. They love privacy, but not because of the lack of space. They do not like to have a shared bathroom or room because they consider it to be not private enough, unlike the Chinese people who think it normal to take a bath in a shared bathroom. The American people love to have a small shower room rather than a big shared bathroom. The understanding of privacy between die American people and the Chinese people is not identical at all.

Witty Sayings:

Privacy and security are those things you give up when you show the world what makes you extraordinary.

—Margaret Cho

What you have when everyone wears the same playclothes for all occasions, is addressed by nickname, expected to participate in Show And Tell, and bullied out of any desire form privacy, is not democracy; it is kindergarten.

—Judith Martin

An American has no sense of privacy. He does not know what it means. There is no such thing in the country.

—George Bernard Shaw

When it comes to privacy and accountability, people always demand the former for themselves and the latter for everyone else.

—David Brinkley

Privacy is not something that I'm merely entitled to, it's an absolute prerequisite.

—Marlon Brando

Privacy on the Internet? That's an oxymoron.

—Catherine Butler

附录Ⅲ 词汇表

A

accessible[əkˈsesɪb(ə)l] adj. 易接近的；可进入的 U5A
achieve[əˈtʃiːv] v. 完成；达到 U4B
acquire[əˈkwaɪə(r)] v. 获得 U4B
adornment[əˈdɔːnmənt] n. 装饰；装饰品 U6A
adverse[ˈædvɜːs] adj. 不利的 U2B
advocate[ˈædvəkeɪt] v. 支持；提倡 U4A
agency[ˈeɪdʒ(ə)nsɪ] n. 代理；代理处 U6B
agent[ˈeɪdʒ(ə)nt] n. 代理人，代理商 U6B
aggressive[əˈgresɪv] adj. 积极的 U2B
aluminum[əˈljuːmɪnəm] n. 铝 U1B
apathy[ˈæpəθɪ] n. 漠不关心；无感情 U6A
apply[əˈplaɪ] v. 应用；运用 U4A
apprentice[əˈprentɪs] v. 当学徒 U6A
approach[əˈprəutʃ] v. 靠近；接近 U3B
armchair[ˈɑːmtʃeə(r)] n. 手椅 U2A
arrange[əˈreɪndʒ] v. 准备 U2A
assistance[əˈsɪstəns] n. 帮助 U2B
attribute[əˈtrɪbjuːt] v. 认为某事［物］属于某人［物］ U2B
auction[ˈɔːkʃn] n. 拍卖 U2A
auspicious[ɔːˈspɪʃəs] adj. 吉祥的 U3B
available[əˈveɪləbl] adj. (东西) 可获得的 U1B
average[ˈæv(ə)rɪdʒ] adj. 平均的；普通的 U6B
avoid[əˈvɔɪd] v. 避免；防止 U3B

B

bargain[ˈbɑːgən] n. 便宜货 U2A
batch[bætʃ] n. 一批 U3A
belt[belt] n. 腰带 U2B
bottom[ˈbɒtəm] n. 底部 U3B
brilliant[ˈbrɪlɪənt] adj. 明亮的；鲜艳的 U3B

C

calamity [kəˈlæməti] n. 灾难 U3B
can [kæn] n. 金属罐 U1A
capitalist [ˈkæpɪt(ə)lɪst] n. 资本家 U5A
cash [kæʃ] n. 现金 U1A
celestial [səˈlestiəl] adj. 天空的 U3A
characteristic [kærəktəˈrɪstɪk] adj. 典型的；特有的 U5B
circulate [ˈsɜːkjəleɪt] v. 传播；流传 U3A
classic [ˈklæsɪk] adj. 经典的；典范的 U4B
client [ˈklaɪənt] n. 客户 U6A
collaborate [kəˈlæbəreit] v. 合作 U6A
combination [ˌkɒmbɪˈneɪʃn] n. 联合；混合 U4A
command [kəˈmɑːnd] v. 命令，指挥；控制 U6A
community [kəˈmjuːnətɪ] n. 社区 U5A
companion [kəmˈpæniən] n. 伴侣；陪伴 U3A
comparison [kəmˈpærɪsn] n. 对比 U2A
composer [kəmˈpozɚ] n. 作曲家；音乐家 U5B
condor [ˈkɒndɔː(r)] n. 大秃鹰 U4B
constructive [kənˈstrʌktɪv] adj. 建设性的；推定的 U5B
contemplate [ˈkɒntəmpleɪt] v. 考虑 U2A
content [ˈkɒntent] n. 主题；主要内容 U3B
continuity [ˌkɒntɪˈnjuːəti] n. 连续性；持续性 U3B
conventional [kənˈvenʃ(ə)n(ə)l] adj. 传统的；常见的 U5B
correlation [ˌkɒrəˈleɪʃn] n. 相互关系 U2B
cradle [ˈkreɪdl] n. 摇篮 U4A
creative [kriːˈeɪtɪv] adj. 创造性的 U5B

D

decorative [ˈdekərətɪv] adj. 装潢用的 U6A
democratic [deməˈkrætɪk] adj. 民主的；民主政治的 U5A
derivative [dɪˈrɪvətɪv] adj. 派生的 U6B
devour [dɪˈvaʊə(r)] v. 狼吞虎咽地吃光 U3B
disadvantage [ˌdɪsədˈvɑːntɪdʒ] n. 不利因素 U2A
discard [dɪsˈkɑːd] v. 丢弃 U1A
disciple [dɪˈsaɪpl] n. 信徒；门徒 U4B
discipline [ˈdɪsəplɪn] n. 训练；训导 U4B
distribution [ˌdɪstrɪˈbjuːʃn] n. 分配；分布 U4A
diversify [daɪˈvɜːsɪfaɪ] v. 多样化 U5B

domestic[dəˈmestɪk] adj. 本国的 U1B
drama[ˈdrɑːmə] n. 戏剧文学；戏剧艺术 U4B
drawback[ˈdrɔːbæk] n. 不利因素 U2A
dynamic[daɪˈnæmɪk] adj. 动态的；发展变化的 U4A

E

eco-minded[ekəuˈmaɪnid] adj. 有环保意识的 U1A
econometric[ɪkɒnəˈmetrɪk] adj. 计量经济学的 U2B
eightfold[ˈeɪtfəʊld] adj. 八倍的；八层的 U4B
elevate[ˈelɪveɪt] v. 提升；举起 U5A
ember[ˈembə(r)] n. 余火未尽的木块 U3B
embrace[ɪmˈbreɪs; em-] v. 拥抱；包含 U5A
embroidery[ɪmˈbrɔɪdəri] n. 刺绣技法 U3A
emotionally[ɪˈməʊʃənəli] adv. 感情上；情绪上 U6A
enlightenment[ɪnˈlaɪtnmənt] n. 启迪；启发 U4A
essence[ˈesns] n. 实质，本质 U4A
evident[ˈevɪd(ə)nt] adj. 明显的；明白的 U5B
exhaust[ɪgˈzɔːst] n. 废气 U1B
expense[ɪkˈspens] n. 费用 U1A
exploit[ˈeksplɔɪt; ɪkˈsplɔɪt] v. 开发，开拓；开采 U6B
explosion[ɪkˈspləʊʒ(ə)n] n. 猛增 U6A
export[ˈekspɔːt; ɪk'-] n. 输出；出口 U6B
extend[ɪkˈstend; ek-] v. 延伸；扩大；推广 U6A

F

fabric[ˈfæbrɪk] n. 织物；布 U6A
fairy[ˈfeəri] n. 小仙人；仙子 U3A
faithful[ˈfeɪθfl] adj. 忠实的；忠诚的 U3A
fascinate[ˈfæsɪneɪt] v. 着迷；迷住 U6A
fatal[ˈfeɪtl] adj. 致命的 U2B
fatality[fəˈtæləti] n. 死亡 U2B
fierce[fɪəs] adj. 凶猛的；凶狠的 U3B
firecracker[ˈfaɪəkrækə(r)] n. 鞭炮；爆竹 U3B
firm[fɜːm] n. 公司 U1B
flourish[ˈflʌrɪʃ] v. 繁荣；茂盛 U6B
freshness[freʃnəs] n. (常指食物)新鲜 U1A
functionality[fʌŋkʃəˈnæləti] n. 功能 U5A

G

garment[ˈgɑːm(ə)nt] n. 衣服；服装 U6B

generate[ˈdʒenəreɪt] v. 使形成；发生 U5A
generation[dʒenəˈreɪʃ(ə)n] n. 一代人 U6A
genre[ˈʒɒ̃rə] n. 体裁 U4B
geographical[ˌdʒiːəˈɡræfɪkl] adj. 地理（学）的 U4A
globalize[ˈɡləʊbəlaɪz] v. （使）全球化；全世界化 U4B
graceful[ˈɡreɪsfl] adj. 优雅的；雅致的 U3B
gradually[ˈɡrædʒuəli] adv. 逐渐地；逐步地 U4B
grocery[ˈɡrəʊsəri] n. 食品杂货店 U1A

H

haggler[ˈhælə] n. 议价者 U2A
hairpin[ˈheəpɪn] n. 发夹 U3A
harm[hɑːm] n. 损害 U1A
harmony[ˈhɑːməni] n. 和声；协调 U5B
hub[hʌb] n. 中心 U6B
hypothesize[haɪˈpɒθəsaɪz] v. 假设 U2B

I

illuminate[ɪˈluːmɪneɪt] v. 照亮；照射 U3B
impatient[ɪmˈpeɪʃnt] adj. 热切的 U2A
improvise[ˈɪmprəvaɪz] v. 即兴创作；即兴表演 U5B
incredibly[ɪnˈkredəbli] adv. 难以置信地；非常地 U5A
indicate[ˈɪndɪkeɪt] v. 表明；显示 U4A
ingredient[ɪnˈɡriːdiənt] n. 成分；（尤指烹饪）原料 U3A
intangible[ɪnˈtændʒəbl] adj. 无形的 U3A
interact[ɪntərˈækt] v. 互相影响；互相作用 U5A
internal[ɪnˈtɜːnl] adj. 国内的；内政的 U4B
invade[ɪnˈveɪd] v. 侵略；侵犯 U3B
invariably[ɪnˈveəriəbli] adv. 总是；不变地 U5B

L

laptop[ˈlæptɒp] n. 便携式电脑 U1A
leather[ˈleðə(r)] n. 皮 U2A
legendary[ˈledʒəndri] adj. 传奇的；传说的 U3A
livelihood[ˈlaɪvlihʊd] n. 赚钱谋生的手段 U1B
longevity[lɒnˈdʒevɪti] n. 持久；长寿 U6A
lunar[ˈluːnə(r)] adj. 月球的 U3A
luxury[ˈlʌkʃ(ə)ri] n. 奢侈品 U6A

M

mainstream[ˈmeɪnstriːm] n. 主流思想；主流群体 U4A
maintain[meɪnˈteɪn] v 维修 U1B
manufacture[ˌmænjuˈfæktʃə(r)] v. 大量生产 U1A
massive[ˈmæsɪv] adj. 大量的；巨大的 U6A
maze[meɪz] n. 迷宫 U2A
meditation[ˌmedɪˈteɪʃn] n. 冥想；沉思 U4B
meld[meld] v. 合并；混合 U5A
momentum[məˈmentəm] n. 势头；动力 U5A
monster[ˈmɒnstə(r)] n. 怪物；怪兽 U3B
multifaceted[ˌmʌltɪˈfæsɪtɪd] adj. 多层面的 U5A
mumble[ˈmʌmb(ə)l] v. 含糊地说话 U6B
mundane[ˈmʌndeɪn] adj. 世俗的；平凡的 U5A

N

novelty[ˈnɒvlti] n. 新鲜事物 U2B

O

obesity[ə(ʊ)ˈbiːsɪtɪ] n. 肥大；肥胖 U6B
occupation[ˌɒkjʊˈpeɪʃ(ə)n] n. 职业 U6B
opera[ˈɒprə] n. 歌剧（剧本）U4B
opportunity[ˌɒpəˈtjuːnətɪ] n. 时机；机会 U6B
originally[əˈrɪdʒənəli] adv. 起初；原来 U4B
output[ˈaʊtpʊt] n. 输出；输出量 U5B
outweigh[ˌaʊtˈweɪ] v. 重于 U2B
overspend[ˌəʊvəˈspend] v. 超支 U1A

P

parlour[ˈpɑːlə] n. 客厅；工作室 U6A
participatory[pɑːˈtɪsɪˈpeɪtərɪ] adj. 供人分享的；吸引参与的 U5A
peak[piːk] n. 顶峰 U1A
perception[pəˈsepʃ(ə)n] n. 知觉 U6B
philosophical[ˌfɪləˈsɒfɪkl] adj. 哲学的 U4A
phone-related[fəʊn rɪˈleɪtɪd] adj. 与手机相关的 U2B
photogenic[ˌfəʊtə(ʊ)ˈdʒenɪk] adj. 上相的；适于摄影的 U6B
pioneer[paɪəˈnɪər] v. 首创；先驱 U6B
popularize[ˈpɒpjələraɪz] v. 使受喜爱；使受欢迎 U4B
portfolio[pɔːtˈfəʊlɪəʊ] n. 公文包；文件夹 U5A

posture [ˈpɒstʃə(r)] n. 姿势 U4A
potential [pəˈtenʃl] n. 潜能；可能性 U6B
preliminary [prɪˈlɪmɪn(ə)rɪ] adj. 初步的；开始的 U5B
previous [ˈpriːvɪəs] adj. 以前的；早先的 U5A
purchase [ˈpɜːtʃəs] n. 采购 U2A

Q

quest [kwest] v. 追求；探索 U4B

R

recommend [ˌrekəˈmend] v. 推荐 U2A
recycle [ˌriːˈsaɪkl] v. 回收利用 U1B
reduction [rɪˈdʌkʃn] n. 降低 U2B
relatively [ˈrelətɪvlɪ] adv. 相当地；相对地 U6B
religious [rɪˈlɪdʒəs] adj. 宗教的；信教的 U4A
repetitive [rɪˈpetətɪv] adj. 多次重复的 U4B
represent [ˌreprɪˈzent] v. 代表；表现 U5A
response [rɪˈspɒns] n. 回答 U2B
retailer [ˈriːteɪlə] n. 零售商 U6B
retire [rɪˈtaɪə(r)] v. 退休 U1B
revolutionize [ˌrevəˈluːʃənaɪz] v. 革命 U2A
rollercoaster [ˈrəʊləˌkəʊstə] n. 过山车 U6A
rooftop [ˈruːftɒp] n. 屋顶外部 U1B
rotate [rəʊˈteɪt] v. (使某物) 旋转 U1B

S

scale [skeɪl] n. 规模 U2A
scare [skeə(r)] v. 惊吓；使害怕 U3B
scholarship [ˈskɒləʃɪp] n. 奖学金 U1A
self-defense [ˌselfdɪˈfens] n. 自卫；正当防卫 U4A
separate [ˈseprət] v. (使) 分离，分散 U3A
shed [ʃed] v. 流；洒 U3A
skyscraper [ˈskaɪskreɪpə(r)] n. 摩天大楼 U1B
slender [ˈslendə] adj. 细长的；苗条的 U6B
solution [səˈluːʃn] n. 解决办法 U1B
sonority [səˈnɒrɪtɪ] n. 响亮；响亮程度 U5B
span [spæn] v. 横跨；跨越 U3A
spare [speə(r)] v. 留出 U1A
spontaneously [spɒnˈteɪnɪəslɪ] adv. 自发地；自然地 U5B

stare[steə] v. 凝视；盯着看 U6B
static[ˈstætɪk] adj. 静态的；停滞的 U4A
status[ˈsteɪtəs] n. 社会地位；专业资格 U4A
stereotype[ˈsteriətaɪp] n. 刻板印象 U1A
stick[stɪk] v. 粘贴；粘住 U3B
stipulate[ˈstɪpjuleɪt] v. 规定；明确要求 U3B
storey[ˈstɔːri] n. 楼层 U1B
strained[streɪnd] adj. 紧张的 U1A
strategic[strəˈtiːdʒɪk] adj. 战略上的；战略的 U5A
summarize[ˈsʌməraɪz] v. 总结；概述 U5B
summon[ˈsʌmən] v. 呼吁 U2B
surface[ˈsɜːfɪs] v. 浮出水面 U6B
sustain[səˈsteɪn] v. 维持；支撑 U6A
swear[sweə] v. 咒骂 U6A
swimwear[ˈswɪmweə] n. 游泳衣 U6A
symphony[ˈsɪmf(ə)nɪ] n. 交响乐；谐声 U5B

T

tattoo[tæˈtuː] n. 文身；刺青 U6A
thematic[θɪˈmætɪk] adj. 主题的；主旋律的 U5B
theory[ˈθɪəri] n. 理论；学说 U4A
threshold[ˈθreʃhəuld] n. 门口 U2B
traditionalist[trəˈdɪʃənəlist] n. 传统主义者；因循守旧者 U5B
traipse[treɪps] v. 疲惫地走 U2A
tray[treɪ] n. 托盘 U1B
treatment[ˈtriːtm(ə)nt] n. 治疗；处理 U5B
trial[ˈtraɪəl] n. 试验；试用 U4B
trigram[ˈtraɪgræm] n. 卦 U4A
troops[truːp] n. 部队；士兵 U3A
tropical[ˈtrɒpɪkl] adj. 热带的 U1B
tuition[tjuˈɪʃn] n. 学费 U1A

U

unprecedented[ʌnˈpresɪdentɪd] adj. 前所未有的；空前的 U4A
unwanted[ˌʌnˈwɒntɪd] adj. 不需要的 U2A
upright[ˈʌpraɪt] adj. 正直的；诚实的 U3A
urban[ˈɜːbən] adj. 都市的 U1B
urgency[ˈɜːdʒ(ə)nsɪ] n. 紧急；紧急的事 U5A

V

variety[vəˈraɪəti] n. 不同种类 U3A
vertical[ˈvɜːtɪkl] adj. 垂直的 U1B
vigorous[ˈvɪgərəs] adj. 充满活力的；精力充沛的 U4A
virtuously[ˈvɜːtjuəsli] adv. 合乎道德地；品性正直地 U5A
vitality[vaɪˈtæləti] n. 生命力；热情 U4B

W

Watt[wɒt] n. 瓦 U1B
weave[wiːv] v. 编；织 U3A
wisdom[ˈwɪzdəm] n. 智慧；才智 U3A
witness[ˈwɪtnəs] n. 目击者；见证人 U3B
worthless[ˈwɜːθləs] adj. 没用的 U1B

附录 IV 短语表

A

a series of 一系列；一连串 U4B
according to 根据 U2B
adapt to 适应 U6B
associate with 与……联系在一起 U5A
at a stretch 一口气 U5B
at the peak of 顶峰 U1A
attribute to 归因于 U2B

B

be characterized by 以……为特征 U4A
be fascinated by 被迷住 U6A
become aware of 知道；发觉 U5A
beg …for 乞讨；恳求 U3A
bid farewell 告别 U3B
branch into 进入 U6A
break the bank 倾家荡产 U1A
but then 然而 U2A

C

cancel out 抵消 U2B
collaborate with 合作 U6A
come across 偶遇；偶然发生 U6B
come out 出现；出版 U4B
connect with 与……连接 U6A

D

date back to 追溯到…… U3A
deal with 处理；对付 U5A
derive from 由……起源；取自 U3A
descend to 降临；下降 U3A
divide into 分成；分为 U4A

drop... off 捎带 U1A

E

equip...with 给……配备 U1B
exert a profound influence on 对……产生深远影响 U4A

F

factorin 计入 U2B
for the sake of 为了 U5B

G

get out of 摆脱；逃避 U6A

H

have...off 休假 U3B

I

in advance 提前；预先 U5B
in contrast to 相比之下 U4B
in keeping with 和……一致 U1B
in the form of 以……的形式 U1B
interact with 与……相互作用；与……相互影响 U5A

M

make ends meet 勉强维持生计 U1A
more and more 越来越多 U1B

N

name after 以……的名字起名 U4A
not necessarily 未必；不一定 U4B
not to mention 更不用说 U1A

P

pass down 使流传 U3A
put down 记下；放下 U5B

R

refer to 指的是 U4B
rule out 排除……的可能性 U6B

S

spring up 迅速出现 U2A
stand out 突出；超群 U6B
swarm into 蜂拥而至 U3B

T

take advantage of 利用 U2A
take a view at 看 U6B
take…into consideration 考虑到 U2B
there and then 在当时 U2A
to name just a few 仅举几例；等等 U5A
together with 与；和……一同 U4A
turn out 证明是 U3B

U

use up 用完 U2A
usher in 迎来 U3B

W

well out 喷涌而出 U5B

参 考 文 献

[1] Peter Harman, Simon Mitton. Cambridge Scientific Minds [M]. Cambridge: Cambridge University Press. 2002.
[2] 葛宝祥, 王利民. E英语教程1 [M]. 北京: 外语教学与研究出版社, 2013.
[3] 葛宝祥, 王利民. E英语教程2 [M]. 北京: 外语教学与研究出版社, 2013.
[4] 葛宝祥, 王利民. E英语教程3 [M]. 北京: 外语教学与研究出版社, 2013.
[5] 李秀清. 21世纪大学艺术英语教程1 [M]. 上海: 复旦大学出版社, 2012.
[6] 陈敏, 刘东霞. A级综合训练教程 [M]. 长春: 东北师范大学出版社, 2013.
[7] 隋铭才. 英语国家概况（上）[M]. 北京: 高等教育出版社, 2013.
[8] 王志茹, 陆小丽. 英语畅谈中国文化 [M]. 北京: 外语教学与研究出版社, 2017.
[9] 廖华英. 中国文化概况 [M]. 北京: 外语教学与研究出版社, 2015.
[10] 束定芳. 中国文化英语教程 [M]. 上海: 上海外语教育出版社, 2016.
[11] 郭铁妹, 张延庚, 杨莉. 艺术设计专业英语 [M]. 北京: 北京理工大学出版社, 2018.
[12] 张克建. 新应用大学英语·基础篇1 [M]. 北京: 外语教学与研究出版社, 2015.
[13] 张克建. 新应用大学英语·基础篇2 [M]. 北京: 外语教学与研究出版社, 2015.